30

To

There's Something About Darcy

best wishes

*

To Jenny

best wishes

[signature] x

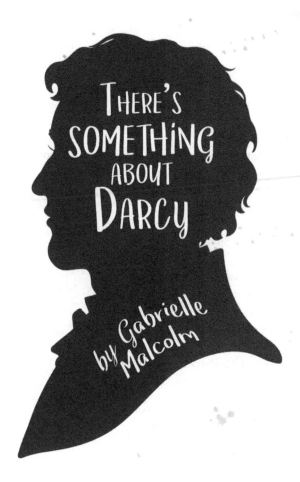

THERE'S SOMETHING ABOUT DARCY

by Gabrielle Malcolm

ENDEAVOUR QUILL

ENDEAVOUR QUILL

First published in 2019 by Endeavour Quill
www.endeavourmedia.co.uk

ISBN 978-1-911445-56-2

A CIP catalogue record for this book is available
from the British Library

Printed and bound in Great Britain by Clays

Cover illustration of Mr Darcy by Laura Barrett at
The Artworks Illustration Agency, 2019

Image of Colin Firth/Darcy merchandise property of Mira Magdo
C E Brock illustration, from *Pride and Prejudice*, 1895
Hugh Thomson illustration, from *Pride and Prejudice*, 1894
Caricature of Beau Brummel by Robert Dighton, 1805
C E Brock illustration, from *Pride and Prejudice*, 1895
F H Townsend illustration from *Jane Eyre*, 1848
Image of Laurence Olivier as Heathcliff from 1939 production of *Wuthering Heights*,
from the Lester Glassner collection, Samuel Goldwyn Pictures
Image of Greer Garson and Laurence Olivier from 1940 production of and *Pride
and Prejudice*, MGM Studios
Hugh Thomson illustration, from *Pride and Prejudice*, 1894
Image of Colin Firth as Mr Darcy from 1995 BBC adaptation of *Pride and Prejudice*
Image of Darcy bust at Chatsworth House property of Gabrielle Malcolm

For my mother, Ann Curry

Contents

Introduction

In the autumn of 1995, a quiet cultural revolution took place, first in the UK and then around the world. It was quiet because it mostly concerned the emotions generated from private reading habits. It was quiet because it arose from Sunday evening television viewing. And it was quiet because it was almost exclusively driven by the reading and viewing habits of women.

Writer and journalist Helen Fielding was one of the first to pick up on this at the time. Through the lens of her column in *The Independent* newspaper, '*The Diary of Bridget Jones*', she scrutinised the week-by-week run of a six-part BBC TV period drama series awaiting the moment the two leading characters would 'get off' with each other. Bridget Jones started life as a caricature of a thirty-something single woman steeped in self-absorption, self-criticism and self-scrutiny – from the number of calories consumed to the size of knickers required in any given social situation. She evolved over the weeks, months and subsequent years into a character that came to lead the vanguard in modern reinterpretations of Jane Austen's *Pride and Prejudice* (1813).

The trigger for this revolution in popular culture, and the object of Fielding's scrutiny, was of course the broadcast of the new BBC TV adaptation of *Pride and Prejudice*, which unexpectedly sent reverberations around the world that still echo today. It was the product of the dovetailing of a specific group of talents: the genius of Jane Austen, the inventiveness of scriptwriter Andrew Davies and the vision of television director Simon Langton, together with a sterling cast headed by Jennifer Ehle and Colin Firth.

One particular scene became etched on the popular consciousness: when Mr Darcy (played by Firth), strides across a field, a wet shirt clinging to his body. Awkward, yet utterly masculine, he strode right into the hearts and dreams of millions.

The result was a television event that has had no serious rivals since, and the birth of an epoch of unprecedented Austen fandom, for the author and her hero. Austen is now unique amongst period novelists in that she occupies a place in contemporary twenty-first century fan culture that very few modern writers can rival. Austen's creations, particularly Elizabeth

Bennet and Mr Darcy, are as much a focus of today's online fan culture as, for example, JK Rowling's *Harry Potter* characters and the *Star Wars* or *Dr Who* universes.

The idea for this book came to me when I was waiting at a bus stop in Bath. Next to me stood a young woman carrying an 'I ♥ Darcy' tote bag. I tracked this item down to the Jane Austen Centre shop, just off Queen's Square. That was my introduction to the notion that there was a demand for Austen and Darcy related things that went beyond the novels and their adaptations. When I heard that Chatsworth House in Derbyshire had to put away the bust of Matthew Macfadyen as Darcy (from the 2005 film version) because visitors kept kissing it, I decided that this urge ought to be investigated.

The fascination with Darcy has grown into a mania, and this book will examine why that is. Darcy now appears in innumerable guises: in fist-fights on screen, slamming his Ferrari into gear in the pages of a romance novel, running a digital media company in San Francisco, as a vampire, a heart surgeon, a neurosurgeon, and even slaying zombies in films and graphic novels. He is especially favoured in the now classic trope of a man emerging – dripping wet – from a lake or pond, wet shirt clinging to his body. Even actors who have never played Darcy use this as a kind of shorthand for masculine gorgeousness. Benedict Cumberbatch, star of *Sherlock* for the BBC and Dr Strange in the Marvel Universe, appeared in a charity photoshoot in 2014 as a 'sexy wet 'n' wild' tribute to Firth as Darcy.

Time travel fantasies undertaken to meet Darcy, updated sequels to *Pride and Prejudice*, modern adaptations and even dragon-taming versions of Darcy (as in *Pemberley: Mr Darcy's Dragon, Longbourn: Dragon Entail, Netherfield: Rogue Dragon*, a three-book series by Maria Grace, White Soup Press, 2016–2018) populate the thriving genre of Jane Austen fan fiction. This is probably one of the most telling and revealing aspects of Austen's modern-day popularity – the huge, ever-increasing, concentrated output of fan fiction. These are stories – mostly circulated online, but many published in print through independent channels – that are based on Austen's original narratives and characters. They explore alternative plotlines, are told from an individual character's perspective or explore 'what if?' scenarios that test the much-loved characters in new and dramatic ways. The figure of Darcy dominates these alternative re-tellings of *Pride and Prejudice*, demonstrating how vivid, personal and meaningful are the relationships between readers and writers of Jane Austen fan fiction, the author and her creation.

The Darcy we know today has a 200-year history behind him. And beyond that history are the influences that might have operated on Austen to create him. He has moved from being the secondary character to Elizabeth, her love interest, to influence later heroic creations. He is now an archetype that defines a whole strand of characters in fiction, drama, media and popular culture. These are identified by a single name – Darcy.

So, what is it that Austen delivers for readers and viewers that turn them into such fans, and superfans, of her novels, her characters and of Darcy in particular? This book will search for some answers to this, and in doing so explore the origins of the character, the depiction of him in the novel and the legacy of his influence.

Colin Firth/Mr Darcy fan merchandise

Chapter 1

"Mr what's-his-name? That tall, proud man"

During the course of *Pride and Prejudice*, Mr Darcy makes so little impression on Kitty Bennet that when he appears at Longbourn in the closing chapters of the novel, she refers to him as 'Mr What's-his-name?' He does not wear a military uniform, so what possible interest could he hold for her?

To be fair to Kitty, there is nothing, throughout the span of the novel, for her to see. Elizabeth and Darcy's romance, whilst the central focus of the novel, is after all a secret one, and most of the characters remain oblivious to it until the very end. However, we, the readers, have been privy to its steady development all along.

Darcy is tall, proud, and of course – rich.

'If *I* were as rich as Mr Darcy… I should not care how proud I was. I would keep a pack of fox-hounds, and drink a bottle of wine every day!'

Pride and Prejudice, Chapter 5, Vol. 1

So announces a 'young Lucas', brother of Charlotte, on learning of Darcy's immense wealth. A boy would certainly not have to worry if he had the life of a Darcy ahead of him.

When he makes his first appearance in the local society of the novel, at the Meryton Assembly, Darcy's background, his property and his attitude and manners immediately become the subject of much gossip. On entering this new society, the first impression he makes on the company is universal. He is rich and he is handsome, he is well-dressed and in the company of fashionable ladies, therefore he *must* be admired. However, the way in which he is initially appraised quickly deteriorates, and hits a low point when, within earshot of Elizabeth, he speaks his mind about her: "She is tolerable; but not handsome enough to tempt me…"

You would think that people would not give this awful, rude man the benefit of their attention. But Austen's point is clear: they do, because he is handsome and wealthy and provides them with a rich seam of gossip to mine. By the dawn of the next day, and chapter, Darcy already fascinates them. After all, as Mr Bennet says to Elizabeth: "For what do we live, but to make sport for our neighbours, and laugh at them in our turn?"

C E Brock illustration, 1895

First Impressions

Mr Darcy's insult to Elizabeth does not turn out to be a mortal wound. The story in *Pride and Prejudice* is in a sense the tale of Darcy's journey back: back to acceptance and approval in Elizabeth's 'fine eyes' and back to the moment when he entered the Meryton Assembly and received everyone's admiration on first impression.

First Impressions was of course Austen's initial choice of title for the novel. She grew and nurtured the characters, and the relationship of Elizabeth and Darcy, over some years. She began in 1796, when she was twenty-one and staying at Goodnestone Park in Kent, her brother Edward's estate. She referred to the manuscript as *First Impressions* in a letter to her sister Cassandra, in 1799.

So, the novel was with her, as part of her life, throughout the first decade of the nineteenth century. Revisions of the manuscript took place later, from 1811–1812, and it was published as *Pride and Prejudice* in 1813, by Thomas Egerton. '*Pride and Prejudice*' is a phrase lifted directly from Frances Burney's novel *Cecilia* (1779); Burney was one of Austen's key influences, with her novels of young women's journeys into the world.

But the story of the foundation of *Pride and Prejudice* began even earlier, during Austen's childhood years at Steventon in Hampshire. This was George Austen's parish and, as the daughter of the vicar, Jane had access to the parish register. It turns out that she enjoyed this access in a mischievous fashion and, probably in her teens, made fictional entries. As the BBC reported in March 2017, Austen listed a marriage between 'Henry Frederic Howard Fitzwilliam of London' and 'Jane

Austen of Steventon.' Another 'Jane Austen' entry unites her with 'Edmund Arthur William Mortimer of Liverpool.'

It is charming and funny to witness this unfolding of the imagination in her early years. This mischievous act reinforces our understanding of the timeline of *Pride and Prejudice* and stimulates speculation about her influences and her invention.

From Stage to Page

Austen was a passionate scholar and historian, and an avid reader from a young age. As well as juvenile works of history and biography, she engaged in home 'theatricals' as a performer and a playwright. Her eldest brother, James, organised the Austen siblings in the barn at the Steventon rectory in productions of Richard Sheridan's *The Rivals* (1775). Austen was involved from about the age of eight. With Sheridan's work and the activity of performing, she could develop her satirical voice.

The influence of Richard Sheridan (1751–1816) on Austen cannot be underestimated. He owned and managed the Theatre Royal, Drury Lane and had a career in politics with the Whig Party. Sheridan's satiric tone and the means by which he fashioned his comedy of manners for the stage can be detected in *Pride and Prejudice* and within the character of Darcy. Getting to know Austen's novels means understanding the significance of such dramas, and the impact of theatricality on her work.

In *The Rivals*, Sheridan created the character of Faulkland, the wittily-constructed figure of a tormented romantic hero. He is in love with the sensible and pragmatic Julia Melville, which is a case of opposites attracting. Julia resembles Charlotte Lucas in many ways, and she understands Faulkland's high ideals and tolerates them as a product of the fashionable poetic view of love at the time.

Faulkland is all seriousness and against frivolity. When he hears that Julia has attended evening parties without him, he is tormented by jealousy and anguished at the idea of her indulging in dances, specifically 'jigs and reels'. He is particularly set against these because of the impulses they might release in people, being folkish and frivolous forms of movement. His response is hilarious in its hyperbole:

> "Hell and the devil!... She thrives in my absence!
> – Dancing!... I have been anxious, silent, pensive,
> sedentary – my days have been hours of care, my nights
> of watchfulness..."

The Rivals, Act 2, Scene 1

He dissects his concerns. He fears that the 'lascivious movement of the jig' will lead to 'quivering warm-breathed sighs' that fill the air so that 'the atmosphere becomes electrical to love'. At this point Faulkland must exit, as he is 'somewhat flurried'.

In Chapter 6, Vol. 1 of *Pride and Prejudice*, a little drama unfolds in Sir William Lucas' drawing room that mirrors this episode. At this evening party Austen lets us in on the secret thoughts of a number of characters. Darcy has begun to notice Elizabeth's 'fine eyes' and tries to get within her orbit. Elizabeth in her turn struggles to accept this attention, and feels nervous and suspicious of his motives. She is afraid that he will insult her again or try to make her feel ridiculous.

The conflict starts to unfold with Charlotte Lucas' interference. She encourages her friend to play the piano and sing. It is as if she knows how Elizabeth's unaffected charm and musical talent might fascinate this superior, difficult man. Austen's expertise in this type of scene is on display here. She manoeuvres her characters around the most mundane of social interactions and makes the atmosphere in her rooms 'electrical'.

Darcy's moodiness starts to show, and interests us. He enjoys Elizabeth's playing. Manners permit him to attend to her as she is performing in a social setting. Then the younger Bennet sisters interfere and demand something livelier. The atmosphere in the room shifts. They pester for 'Scotch and Irish airs' to liven things up. These are the very same 'jigs and reels' so feared by Faulkland.

Elizabeth leaves the instrument, so Darcy can no longer gaze upon her. He is frustrated, so at his next interaction he snaps at Sir William. Ever the gracious host, Sir William has only tried to make conversation with Darcy and commented: "There is nothing like dancing after all – I consider it as one of the first refinements of polished societies…" Darcy retorts perhaps too harshly to this. "Certainly, sir, and it has the advantage of also being in vogue amongst the less polished societies of the world. Every savage can dance."

Such very superior dancing is not often seen.

Hugh Thomson illustration, 1894

A Social Performance

This cutting reply is undeserved, and it both betrays Darcy's moodiness and shows a slippage of manners. Charlotte's suspicions are aroused at this fracture in Darcy's acceptable social performance. Austen helps the reader to detect that, perhaps, she sees the possible first glimmerings of Darcy and Elizabeth's mutual attraction. They make each other nervous and irritable. This is all managed expertly in this scene. Austen demonstrates her accomplishment with nuanced social drama and shows how Faulkland was a useful model for Darcy. Sheridan himself recommended *Pride and Prejudice* to his friends as one of the 'cleverest' things he had ever read.

Performance on the social stage was important, and Austen could channel that. In the cultural framework of her time there were many important social actors. Fashion and fame both played their part in Austen's invention of Darcy.

The man possessed of the brightest celebrity trajectory across the first decade of the nineteenth century, contemporary with Austen's career, was gorgeous George 'Beau' Brummell (1778–1840). Brummell is remembered for his friendship with the Prince of Wales and the influence he had upon men's fashion. For a short period, from 1800–1813, he enjoyed great favour and access at court, but he fell from grace quite spectacularly and had to retire to an ignominious exile in

France. He lived on for many years in debt and drunkenness; the competitive, expensive world of London and Royal society ultimately ruined him.

As a young officer in the Prince of Wales' personal regiment, Brummell drew attention for his wit, charm and good looks. He was never titled or particularly wealthy, with only a modest inheritance and rank. However, by rejecting the prevailing overly decorative and foppish male fashions of the late eighteenth century, he made an enduring mark.

Brummell instructed his tailors to abandon frock coats and short breeches with hose, and instead to favour long trousers, neatly-cut coats and an elaborate cravat, the forerunner of the necktie. He championed the leaner line, simpler cut and practical attire of the sportsman, the gentleman farmer and the huntsman, to produce the new style of the 'dandy'. This is the attire typically associated with Austen's leading men, and Darcy in particular.

To imagine Darcy in any other type of clothing, more akin to the conventional late-eighteenth century style, would feel inappropriate now. All adaptations of the novel have kitted him out in the more Brummell-inspired active wear of the early nineteenth century gentleman. It fits with the perception we have of him, as one capable of riding unmade roads from London to Derbyshire and of going in pursuit of Wickham in the backstreets of Georgian London.

Tight riding breeches have done nothing to harm Darcy's reputation. Slim, tailored trousers as everyday wear made for a practical garment and retained an air of elegance. The practicality of the suit did not prevent Brummell from taking five hours to perform his toilette, nor from requiring his boots to be polished with champagne.

Beau Brummel by Robert Dighton, 1805

Within 'five minutes' of Darcy's appearance at the Meryton Assembly he has impressed the company. This comes about because of the 'fashion' of his party, made up of the Bingleys and Hursts. The desire to make the best possible first impression, on entry to a room or at first sight, was crucial in Georgian society. The poet Lord Byron (1788–1824) was born with a club foot, of which he was very self-conscious. In order to preserve his image of fashionability and confidence, he arrived early for evening parties so that when others entered the room he would be leaning or seated, and they would thus not observe him limping in. At White's Club in St James', London, Beau Brummell ensured that only the most elegant and fashionable members were allowed to sit with him at the front of the bow window, so that passers-by could marvel at their finery and fashion.

There are sparse, but telling, descriptions of Darcy's look in the novel. He is seen thus: his 'fine, tall person, handsome features, noble mien…'. It is all we get, along with probably the most important fact, the ' …report of his having ten thousand a year.' Handsome, superior and wealthy, the ' … gentlemen pronounced him to be a fine figure of a man, the ladies declared he was much handsomer than Bingley…'.

" …Handsomer Than Bingley…"

Poor Bingley, forever in Darcy's shadow and under his influence. This clear social, financial and – it must be said – physical superiority, along with his estate at Pemberley and frequent trips to London, mark Darcy out as a man of fashion and status. Therefore, he has been characterised most often as the Brummellesque modern Georgian/Regency gentleman. That look from the first decade of the nineteenth century, the newly-besuited man of fashion, fits our understanding of the 'fine, tall,… handsome,… noble' patrician.

Simon Bent's TV drama *Beau Brummell: This Charming Man* (2006) starred James Purefoy as the charismatic and deeply troubled leader of fashion. This dramatisation revelled in the male fashion of Regency high society, when an unpaid tailor's bill could lead to one's social downfall. The Prince Regent (Hugh Bonneville) protects Brummell from debt collectors and rivals, for a time. But *This Charming Man* shows the competitive and pressurised world of Georgian society and the way in which it ground people down.

Financial problems beset Brummell, and the Regent's patronage ebbed away. By 1811 his influence had waned, and then came the notorious put-down. The Regent 'cut' Brummell at a party. This was the means of giving someone notice that their presence was no longer required at court, and allowed royalty to avoid having to make direct, embarrassing rejections of those who were out of favour. Brummell, however, did not take it lying down and retorted, within earshot of the Regent, to his companion: "Alvanley, who's your fat friend?"

So, Brummell was cast out. The Regent was very self-conscious of his size and looks, and jealous of Brummell. As one Australian reviewer of *This Charming Man* pointed out: 'The moral of the story is all can be fine and dandy until you tell someone they're fat.' Even the most artfully-tailored clothes could not disguise Prinny's massive girth.

Living in A Material World

The fine figure that Brummell presented was his ticket to high society, but it could not keep him there indefinitely. Without an income, his downfall was inevitable. Wealth not only provided entry to the world of fashion, it kept trouble from your door and was a buffer against scandal and rejection. Darcy, the 'tall, proud man' has the resources to be a protector and problem-solver. He has the poise and fashion of a Brummell, but Austen endowed him with the means to rise above it all.

Austen is sometimes accused by her detractors of neglecting to mention national crises and political issues in her novels. She makes no *direct* reference, for example, to the Napoleonic Wars. Her novels, some say, are not of the *real* world, she only depicts a sheltered bubble of society. Recently, however, that judgment has been challenged by, amongst others, Paula Byrne in her book *The Real Jane Austen: A Life in Small Things* (2013). Byrne tells us that Austen's novels were 'grounded' in the world of the early nineteenth century because they drew upon the real people, places and events of her life. She showed, for example, a keen sensitivity to the culture of the British navy in both *Mansfield Park* and *Persuasion,* and of the social impact of regional English militia in *Pride and Prejudice*, of course. Two of Austen's brothers served in the navy and rose up through the ranks to occupy important roles. Her world, from time to time, would have been populated by men in naval and military uniform.

Her brother Frank (Francis William) Austen joined the navy when he was only twelve, in 1786. This was not unusual in the eighteenth century. Britain's power was its navy. Frank went on to command a series of different ships and served in the Napoleonic Wars and the War of 1812. He was knighted in the 1830s and rose to become Admiral of the Fleet in the 1860s. But this was long after his younger sister had passed away. She did not live to see her brothers' impressive careers. She knew Frank as a young lieutenant in the 1790s, promoted to captain in the early 1800s. He was a well-liked officer, known for his sympathy and care for his crew. We can detect his influence in the characterisations of Captain Wentworth and his comrades in *Persuasion*.

Charles Austen (1779–1852), the youngest of the Austen sons, followed his brother into the navy in 1791 and eventually rose to the rank of Rear Admiral. He married the daughter of the Attorney-General of Bermuda. In the relationship and correspondence between Fanny Price and her brother William in *Mansfield Park* there is the mark of authenticity, based as it is on Jane's long-distance relationship with her brothers.

A Patchwork Composition

If Austen was not overtly concerned with wider political issues in her novels, we can clearly see where social and cultural issues impacted her on a personal level, and led her to include certain of these in her writing. Society, fashion and theatre remained important to her and provided significant material.

The Bodleian Library at Oxford launched a project in 2011, to examine Austen's surviving manuscripts. They acquired and focussed on the manuscript for the unpublished, unfinished novel *The Watsons*. In his May 2013 blog for *The Spectator*, (https://blogs.spectator.co.uk/2013/05/jane-austens-pinny) Christopher Fletcher, the library's Keeper of Special Collections, commented that of particular interest for the scholar and bibliophile was Austen's technique of using dress-making pins to attach pieces of paper to amend text and make corrections. Austen's form of editing seems to have been a 'cut and pin' method. As Fletcher rightly asks about these humble pins, 'Is it not poignant to think that those patching together and preserving evidence of Jane's textual struggle may once have fixed her pinny?' This echoes Byrne's study of Austen's world of small things and material culture.

Austen's use of regular dress-making pins is an example of her tendency to employ things that she had to hand. Being familiar with domestic chores, pins and the like were amongst the tools of her trade. They give us, as Fletcher reminds us, a flavour of the period and Austen's working methods. And he tells us that Lord Byron (1788–1824) joked about the habit women had, of storing their pins in copies of his poem *Don Juan* (first published in 1819): 'Which surely were invented for our sins/Making a woman like a porcupine/Not rashly to be touched'.

We also know of 'Mrs Joe' (Gargery) from Dickens' *Great Expectations* (1860) and her reputation for spikiness and harshness. Pip's memories of his early nineteenth-century childhood on the Kent marshes involve being raised 'by hand' by a sister who was 'tall and bony, and almost always wore a coarse apron, fastened over her figure behind with two loops, and having a square impregnable bib in front, that was stuck full of pins and needles.'

This personal touch to her editing holds a sense of magic for readers of Austen. It is amazing to think that the pins that held her pages in place were once fixed on the front of her apron. The magical feeling of connection across time with the author is also awakened with our feelings around the young

Jane making fictional entries in her father's parish register at Steventon. For an early twenty-first century scholar, reader and fan, these two images bookend the author's life. The mature writer, running a household at Chawton with her mother and sister, interspersing everyday chores such as dress-making with her writing and editing, is the successor to the little girl at Steventon, mischievously concocting fantasy marriage entries in her father's official records.

In childhood she borrowed the name of Fitzwilliam, that would become the first name of her most famous hero, Darcy.

Hero, Protector, Nobleman, Bastard?

Darcy is simply 'Darcy' to his friends, social circle and relatives – Colonel Fitzwilliam and Lady Catherine De Bourgh. Darcy is related to nobility through his mother and aunt, even though he himself never has a title. He does, however, have a 'noble mien'.

'Fitzwilliam' is from the Norman French and Germanic languages. Fitz means 'son of' and 'Wilhelm' can be translated as 'protector'. From Tudor and Stuart times Fitz was also ascribed to the illegitimate sons of kings and nobility (Fitzroy, Fitzhenry, Fitzherbert). Was Austen implying that Darcy was descended from royalty, but from the wrong side of the sheets?

'Fitzwilliam Darcy' certainly rings with patrician respectability and dignity, established property and money. Austen chose her language carefully, and the attention to the name conveys an impression of historic pedigree. It carries with it a tradition of Norman French and landed gentry. D'Arcy refers to an inhabitant of the town of Arcy in La Manche. It has different variants and spellings: Dorcey, D'orsay and d'Orsai. William de Arcai was a knight granted land in Lincolnshire by William the Conqueror. He was succeeded by William Daresai, who was later succeeded by Roger Arsi, and eventually Thomas Darcy – with the familiar spelling.

Darcy is distinguished, via this etymology, as a figure of authority with an extended Anglo-Norman heritage. There are also associations with the Irish Protestant landed gentry. With this there might be a nod towards Thomas Lefroy, a young man from Austen's past. In Gaelic, O'Dorchaidhe (O Dor-kay-da) means 'descendant of the dark one'. A stern, brooding, tall, dark, and handsome hero? The romantic significance of the Irish connection probably meant a lot to the author thanks to her friendship with Lefroy.

So, as we investigate Austen and her famous hero in a social, cultural and historic context we discover various factors that come into play when thinking about his origins. He has, perhaps, a 'right' to be proud according to Charlotte Lucas, with his 'fortune' and his 'favour'. He does have great attributes as we will discover, as well as distinct flaws. This makes him an interesting, enduring character who has a versatility that might not be obvious at first.

Colin Firth, in an interview for *The Making of Pride and Prejudice* (BBC Books, 1995) described the clarity with which Darcy's character comes across in the novel. Austen's depth and tone helped Firth (and the viewers) to see Darcy as a fully-developed figure. What Firth found interesting was the complexity and truth that lay beneath the surface of the character. He knew that Jane Austen had an instinctive grasp of Darcy's inner self; even though she did not always express it, it could be discerned, and we can see it in Firth's performance. Her great ability with character gives them an internal and external life that, two centuries on, can be understood and acted.

This complex character has, since his creation, been broken down, reimagined and reinvented in various ways. For 200 years he has been with us in popular culture and is now such a familiar figure he has gained archetypal status in the early twenty-first century. He is an archetype that can be repeated in different stories and remain recognisable. There are shorthand ways now, of instantly supplying us with the idea of Darcy in different media, literature, folklore and drama. This is what the following chapters will examine, beginning with the literary formulation of him in *Pride and Prejudice*, and taking in Austen's influences from other novelists.

Darcy's versatility, from Austen's clever use of culture, history and society, means that he has a capacity for growth. We are now excited by the places in which we find him. For example, in the form of the ice dance pairs competition at the South Korea 2018 Winter Olympic Games. There, the German couple Joti Polizoakis and Kavita Lorenz performed to Dario Marianelli's soundtrack from the 2005 *Pride and Prejudice* film. Lorenz was attired in a gauzy empire line dress as Elizabeth, and Polizoakis in an open-neck white shirt as Darcy.

Or in the BBC Radio 4 programme *More or Less*, in February 2018. This show asked questions about statistics and the accuracy of figures, and they put forward the challenge: 'Just how much is Mr Darcy's £10,000-a-year fortune worth today'? And the conclusion? In excess of £800,000, but it's the proportion that counts. In line with early nineteenth-century population statistics, Mr Darcy's wealth and property are proportionately worth more, as there were far fewer people in the country. So, he *would* be amongst the super-rich billionaire class. One of the richest men in the country, then and now.

Instantly recognisable, he appears across the ages as the Gaelic 'dark one', or the 'protector' from medieval Germanic and French romances. And like those heroes he can have troubled and conflicted feelings about love, honour and duty. Darcy is also the modern hero at the dawn of the nineteenth century, having to deal with the expectations that such a society imposes on him and informing others that come after him. We will see this played out in version after version of the character.

Marilyn Brant, the best-selling author of romantic fiction and Jane Austen fan fiction, offered reasons for this in a blog post for the website *Austen Variations* in April 2015 (https://austenvariations.com/holding-out-for-a-hero-by-marilyn-brant), when she discussed the fictional heroes that 'stay with us.' She praises Darcy's willingness to make sacrifices and love 'without hesitation – and without any expectations of credit.' She admires his strength of mind and character and how he goes about protecting Elizabeth, making plans in the background to rescue reputations. Thus, she enjoys using the Darcy-type in her fiction.

Tall and proud he might be, according to Kitty, but his name is now forever embedded in our collective imaginations. Historical novelist Amanda Grange recognised this when she recreated Darcy as *Mr Darcy – Vampyre* (2009). In an article for the *Historical Novel Society Magazine* (2010) she summed things up: '[Darcy] is over 200 years old and yet is forever young and handsome and still has the power to attract women…'.

Chapter 2

"What does Mr Darcy mean?"
The hero in the novel

Darcy could have maintained his unassailable social position and married someone within his social sphere. He does not need to marry. He does not need to compete, negotiate or compromise in the marriage market. However, he does choose, according to his heart – and he chooses Elizabeth.

Austen focused her narratives on the upper and middle classes, at a time when there was a great deal of fluidity in British society. Populations were in transition, moving from rural areas to the ever-expanding industrial centres around cities. To maintain a life in the countryside and select a place 'in town' for the season was a mark of high status. People were eager to manage such a lifestyle, and for a family like the Bennets, with five daughters, fortuitous marriages were the only hope.

A Woman's Place

This urgency to marry is the driving force behind Mrs Bennet's overactive tongue and excitement when she discovers that Jane has caught Mr Bingley's eye. But the mother's over-eager presumptions drive a wedge between Elizabeth and Darcy. He lives removed from this anxiety, but Mrs Bennet experiences it from day to day as she balances a household budget and lies awake at night, worrying about marriage prospects for five daughters and the threat of disinheritance. Privilege is everything.

Miss Bates, Mrs Norris, Jane Fairfax, Mrs Dashwood and her daughters and Mrs Smith of Westgate Buildings in Bath – across her novels, Austen's collection of female characters who live in reduced circumstances is wide-ranging. They live with the ever-present dangers, ambiguities and insecurity of widowhood, orphan status, spinsterhood, disinheritance, ill-health and disenfranchisement of different kinds. The Bennet girls are in this precarious position – a heartbeat away from losing their home to a male cousin.

So, life with a Mr Darcy was insurance for the whole family against ruin and disinheritance. Elizabeth's marriage is equivalent to marrying into aristocracy. Her social elevation is that emphatic. Her union means protection, and a buffer against their loss of Longbourn. No one need fear the future once she is mistress of Pemberley. Lydia knows this, and so she can pester for supplements and loans she will never pay back. It will also mean that Kitty and Mary are exposed to good prospects and influences.

Austen maintained this thorough exposition of social mobility in the world of her novels. In *Pride and Prejudice* she underlines Elizabeth's stratospheric rise in the marriage ranks when Lady Catherine visits Longbourn. Darcy's aunt must actually inconvenience herself with travel into Hertfordshire, so incensed is she at the rumours of Darcy's attachment. She is on an earnest mission to prove her point: Elizabeth is unworthy and will pollute the 'shades of Pemberley' because of her low birth and her sister's marriage to Wickham.

"...An Object of Some Interest..."

As we move through the novel, we can see Darcy's conduct towards Elizabeth and others changing, laying the foundations for his aunt's suspicions.

He is one type of man at the beginning: aloof and privileged, proud and seemingly self-possessed and only willing to condescend if he chooses to. Elizabeth feels a keen sense of the 'ridiculous' in her first encounters with him. Jane and Charlotte are the only people prepared to give him the benefit of the doubt. Charlotte sees that such privilege can be an impediment to happiness.

Elizabeth is so concerned with other people's business and the outcome of Bingley's attentions to Jane that '[She] was far from suspecting that she was herself becoming an object of some interest in the eyes of his friend.'

We then join the narrative of Darcy's interior dialogue and reasoning. This is something Austen used to create positions and counter-positions throughout the novel and enabled Colin Firth, as he admits, to find the fluidity and logic in the man's character.

'Mr Darcy had at first scarcely allowed her to be pretty; he had looked at her without admiration at the ball; and when they next met, he looked at her only to criticise. But no sooner had he made it clear to himself and his friends that she had hardly a good feature in her face, than he began to find it was rendered uncommonly intelligent by the beautiful expression of her dark eyes.'

Pride and Prejudice, Chapter 6, Vol. 1

The turning point in the first volume comes here. Austen shows Darcy's feelings for Elizabeth creeping up on him. She shows that he has a lack of worldliness and experience where relationships are concerned. Confused and contradictory feelings are at the root of his first impressions. Just as he denies any attraction, there it all is: intelligence, 'expression', a 'light and pleasing' figure and 'easy playfulness'. His helpless susceptibility to Elizabeth's personality and wit makes him more attractive to readers. Plus, to make him even more appealing, these feelings are unknown and unsuspected by Elizabeth.

For Elizabeth to attract the Master of Pemberley could be not be further from her mind, because ' ...to her he was only the man who made himself agreeable nowhere, and who had not thought her handsome enough to dance with.' The idea of a secret passion, harboured by a brooding, handsome man, is very exciting. The tension and interest begin to build.

Darcy's first, tentative steps towards being in her company take place soon after their first meeting and his slight towards her. At Sir William Lucas' evening reception, Darcy listens in on Elizabeth's conversation. She suspects he has an ulterior motive – to ridicule her. However, the resulting impression on the readers is sweet and endearing. We are susceptible to this earnest, awkward side to his courtship. Elizabeth is the object of his fascination, but he allows his pride to get in the way. It is also his lack of social graces, till now masked by his superior demeanour, that come to the reader's attention.

Elizabeth is alert and perceptive, but not that good at interpreting signals sent her way.

"What does Mr Darcy *mean*," she said to Charlotte, "by listening to my conversation with Colonel Forster?"

Charlotte, wisely, gives her response: "That is a question which only Mr Darcy can answer."

"But if he does it anymore I shall certainly let him know that I see what he is about. He has a satirical eye, and if I do not begin by being impertinent myself, I shall soon grow afraid of him."

Growing and Changing

Darcy's story arc is one of personal development and the growth of self-knowledge, so that he gains insight into his feelings and the conflicting emotions that so trouble him. But first he has to undergo an ordeal. Whilst considering his feelings for Elizabeth, after she has rejected his request for a dance at Sir William's evening party, he is 'accosted' and interrogated by the rival for his feelings, Miss Bingley. She tries to gain his attention by an appeal to his snobbery:

> "I can guess the subject of your reverie."
> "I should imagine not."
> "You are considering how insupportable it would be to pass many evenings in this manner – in such society; and indeed… What would I give to hear your strictures on them!"

Miss Bingley is accustomed to hearing Darcy's thoughts on society and manners. This time, however, a change has come over him.

" …My mind was more agreeably engaged. I have been meditating on the very great pleasure which a pair of fine eyes in the face of a pretty woman can bestow."

Pride and Prejudice, Chapter 6, Volume 1

Miss Bingley immediately responds with hope. Poor Miss Bingley. She needs to know *who* it is that has so bewitched him, and 'Mr Darcy replied with great intrepidity, "Miss Elizabeth Bennet."' This passage is Austen at her best, so much so, that we feel sympathy for Miss Bingley momentarily. Darcy admits the truth with great 'intrepidity' which makes this a point-of-no-return in the novel. Such a disclosure to Miss Bingley means Darcy will have to defend his choice. What has been said, cannot be unsaid.

This episode was an absolute gift for directors and screenwriters. It translated beautifully into dramatic form, with just the right beats for performance, in the 1995 adaptation. Miss Bingley (Anna Chancellor) flashes Darcy a wide-eyed, fluttering look before Colin Firth as Darcy dashes her hopes with the mention of Elizabeth Bennet. Caroline, however, will not be put off. At every opportunity after this she pursues the topic of Elizabeth and the Bennet family: "You will have a charming mother-in-law, indeed, and of course she will always be at Pemberley with you."

Darcy refuses to rise to her provocations, and so 'her wit flowed long'. Austen just tells us the outline, and it is left up to the reader to imagine Miss Bingley's venom. Austen liked to give us space to do this. Miss Bingley has already described '*these* people' with spiteful relish at the Meryton Assembly: 'The insipidity and yet the noise; the nothingness and yet the self-importance…!" We perceive the wide social gulf between Darcy's circle and Elizabeth's family and society. This makes their narrative all the more compelling.

The next time Darcy sees Elizabeth, she is even more vulnerable to snobbish criticism. She arrives at Netherfield with 'weary ankles, dirty stockings, and a face glowing with the warmth of exercise.' Austen contradicts the notion of conventional beauty. To be flushed with exertion was not an attractive quality in a woman of the early nineteenth century. Clean linens and a pale complexion were signs of privilege and rank. Working class women needed to perform menial tasks and walk out of necessity, without cover from the elements. Think of Mrs Bennet's excitement at the prospect of 'carriages' once Jane marries Mr Bingley.

Elizabeth *chose* to walk to Netherfield and arrive in this unseemly condition. Bingley, Miss Bingley, the Hursts and Darcy receive her in a polite fashion – at least to her face. Tension crackles in the room. Austen reveals the thoughts of those present, one by one. Thanks to Austen's free indirect prose style it is as though she is in the room with them and mediating those thoughts to us. She lets the reader in on their feelings.

Bingley is 'pure good humour and kindness.' Miss Bingley and her sister make their impressions of Elizabeth's undignified entrance very plain, Mr Hurst, by contrast 'was thinking only of his breakfast.' Darcy, significantly, *says* nothing at first. Austen offers up, instead, his conflicted, internal emotions: '…divided between admiration of the brilliancy which exercise had given to her complexion, and doubt as to the occasion's justifying her coming so far alone.'

Town Versus Country

Miss Bingley closely monitors Darcy and Elizabeth during the Netherfield episode. She is alert to his every mood and reactions to their house guest. She aims her attacks at 'Eliza', and Darcy must endure them: '[Elizabeth's] manners were pronounced to be very bad indeed, a mixture of pride and impertinence; she had no conversation, no style, no beauty.' This is a great test for Darcy. Caroline draws an admission from him that he would find Elizabeth's 'exhibition' of behaviour unacceptable in his sister, Georgiana. The word 'exhibition' is calculated to drill into his sensibilities. Miss Bingley piles up layers of blame and insult, 'her wit flowed' again:

"To walk three miles, or four miles, or five miles, or whatever it is, above her ankles in dirt, and alone, quite alone! What could she mean by it? It seems to me to show an abominable sort of conceited independence, a most country-town indifference to decorum."

Pride and Prejudice, Chapter 8, Vol. 1

Here, she highlights the difference between town and country – *her* metropolitan mindset versus 'Miss Eliza Bennet's' rustic lack of decorum. What can one expect from such a bumpkin as Miss 'Eliza'? Miss Bingley loves to use this over-familiar contraction of her rival's name. Darcy manages to silence her, however, with a reiteration of his admiration for Elizabeth's 'fine eyes' – 'brightened by the exercise.'

The Bingley/Hurst/Darcy circle have been used to demolishing others with their drawing-room conversation. Darcy has a hard time resisting their snobbery.

'"I think I have heard you say, that their uncle is an attorney at Meryton."

"Yes; and they have another who lives somewhere near Cheapside."

"This is capital," added her sister, and they both laughed heartily.'

Bingley finds this cruel, and says so, but Darcy promptly subscribes to this view.

"If they had uncles to fill all Cheapside," cried Bingley, "it would not make them one jot less agreeable."

"But it must very materially lessen their chance of marrying men of any consideration in the world," replied Darcy.

Pride and Prejudice, Chapter 8, Volume 1

Irony is heaped upon irony as Darcy falls deeper in love with Elizabeth.

At Netherfield, Elizabeth is Cinderella to Miss Bingley and Mrs Hurst as the ugly sisters. Eventually, they draw Darcy out on his views about 'accomplished' women. He talks about the 'capacity', 'taste', 'application' and 'elegance' of the truly accomplished woman. Elizabeth sees this as simply disparaging herself, and others who do not meet that level. He tries to remedy how she interprets his words, making a hasty, clumsy comment about the 'improvement of [the] mind by extensive reading.' Any attempt at praising Elizabeth is lost, however, in the 'decorum' of the snide inflections of drawing-room conversations.

Austen embeds irony in these examples of social discourse and mannered exchanges. In seeking to belittle Elizabeth, Caroline Bingley only affords Darcy more opportunities to compliment her. There are some turning points here. Darcy is forced to rethink his definitions: what *are* manners and socially superior modes of behaviour? Mr Darcy has to ask himself, what he *means*. He has to question everything. In trying to make Elizabeth feel intimidated and undermined, Caroline and Mrs Hurst only reveal their own crassness and elevate the visitor in Darcy's estimation.

When Elizabeth leaves the room, Caroline pronounces upon her 'paltry device(s)' and 'mean art(s)' to gain the attention of men. The tension in the Netherfield salon mounts. Darcy is the immensely valuable prize that she competes for, and she can feel her chance with him slipping away, so Miss Bingley resorts to more and more desperate measures, until Darcy has to speak up. The cracks in his façade start to show in order to silence Elizabeth's detractor: " ...there is a meanness in all the arts which ladies sometimes condescend to employ for captivation. Whatever bears affinity to cunning is despicable."

Well, that certainly told *her*.

Darcy is a master of the put-down and closes the door firmly on Caroline's hope that she might secure him. This time at Netherfield is a time of trial for the future lovers. Darcy realises that Elizabeth could be an eligible match, but then Austen punctures this with a perfectly-timed visit from Mrs Bennet and her other three daughters.

The mother weighs in vociferously to the conversation and immediately clashes with Darcy. She pushes things further and is then 'offended by his manner of mentioning a country neighbourhood'. This is a wonderfully witty exchange, about class consciousness and the town and country divide, similar to Caroline Bingley's remarks about Elizabeth's 'country-town indifference to decorum'.

The Mother-in-Law Problem

The voluble, incautious Mrs Bennet versus the dour Mr Darcy – a debate that reintroduces all the doubts into Darcy's mind. Mrs Bennet is a whirlwind that impacts on all the society around her and represents the ultimate test for Darcy. Her mother's comments cause Elizabeth to blush, and Miss Bingley homes in on her discomfort, sensing a victory. She throws an 'expressive smile' in Darcy's direction. This serves to reinforce her earlier remarks about the 'nothingness' of such as the Bennets.

Mrs Bennet, however, runs on with her chatter. In Darcy's eyes she might be crass and outspoken, but she is not snide or spiteful. She indulges in her customary bragging about such things as keeping a cook. But however vulgar, gossipy or blunt she might be, we quickly recognise that Austen is drawing our attention to *relative* status and manners. Darcy has witnessed the Netherfield ladies taking *pleasure* in their superiority over others, and for the first time it troubles him. He is still battling with his pride by the end of the Netherfield episode.

Darcy is on a steep learning curve throughout the novel. His aloofness and disdain for his social inferiors have carried him through life, thus far. However, the agents of change are at work on him, and he finds that he needs to figure out how to gain the approval and love of someone he really values.

Mrs Bennet, Kitty and Lydia test his patience, constancy and maturity. Mary tests others with her piano recitals. The two youngest Bennets blurt out their wish that Bingley hold a ball at Netherfield. When they leave, Miss Bingley and her sister try to draw Darcy out again on the subject of the Bennets' vulgarity, but 'he could not be prevailed on to join in their censure of [Elizabeth or her relations' behaviour], in spite of all Miss Bingley's witticisms on fine eyes.'

Darcy tries to find opportunities to engage with Elizabeth, but in so doing he becomes critical of Bingley. Elizabeth's sense of fairness sees her leap to his defence. She fearlessly tackles Darcy on his opinions and challenges his point of view, clearly something he is not used to. Bingley admits, in front of the company, that he is afraid of Darcy:

" …if Darcy were not such a great tall fellow, in comparison with myself, I should not pay him half so much deference. I declare I do not know a more awful object than Darcy… at his own house especially, of a Sunday evening when he has nothing to do."

Pride and Prejudice, Chapter 10, Vol. 1

Darcy is tall and quite scary. The popular archetype that has emerged from Austen's original is additionally based on prevailing types of the hero from history, poetry, drama and politics. That Darcy was a fashionably tall person, possibly a dandy of a gentleman, with a powerful physical presence, means that he could dominate the room. He appeared in the final novel of 1813 as the product of years of meticulous planning and composition. Austen had a complete draft of *First Impressions* in 1796–97 and then revised it over the intervening years until 1811, when a completed draft of *Pride and Prejudice* went forward for publication.

The Man Alone

The Romantic movement of poetry, art, performance and philosophy characterises the period of Austen's literary development. She was a contemporary of the poet George Gordon, Lord Byron (1788–1824), the 'English milord' as he was known in Europe, who was supposedly 'mad, bad, and dangerous to know' as one of his many lovers, Lady Caroline

Lamb, allegedly said of him. The reputation ascribed to him has lived on, long past the considerable popularity of his works. He was instrumental in the creation of the archetypal tormented, mad and maddening Romantic poet.

Whilst Byron was clearly complicit in generating this celebrity reputation, he was also a skilled and dedicated poet whose output included many long narrative poems. He could articulate the vision in his verse. Byron embarked on his Grand Tour in 1811, and on his return published the autobiographically inspired work *Childe Harold's Pilgrimage* followed by his series of *Turkish Tales* in 1813. These included *The Bride of Abydos*, *The Giaour* and *The Corsair*.

Byron's poems were considered scandalous, and he became the most famous poet of the Movement, as well as part of the same social set as the Prince Regent and Beau Brummell. In *This Charming Man*, Byron and Brummell are even shown as lovers. Byron was known for his passions and fascinations with many different men and women.

So, as contemporaries, Austen and Byron could not have been more different. However, they were both influenced by theatre, melodrama, comedy of manners and Gothic tales of danger and threat. They created heroes that were equally representative of the zeitgeist.

In *The Corsair*, the hero Conrad the pirate is comparable to Darcy, being 'Scarce seen to smile, and seldom heard to sigh'.

The unsmiling, difficult and *lonely* hero in Byron's imagination became a dangerous, threatening and somewhat sinister character. He is the product of the revolutionary and early industrial age – a stateless, rootless man of determination and cynicism.

> 'Lone, wild, and strange, he stood alike exempt
> From all affection and from all contempt.'
>
> The Corsair, Canto 1, XII

What came to be known as the 'Byronic' hero of the nineteenth century emerged from this portrayal of complex, thoughtful and troubled souls. The origins are in Shakespeare with *Hamlet* and in the German Romantic tradition from myth and folklore, and such modern works as Johann Goethe's *Werther* (1774). This was hugely influential on the English Romantic movement and directly influenced Byron's poetry, Jane Austen's novels and later, the novels of Emily Brontë.

Werther is the troubled and sensitive artist-hero. His story is told in the form of letters to a friend. Austen was familiar with this epistolary form; the second half of *Pride and Prejudice* is dense with written correspondence that conveys information and enables deep disclosure, from Darcy above all. It is *the* means by which he can properly articulate his feelings.

Instead of an artist, a prince, a buccaneer or a 'mad, bad' poet, Austen used a member of the landed English gentry as the difficult, troubled young man, closed off from his feelings. He has the tendency to become an intimidating 'awful object', according to Bingley, when he is bored. Here, Austen gestures towards a description of Darcy that resonates with Goethe or Byron, but as is her custom, she includes something of a parody. Bingley draws attention to the bored, difficult Darcy rattling about in his enormous stately home on a Sunday afternoon. He is an intimidating, awful creature in breeches, an image which goes some way to justifying Elizabeth's finding him 'ridiculous'. Darcy's seriousness, Bingley's description and Austen's tone combine to send up the character. Like Sheridan's Faulkland in *The Rivals* with his horror at 'jigs and reels', Darcy's earnest disapproval is easily mocked. Therefore, by contrast, Elizabeth's 'lightness' appears all the more attractive to him. She is the light and he is the shade in their romance.

When Bingley describes his friend as that 'awful object' – although it is done with humour and affection – Elizabeth 'thought she could perceive that [Darcy] was rather offended; and therefore, checked her laugh.' This is a moment when *she* learns to appreciate *his* mood and decides against even light-hearted mockery. She notices 'how frequently Mr Darcy's eyes were fixed on her.' What would it mean, she asks, to 'be an object of admiration to so great a man…?' A connection forms between them.

Austen then surprises the reader – and Elizabeth – when Miss Bingley 'varied the charm of her evening playing by a lively Scotch air.' It's those 'jigs and reels' again. Did Miss Bingley do it on purpose to see Darcy's reaction? In contrast to Sir William's soiree, this time,' ...Mr Darcy, drawing near Elizabeth, said to her – "Do you not feel a great inclination, Miss Bennet, to seize such an opportunity of dancing a reel?"'

This raises the tension in the room. The 'electricity' crackles between them. Mr Darcy, the man who thinks dancing is 'savage', has a spur of the moment 'inclination' to dance a reel, of all things! This is a milestone of change in his behaviour. Elizabeth refuses, but with such 'a mixture of sweetness and archness in her manner' that 'Darcy had never been so bewitched by any woman as he was by her.' He is lost, as Elizabeth has probably forgiven him now for the slight at the Meryton Assembly, and Miss Bingley's hopes are dashed forever.

The Inner Struggle

Darcy's struggle in the novel is one of trying to resist the charms of a woman of inferior birth and status. At times he grows confident in his power to succeed, only to find it diminish again. This part of the story is Darcy's 'bildungsroman', his narrative of growth – from inexperience to maturity, from ignorance to knowledge. This was a mainstay of the eighteenth century, with Goethe's *Werther*, Voltaire's *Candide* (1759), and Laurence Stern's *Life and Opinions of Tristram Shandy, Gentleman* (1759). All were hugely popular, fashionable and influential, and some had an inflammatory effect on society.

The 'bildungsroman' describes the coming-of-age exploration of the world, with title characters that experience an education and in particular a search – for emotional authenticity, real values and true relationships. Henry Fielding, with *Tom Jones* (1749) – one of Austen's favourites – and Laurence Stern, for example, examined what it meant to be a gentleman in the modern Enlightenment Age. Was it achieved by birth or behaviour?

Darcy's story, in this light, is one of development and education. We can compare his attitudes and behaviour at the outset of the story, with reference to dancing and accomplishments for example, with the man he becomes by the end. No longer as anxious or tongue-tied, proud or dismissive, he is able to approach Mr Bennet in the inner sanctum of his library to ask for Elizabeth's hand. He remains handsome and rich, but shows he is capable of growth and change and braving social disapproval, particularly from his aunt. Elizabeth is good for him. Some of her defiance has rubbed off on him, and she has helped him to confront and admit to his flaws and do something about them. Their time together at Rosings and Hunsford has been crucial to this, of course.

Central to the story's climax is the proposal he makes to her at the home of Charlotte and Mr Collins. Elizabeth is in the little sitting room that her best friend uses as a place of sanctuary from her husband and the overbearing influence of Darcy's aunt Lady Catherine de Bourgh. Into this place of female privacy strides Darcy.

Austen entertains us by having him visit a few times, and 'he frequently sat there ten minutes together without opening his lips.' It is very amusing to chart this steady conquest of nerves as he bounces back and forth between Rosings and the Hunsford parsonage. He makes small talk and falls back on that social staple of enquiring after the health of Elizabeth's family. Charlotte interrupts one of these stilted exchanges and says afterwards: "My dear Elizabeth, he must be in love with you, or he would never have called on us in this familiar way."

Charlotte Collins helpfully becomes our lead in the novel's narrative and the subtext of the characters' feelings:

'Mrs Collins knew not what to make of him... she would like to have believed this change the effect of love, and the object of that love, her friend Eliza, she set herself seriously to work to find it out.'

Pride and Prejudice, Chapter 9, Vol. II

At the same time, Darcy's cousin Colonel Fitzwilliam is showing 'pleasantness' to Elizabeth. He clearly admires her, and we might see the possibility of her making a match with him. Charlotte considers it and fantasises about a 'planned' marriage. However, amusingly, she weighs up the 'advantages' between the two wealthy cousins. She ponders that 'to counterbalance' the advantages of the Colonel, 'Mr Darcy had considerable patronage in the church.' Ever pragmatic, Charlotte looks out for *her* family's future.

Mr Darcy is the most powerful force in his family. Colonel Fitzwilliam must be 'at his [cousin's] disposal' for travel arrangements and family 'business'. Elizabeth recognises the impact Darcy has on those around him: "I do not know anybody who seems more to enjoy the power of doing what he likes than Mr Darcy." She also educates Colonel Fitzwilliam about the relative degrees of social power and agency. He complains about 'self-denial and dependence' to which Elizabeth responds in her amused and candid fashion: "Now, seriously, what have you ever known of self-denial and dependence? When you have been prevented by want of money from going wherever you chose, or procuring anything you had a fancy for?" One of Elizabeth Bennet's functions in the novel is to educate the Fitzwilliam and Darcy cousins on the *real* meaning of 'dependence and self-denial'.

In return, Colonel Fitzwilliam relates to Elizabeth the actions that Darcy undertook to rescue Bingley from a huge mistake (poor Jane): "I understood that there were some very strong objections against the lady." He says this whilst finding her sister the most charming and pleasant of company. Elizabeth, stunned and wounded, feels her indignation rising at Darcy and his 'interference' in her sister's life. Her 'agitation and tears' on that subject cause her to feel a headache coming on, and so she retires to Charlotte's sitting room.

Anxiety, indignation and antagonism grow in Elizabeth's breast. Darcy is more and more on her mind. She muses on Jane's letters that reveal how the Bingley family has snubbed her. It is from this point in the novel that letters play a bigger and bigger role in the narrative. Austen positions her characters to create the maximum drama. Into this tense situation Darcy intrudes once more, to Elizabeth's astonishment as she seeks some sanctuary in Charlotte's sitting room.

Within a few short sentences Austen moves the novel into its climactic scene. Once Darcy has declared his feelings there is no going back. This declaration comes as a surprise to Elizabeth and the first-time reader. Perhaps the reader – along with Charlotte – could have discerned this approach, but it is the intensity of his feelings that startle both the reader and the heroine:

"In vain have I struggled. It will not do. My feelings will not be repressed. You must allow me to tell you how ardently I admire and love you."

Pride and Prejudice, Chapter 11, Volume 2

Here we have it: the 'ardent' admiration and love; a struggle that has required all his strength but against which he is helpless. Darcy is compelled to make the forthright announcement that his feelings will not be repressed any longer.

"*You must allow me to tell you how ardently I admire and love you.*"

C E Brock illustration, 1895

Austen gets it just right. This is the internal struggle that the hero has had to undergo, with only the occasional glimmer in the free indirect narrative, to indicate the intensity of it. Now, the full force of this comes across and offers a rationale as to why Darcy is such a popular, enduring character. This is why the 'mania' for him is justified. It is Austen's winning formula of literary and romantic alchemy, lightning in a bottle: the perfect appeal to the widest possible audience for the longest time.

Pride Comes Before a Fall

Darcy's passionate announcement is the only element of direct speech that Austen gives to him in this exchange as part of his sudden proposal. The rest is reported speech. The impact is with the first words and the short, clipped sentences: "In vain have I struggled. It will not do." The rest of the declaration descends, unfortunately, into a diatribe on 'difference', 'inferiority' and 'pride'. He completely ruins it after a very promising beginning. First genuine feeling, and then – pride takes over. We do not need to hear the detail of this, we can focus on the first earnest expression of love, instead.

Many of Austen's heroes are not known, of course, for the security and certainty of their first choices for matrimony and their wisdom over romantic dalliances. The novels are peppered with their mistakes, blunders and clumsiness with relationships.

Edward Ferrars, in *Sense and Sensibility*, must rectify his impulsive attachment to Lucy Steele. His brother's passion comes to his rescue and saves him from this entanglement, so that he is free to declare his love for Elinor Dashwood. Those Ferrars brothers are incurable romantics. Willoughby, by contrast, is more manipulative and cruelly raises and then dashes Marianne's hopes. In *Emma*, the elusive Frank Churchill maintains an elaborate smokescreen to disguise his attachment to Jane Fairfax. This causes Emma to misunderstand his intentions towards her. Edmund Bertram, in *Mansfield Park*, falls hard for the allure of Mary Crawford until he has to admit that she does not have the makings of a clergyman's wife. It comes as no surprise, therefore, that Darcy's first proposal is met with rejection.

Neither he nor Elizabeth holds back in their sarcasm and disdain for one another. There could not be a worse beginning to any relationship. However, Darcy, like Captain Wentworth in *Persuasion*, is constant. In the sitting room at Hunsford, Austen shows her skill at portraying the escalation of conflict. When direct speech resumes, Elizabeth accuses Darcy of the very worst fault imaginable. The argument escalates to become more and more personal and he cannot believe he is accused of lacking gentlemanly manners and of possessing: 'arrogance,… conceit, and… selfish disdain of the feelings of others…'. She declares: ' …I had not known you a month before I felt that you were the last man in the world I could ever be prevailed upon to marry.'

Elizabeth's reply is a detailed demolition of Darcy's treatment of her, and the wider society of Meryton. Austen allows Elizabeth to run on this time. Her astonishment at the revelation of Darcy's feelings, and her reaction to him, lasts all night and well into her walk the next day. We remain with Elizabeth and the 'tumult of her mind'.

We are left to guess how Darcy has been feeling, until he approaches her with: "Will you do me the honour of reading that letter?" And then he is gone. Austen provides us with his explanation, as composed overnight. It is his commentary of events and an exposition of his internal conflict. This harks back to influences from the eighteenth-century writers of the epistolary novel, such as Samuel Richardson. The opportunity to reflect and compose an explanation is a useful one for elaborating on characters' motives and for moving action forwards. It also echoes William Wordsworth's principle for composition in poetry, 'emotion recollected in tranquillity…' from his Preface to the *Lyrical Ballads* (1800).

Rags-to-Riches and Virtue Rewarded

Darcy's letter, as it turns out, is emotional, heart-felt, honest and detailed. His frank disclosure encourages a turning point. It was painful for him to reveal the truth about his sister and

Wickham. It is equally painful for Elizabeth to read, because of the disappointment she feels for Jane. They are equally devoted to their closest siblings. The letter signals the start of the shift in their relationship. From this point on they are drawn closer together even when apart. Their futures are intertwined. The discussion about the art of letter-writing that took place at Netherfield, Austen shows, pays off for Darcy in the long run.

Elizabeth's feelings begin to reform, and Austen brilliantly describes and dramatises the process of their growing relationship in the rest of the novel. The steady arc of their love is one of the masterpiece achievements in her prose. The letter is the admission of prejudice – towards Jane and the Bennets – and an explanation of his justifiable dislike and distrust of Wickham. Both Elizabeth's and Darcy's characters are re-shaped during the ensuing chapters. Theirs is a resounding narrative of growth, change and the discovery of romantic compatibility.

Austen, amongst numerous influences, found the famed serial novels of Samuel Richardson to be immensely helpful for her compositions. In *Pamela; Or, Virtue Rewarded* (1740) the low-born, young (she is only fifteen at the time) servant is the target of her employer, 'Mr B'. At the centre of this scandalous and ground-breaking novel is his attempt to control and rape her. Pamela, in her 'virtue', and as a departure from the expected scenario, manages to resist him and thus, thanks to her good character, she has a powerful effect on him. He realises that she is worth more and decides to make her his wife. 'Mr B' admits that she is superior in character to him.

In the second volume of *Pamela* her story develops. She becomes the wife of a gentleman and shows her resilience and strength of character in the face of snobbery and derision from her husband's class. She has to acclimatise to this new world. The novel had a huge impact on the public, prompting many imitations and sparking a fashionable 'mania' for all things 'Pamela'. It was a detailed novel of character and relationships, creating the model for other works to come. Austen used this 'rags-to-riches', Cinderella-type framework in *Pride and Prejudice*.

The tale of Cinderella was a familiar narrative popularised by Charles Perrault. He published a refinement of the folktale, *Cinderella; Or, The Little Glass Slipper*, which was translated into English in 1729. Austen lavished more detail on her characters and more emotional insight into her expansion of the fairy-tale framework in a modern novel. Perrault, to Richardson, to Austen – the story developed and furthered the critique of the marriage contract in society. Prince Charming, to the dubious 'Mr B', and on to the courageous Darcy. But Darcy also occupies the subordinate role, of the lover who is spurned and then has to redeem himself. This exhibits Austen's superior take on the narrative and demonstrates the enduring effectiveness of her hero.

As a young woman of twenty, Austen committed to the subscription scheme in support of the publication of Frances Burney's new novel *Camilla* (1796). In what Jocelyn Harris ('Persuasions Online', Jane Austen Society of North America, Winter 2014) aptly called an 'early form of crowd sourcing', Burney looked to her fans, including Austen and her circle of friends, to pledge a guinea apiece to get her new four-volume novel out.

Camilla, like Burney's earlier *Cecilia* (1782), is about the romantic trials and matrimonial concerns of a group of young people. Also, in *Evelina* (1778) Burney returned to the comic romance of an outsider heroine who is raised up and must shop, dress and learn how to conduct herself according to upper class social rules. It is subtitled *The History of a Young Lady's Entrance into the World*, and on making this entrance, Evelina immediately catches the eyes of both the gallant Lord Orville and the caddish baronet Sir Clement Willoughby. No doubt Austen recalled this Willoughby when naming Marianne's duplicitous suitor in *Sense and Sensibility*. Early in the story Orville and Evelina share a dance, during which time they lay the foundations for their romance.

As a result of the influences of Burney, Richardson and Sheridan, Austen used the potential of romantic rivalry to explore the comic possibilities of manners and public conduct. From Burney, Austen also took the 'sentimental' tradition of literature and imprinted her particular mark on it.

The sentimental novel involved the union of satire with moral lessons to produce deep feeling in the readers. In this tradition, the heroine is often caught in a tangle between two men that she has feelings for, and she must discover which one is worthy to be a suitor. It often involves some risk and moral threat to her virtue. This is Elizabeth's situation in *Pride and Prejudice*, when she becomes concerned with Wickham's plight at Darcy's expense.

The 'serpent in the garden' of these moral tales is usually in the form of a young man seeking to seduce an innocent young woman out in the world. It is part of his amusement to systematically seduce her, strip her of fortune and reputation and abandon her. Chancers, rakes and fortune hunters abound in the sentimental novel and in Austen's works.

Austen showed in *Sense and Sensibility* and *Pride and Prejudice* the distressing and devastating consequences of seduction and elopements. When Darcy frustrates Wickham's plan with Georgiana, he shifts his focus to another county and targets Lydia. Darcy then has to make it his mission to combat Wickham, because of his ruinous and painful impact on different families. The abandoned, 'fallen' young woman (aged perhaps no more than fourteen) even if an heiress, had nowhere to turn and risked poverty and prostitution. Drama, romance, and a satisfying resolution of 'virtue rewarded' and true love gained, gave Austen's readers the sought-for ending.

Austen built upon the established sentimental tradition and used the foundation created by other novelists to reach her readers. She also borrowed references directly from them. For example, the dual structure of *Pride and Prejudice* comes straight from Burney, inspired by Dr Lyster in *Cecilia* with: "The whole of this unfortunate business… has been the result of *Pride and Prejudice*." Not only that, in *Cecilia* we meet Lady Margaret Monckton and her scheming companion, Miss Bennet.

A World of Threat and Anxiety

To Austen's influences, Burney, Richardson and Sheridan, we must add Ann Radcliffe – *Mrs* Radcliffe. She was perhaps the most important role model and gave Austen a template for both her writing and her career as a female novelist. So important was this influence that in the film *Becoming Jane* (2007), which was based on the 2003 critical biography Becoming Jane Austen by Jon Hunter Spence, a 'What if?' scenario was dedicated to a meeting between Jane (played by Anne Hathaway) and the reclusive Radcliffe (Helen McCrory). There is no evidence that they actually did meet in real life. In this fictional sequence, McCrory's Radcliffe is a slightly dreamy, distracted woman. She is not quite in touch with reality, it seems. Perhaps this is the price you pay as a novelist of the intense Gothic, romantic school?

Hathaway's Jane is a passionate fangirl who meets her idol and wants to know how she does it. She comes away slightly bemused and even disappointed. Never meet your heroes. Screenwriters Kevin Hood and Sarah Williams, and director Julian Jarrold, represent with this imagined scene the steep learning curve Jane Austen engaged in as a writer throughout her twenties. They show her transition from avid reader and idealistic fan to capable, inspired and mature artist.

If Burney gives Austen a model for rags-to-riches romantic comedy and Sheridan provides a model for social satire, dialogue and irony, then Radcliffe cemented the template of the brooding, difficult, tortured hero. There are brooding types and then there are Radcliffe's brooding types. She delivered on this every time. In *The Romance of the Forest* (1791), Louis de la Motte is a young soldier who deserts his regiment and meets the beautiful Adeline. He pines with unrequited love for her. She is in love with the gallant Theodore, the estranged son of a nobleman, who she nurses back to health in a remote inn. Both young men risk their lives, repeatedly, for the foundling Adeline, as they protect her from the evil machinations of the sinister Marquis de Montalt. In Radcliffe's most critically acclaimed work, The *Italian* (1797), she created Vincentio and Ellena, the tormented couple who are hounded by the villain Schedoni. Vincentio must go to great lengths to retrieve Ellena from the series of convents in which she is imprisoned by her scheming uncle the Count di Marinella, disguised as the monk Father Schedoni. Vincentio is torn between his family honour and love for the low-born Ellena. He remains constant, however, until she is proven to be of noble blood. The villains in these tales represent a type that Byron found useful in his poems, whose jealousy, greed and corruption drive the action.

Radcliffe's novels represent a pinnacle of the Gothic movement. The Gothic in literature and drama involves the supernatural – forms, creatures and forces – bleeding into everyday life. The cracks in reality open, and other-worldly things enter. The forms these things take vary according to the different social anxieties and ills at the time of writing. It might be something foreign, diseased, infectious and sinister, or it might be something changed, transformed, disguised or metamorphosed: a man into a wolf, or an evil foreign interloper preying on innocent young flesh. We are presented with extended metaphor for lust, vengeance and invasion.

Austen used this Gothic sensibility as a driving force for Catherine Morland's imagination in *Northanger Abbey*. The Gothic also informs the real-world threats and jeopardy for young women in *Pride and Prejudice*. It translates into the story in the form of snobbery, seduction and disinheritance. Threats hang over the Bennet sisters, and this makes Darcy all the more useful as a hero. He is mobile, active and knows the ways of the world. The Gothic form influences the resolution of Darcy and Elizabeth. It helps create miraculous confluences of events, the product of fateful and fortunate coincidences that render the conclusion all the more powerful.

When she encounters Darcy at Pemberley, the hero in his home environment, this marks the start of their redemption and the confluence of their pathways towards one another. Elizabeth shows how comfortable and secure she is with her Aunt and Uncle Gardiner. She demonstrates her sympathy and affinity for Georgiana – the former target of Wickham's cruel fortune-hunting. The introduction to Pemberley transforms Elizabeth and offers a deeper insight into Darcy's nature.

The hero is in harmony with his home estate and shown at his best. Elizabeth recognises that this could have been her life. Had she accepted him, she would have been mistress of this grand estate. He offered that up, and she refused.

One of the things that make Austen's characterisation so entertaining is the time she devotes, after Darcy's proposal, to Elizabeth to allow contemplation of her decision and realise what she has refused. She admits as much, though. When Darcy questions her about the moment she realised her feelings for him, she tells him it was when she first saw his grounds at Pemberley. Halfway through the action he is refused, and so the two must work their way back towards this resolution. It creates a deeper, mature, more abiding sense of their relationship. The fairy-tale basis diminishes, and a modern novel of social and psychological insight emerges.

Elizabeth, the well-travelled heroine, makes her way into Darcy's territory and finds to her astonishment that a real home awaits her. In his own home he is a kinder, more charming man and a much more gracious host than she dared to imagine, or than Bingley led her to believe back in Volume 1. The Gardiners – the very 'Cheapside' relatives so disparaged at Netherfield – are treated as honoured guests. Prejudicial attitudes are shown to be what they are: hollow and meaningless. Family pride is superficial unless accompanied by love and loyalty. Darcy, Elizabeth, Georgiana and Aunt and Uncle Gardiner form a neat, contented family party. A prospect of things to come, we hope.

A Bright Future

This visit is the springboard for the union of the couple, as it shows the flipside of their characters, based on kindness and familial attachments. However, like all good novels of the period, their love must be put to the test once more. Lydia obliges. The time at Pemberley, comprised of pleasant dinners, musical evenings, conversation and fishing, is cut short with the arrival of another letter.

The scandal with Wickham unfolds, and Elizabeth believes that all is lost. This lowest ebb, however, sees Darcy spring into action. He is motivated and 'turns' to show a further aspect to his personality. This is not sinister or Gothic, rather it shows his determination and devotion. His response to the scandal is that of a gallant hero, despite – in fact because of – his unrequited love. Later, he explains to Elizabeth why he did so many favours for Lydia, the Bennet family and his enemy Wickham, once she has discovered what happened:

> "'If you will thank me,' he replied, 'let it be for yourself alone. That the wish of giving happiness to you, might add force to the other inducements which led me on, I shall not attempt to deny. But your family owe me nothing. Much as I respect them, I believe, I thought only of you.'"
>
> *Pride and Prejudice*, Chapter 16, Vol. IV

The world suddenly opens up for Elizabeth, and the sun breaks through the clouds – a golden future awaits her. Darcy has come through for her, rescued her whole family, and he is more in love with her than ever.

Darcy's ability to change his views, modify his opinions – for example, developing respect for the Bennet family – and learn from his mistakes have powerfully impressed readers for the past 200 years. He grows and transforms before our eyes. He is reinvented throughout the course of the narrative into an ideal form of a man.

At the outset, his flaws are evident and examined in excruciating detail by Mrs Bennet especially. These are steadily corrected as he grows in affection for Elizabeth. For example, he realises that his aunt, Lady Catherine, is just as vulgar and outspoken as Mrs Bennet can be, and actually crueller in her derision and manipulation of others, and her boastfulness. She can, for example, dismiss Mrs Bennet in the woman's own home. Just because you are rich and have a title does not automatically make you gracious.

Darcy learns that being too proud to divulge family secrets can jeopardise other, innocent, people. He comes to appreciate that pride in one's heritage, status and achievements must be tempered with some modesty, humility and love. Otherwise, happiness is liable to elude one.

Happiness and contentment are the outcome for the eldest Bennet girls and their suitors – the 'deserving' couples. And Darcy, in this manifestation, is the epitome of male attractiveness and fictional romantic heroism. He appeared in Austen's novel at a crucial cultural intersection in the early years of the nineteenth century. She created a great model, poised to take on the new century. The modern, golden age period of novel-writing in the nineteenth century witnessed a proliferation of this type of hero.

She drew upon different influences to create a character that works brilliantly as he challenges and entertains the reader.

Taking some of the best elements of the intrigue, secrecy and coincidence from Gothic tales, Austen set about elevating the social and romantic novel. Darcy is a robust, mobile, effective figure. He is a fashionable society gentleman who presents as aloof and difficult, but who can nonetheless feel intensely and commit those feelings to paper.

Ultimately, Darcy comes across as charming, endearing and inadvertently amusing. His response to Elizabeth's change of heart at the end of their story is adorable, especially after her accusation of his lack of gentlemanly behaviour – that still really smarts. But he learned to meet that with constancy and passion, qualities that makes him enduringly popular in the original novel.

"You are too generous to trifle with me. If your feelings are still what they were last April, tell me so at once. My affections and wishes are unchanged but one word from you will silence me on the subject forever."

Chapter 3

'The man of family pride': Darcy's descendants in the nineteenth century

'Why do you like Miss Austen so very much?'

Charlotte Brontë (1816–1855) had mixed feelings about Jane Austen and her novels. Although only a couple of decades separate their writing careers in the first half of the nineteenth century, their voices could not be more at odds with one another. Brontë remained unconvinced by Austen. She was not the only one in the decades after Austen's death to feel this way, either. Appreciation of the 'Lady' author of *Pride and Prejudice* was by no means universal. At the outset, reception of Austen's novels from many quarters were concerned with different qualities and features of her writing.

The *British Critic* magazine, for example, was a conservative High Church review, founded in reaction to French

Republican politics. In 1811, it was taken on by proprietors Joshua Watson and HH Norris, who were part of the High Church pressure group with the worthy, rather wordy, title of the Hackney Phalanx for the Preservation of Anglican Orthodoxy. Their magazine reflected this worthiness and was in the position, in 1813, to review *Pride and Prejudice*.

The *Critic* deemed the novel a success but was not overly forthcoming with its praise. The conservative tone extended throughout the reflections and demonstrated the fact that the editorial policy encouraged literature of an improving type, with a clear moral message. A novel, they reckoned, had a job to do. The anonymous reviewer had 'perused' the novel with 'much satisfaction and amusement,' and felt sure that with such encouragement and a 'successful circulation' the author would be induced towards 'similar exertions'. We are all certainly very glad that Austen took this as encouragement.

Pride and Prejudice in the Nineteenth Century: Austen's Harmony and Pace

Readers of the early nineteenth-century novel had an unprecedented variety of material available. The response of reviewers to *Pride and Prejudice* is in part thanks to the extent to which Austen modified her use of drama and strong emotion, in contrast to the highly-charged works of the eighteenth to nine-teenth century 'sentimental' tradition. These include works by her favourites, Samuel Richardson (with *Clarissa*, 1748) and Ann Radcliffe. Austen's prose is controlled. Her work offered something of a welcome change from what had been the prevailing fashion in writing for many decades, to produce novels of 'feeling'.

Alternatively, some of the negative criticism levelled at Austen drew attention to this 'simplicity' and scarcity of emotion and her lack of 'variety'. She had, according to some reviewers, a shortage of characters in her 'dramatis personae'. This relatively economical use of characters, focusing on a limited social circle, is one of the features of her writing for which she is either still praised or (more rarely, now) disparaged.

Did Austen focus too much on a small section of society, in their bubble of privilege? Even if we think that her society *is* limited, her small cast of characters is not disappointing. For the early nineteenth-century reader they stood up to close scrutiny as contemporary figures, and they still endure today. The repeated descriptions of 'well-drawn', 'sustained' and 'natural' chime out from the pages of contemporary magazine and newspaper reviews.

According to the *British Critic* Austen 'supported' her characters with 'vigour' and 'spirit'. The strength of her composition was never in doubt. There seemed to be a penchant for jauntiness and pace amongst these critics. They liked a novel with movement and energy, and a scheme something like a well-structured piece of music. Austen offered careful phrasing, harmony, resonance and well-balanced prose.

The *Critical Review* of 1813 described the many points in *Pride and Prejudice*'s favour, in particular the strength of the character portrayals. These the reviewer likened to those in Shakespeare. He found Elizabeth – the witty and 'arch' counterpoint to Darcy's aloofness – to be similar to Beatrice in *Much Ado About Nothing*. Her story showed the points of development and the overall movement of the whole novel:

'There is not one person in the drama with whom we could readily dispense; they have all their proper places; and fill their several stations with great credit to themselves, and much satisfaction to the reader.'

The Critical Review, 1813

The comparison with the theatre and 'drama' is a frequent one amongst contemporary critics of Austen. The frame of reference is that of the stage, so that potential readers considering *Pride and Prejudice* could be reassured that the novelist understood scene-setting and how to entertain. As an expensive item, a novel had to be worth the investment.

Drama plus social order were thus admirable features of

Austen's work, and excellent lessons could be learned from the plight and predicaments of the Bennet family. There is a definite underlying sense of moral issues addressed, and throughout her work there is a pleasing sense of right and wrong. With few exceptions we see corruption punished and fairness for the just.

The Argument for Genius

Austen's work grew in stature and reputation as the nineteenth century progressed and more people became familiar with her novels. Readers appreciated the skill of her characterisations. In his diary of 1819, the lawyer Henry Crabb Robinson described how impressed he was with the 'thick-headed servile parson' Mr Collins, the convincing contrast between the characters of Jane and Elizabeth, and the authenticity of the dialogue.

Twenty years on and Austen, largely thanks to *Pride and Prejudice*, was included in the article 'Notes on English Novelists' in the *Athenaeum* journal of 1833. In this, her works were unequivocally described as 'genius'. Her reputation was gathering strength, as critics began to use her as a measure for popular, refined, well-crafted prose. They were both entertained and impressed by her. The great 'Wizard of the North', novelist Sir Walter Scott (1771–1832), with *Ivanhoe* (1819) and *The Bride of Lammermoor* (1819) amongst many others to his credit, writing in *Blackwood's Edinburgh Magazine* used Austen as the yardstick by which to evaluate the talents of other writers. He described Maria Edgeworth (1768–1849), the great Irish novelist, in terms of how she compared to Austen.

In the *Edinburgh Review*, Thomas Lister considered Austen's, by that time widely acknowledged, greatness and her 'natural' style. He thought those readers that might desire something more 'robustious' [sic] were not aware of the fact that: 'the highest triumph of art consists in its concealment.'

> '[Austen's] works, like well-proportioned rooms, are rendered less apparently grand and imposing by the very excellence of their adjustment.'
>
> *Edinburgh Review*, 1830

The perfect Georgian proportions, then. The balance and harmony to be found in her prose, like architectural measurements, worked their charm.

Edgeworth, Catherine Gore (1798–1861), Mary Brunton (1778–1818) and Harriet Martineau (1802–1876) were more prolific than Austen but are now largely forgotten outside academic and scholarly circles. They were, and are, often compared – favourably and unfavourably – to Austen. Martineau was considered more 'masculine' in her literary style; a term considered a compliment for a female novelist of the time.

Austen was accorded huge praise, however, by critic and philosopher G H Lewes (1817-1878) who called her the 'prose Shakespeare'. Lewes was unswerving in his views on literary excellence. He lived, unmarried, with Maryanne Evans (George Eliot, 1819–1880) from 1854, and was a famous religious sceptic and critic of the contemporary social order.

As a great champion of Austen's work, he saw himself as an advocate of the new. Her refined depiction of 'human nature' created a standard by which other novelists, especially her female contemporaries and successors, were judged, and make no mistake – literature was appraised along masculine and feminine lines and sensibilities throughout most of the nineteenth century.

Walter Scott conceded that Austen out-performed him when it came to subtlety of prose, and the actor/manager William Macready (1793–1873) described his 'high opinion' of her:

'[Austen] does not probe the vices, but lays bare the weaknesses of character; the blemishes on the skin, and not the corruption at the heart, is what she examines.'

William Macready, diary entry, 1834

It is up to readers to pass judgment in the end as to how far she investigates the human heart and its nature, reinforced always by her robust structure and the clarity of her prose.

Throughout the 1830s and on into the 1840s, praise for her grew and her reputation was cemented.

Human nature, humour, vigour, subtlety, wit and completeness were all praised, along with her ability to depict character. But what of her hero of *Pride and Prejudice*? Did readers, critics, and fellow authors regard Darcy with the same admiration they had for Elizabeth?

Passion Over the Pennine Hills

Darcy was 'the man of family pride' according to the contemporary *Critical Review* (1813), and a figure of 'the greatest reserve and hauteur.' He did not, it seems have the same appeal that he now holds for fans in the early twenty-first century. Despite the praise heaped on Austen by so many prominent admirers in literature, publishing and theatre, Darcy seems to have passed them by. It was her heroines and the command and understanding she had of her milieu that garnered most praise.

Lewes' great admiration, comparing her skill to that of Shakespeare, Goethe and Molière (again, the poetic and theatrical comparisons), encouraged Charlotte Brontë to seek out the 1833 Bentley edition of *Pride and Prejudice* in 1848. There are a couple of interesting aspects to note in this. Firstly, Lewes' glowing critique of *Jane Eyre* (1847) in Fraser's Magazine persuaded Charlotte to trust his literary taste. He admired her work; therefore, he must offer good advice on other reading matter. Second, it is worth pointing out that Charlotte and her sisters, it seems, had not yet read Austen's novels. They were not standard reading for the usually voracious bibliophiles of the Brontë family.

Despite their altogether well-read, well-tutored background, it seems strange that up until this point Charlotte was not informed about such a recent novelist. As conversant as she, Emily (1818–1848), and Anne (1820–1849) were with narrative forms – of Scott, Shakespeare, and Goethe – and philosophic and religious texts, Austen had not yet featured.

The evenings that the Brontës spent around their parlour table in the Haworth parsonage are famous in literary history. They would be in the throes of what Emily called their 'scribblemania' of composition. They started out with tales in their childhood, the juvenilia of the 'Glass Town Federation' stories. Charlotte and brother Branwell (1817–1848) wrote the narratives of 'Angria' and Emily and Anne about 'Gondol'. Dramas, poetry and history make up these detailed fantasies.

Charlotte and Branwell developed a competitive, destructive rivalry between their two main protagonists: Charlotte's Arthur Wellesley, the Duke of Zamorna (clearly based on Wellington, the nation's hero) and Branwell's Alexander Percy, the Earl of Northangerland. However, this name suggests that

Branwell, at least, might have been familiar with Austen's novels, if only *Northanger Abbey*.

Still, Charlotte claimed no knowledge of Austen and, when she did finally read *Pride and Prejudice*, could not agree with Lewes about the greatness of the work. She asked: 'Why do you like Miss Austen so very much?... I am puzzled on that point.' And Charlotte's famous reaction continues, damning Austen with faint praise, when on reading the novel:

'And what did I find? An accurate daguerreotyped portrait of a commonplace face; a carefully fenced, highly cultivated garden, with neat borders and delicate flowers; but no glance of a bright vivid physiognomy, no open country, no fresh air, no bonny beck. I should hardly like to live with her ladies and gentlemen, in their elegant but confined houses. These observations will probably irritate you, but I shall run the risk.'

Charlotte Brontë, Letter to GH Lewes, 1848

William Thackeray (1811–1863), George Sand (1804–1876) – the wit and passion of these writers spoke to Charlotte, rather than the elegant confinement of Austen. She wrote to editor WS Williams at her publisher's, Smith, Elder & Co:

' …anything like warmth of enthusiasm; anything energetic, poignant, heartfelt, is utterly out of place in commending these works: all such demonstration the author's characters would have met with a well-bred sneer, would have calmly scorned as outré and extravagant.'

Charlotte Brontë, Letter to Williams, 1850

Darcy is one that she likely imagined sneering. Charlotte conflates the attitudes of the characters and the author. She thinks of Austen as fenced in and passionless, in contrast to *her* passion and that contained in *her* fiction.

However, Edward Rochester and Darcy have so much in common: they are strong, imposing, wealthy and difficult. Their similarities are clear. They are powerful, heroic figures that defy social expectations and conventions for the women that they fall in love with. They are seen to stoop far below their station for love. Sometimes, it seems the only thing separating them is the Pennine Way.

Charlotte was determined to inject passion into her characters. And she certainly did that. *Jane Eyre* sets a standard for nineteenth-century characters as complex and challenging. It is full of twists and turns and difficult growth. The novel is a bildungsroman for the female protagonist, but the learning and growing is not confined to Jane alone.

In the hands of writers such as Charlotte Brontë and Austen

the rags-to-riches, low to high romance story involves riveting emotional insight and development. That is probably why such debate still continues about the respective qualities and power of *Jane Eyre* and *Pride and Prejudice*, Jane and Elizabeth, Rochester and Darcy. Do you favour the patrician, commanding, brooding hero on the northern edge of the Pennines in Yorkshire, or the patrician, commanding brooding hero on his estate among the Derbyshire Peaks?

'Womanly and Literary'

In 1852, the *New Monthly Magazine* reported on the 'female novelists'. This was one of many articles across the period (including those published in *Blackwood's Magazine* and the conservative *Christian Remembrancer*) that considered the gender differences between male and female writers and analysed their approaches to fiction.

The *Monthly* informed readers that writing novels was 'attractive' to women because it falls 'within the scope of those faculties, which are, generally speaking, characteristic of the fair sex.' This is one of those comments that lead us to characterise the Victorian period as a conservative and repressive one, especially where women were concerned.

And, true, the role of women outside the home was certainly

limited as far as the middle and upper classes went. However, the gender-specific terms and discriminatory remarks of a few conservative, and sometimes vehemently reactionary, critics should not set the tone for the whole period. That would diminish the achievements of so many female writers. The writing of George Sand, Harriet Martineau, Elizabeth Barrett Browning (1806–1861), Mary Braddon (1835–1915) and Elizabeth Gaskell (1810–1865), as well as the Brontë sisters, dealt with women's sexuality, agency and determination to shape their lives, for better or worse, in new and challenging ways.

The anonymous critic in the *Monthly Magazine* continues with more emphatic remarks on the male–female differences that were perceived to exist between writers. There is proof 'that clever women can write, and have written, very clever novels…'. Austen is the figurehead that rose above others. She 'is perfect mistress of all she touches, and certainly touches nothing without embellishing it – if not with the embellishments of idealism and romance, at least with the fresh strokes of nature.'

We are back to 'nature', again. As a female writer, she can discern the flow of life and the patterns of human behaviour. Admiration for Austen continued to build, with politician and historian Thomas Macaulay (1800-1859) coming out resoundingly in her favour and Lewes growing more passionate in his praise. Lewes, in the *Westminster Review* of 1852, for example, wrote that 'First and foremost, let Jane Austen be named the greatest artist that has ever written, using the term to signify the most perfect mastery over the means to her end.'

He wrote that Austen developed her characters for a world that she knew because she was clever enough not to risk the depiction of 'worlds of passionate existence into which she has never set foot,' such as married life and sexual relationships, we can assume. She was, for Lewes, 'at once womanly and literary.'

Austen met with approval during the Victorian period for her many qualities, and for reasons that resonated with the fashions of the age. Her nephew James Austen-Leigh published *A Memoir of Jane Austen* in 1869. It was a selective narrative of her life and career. Her sister, Cassandra, chose to destroy some of her letters, so the bulk of the memoir was made up from surviving correspondence and the memories of those who knew her when they were children. Hence, the image of 'dear Aunt Jane' that persisted into the twentieth century.

This biographical reading of her has somewhat coloured and divided opinion since. The cosy 'Victorianisation' of Austen jars with her satirical voice and ability to depict scenes with such clever irony. Perceived through her family's filter of respectability, or that of Charlotte Brontë's irritation, we can see the different ways in which Austen was read in the nineteenth century.

The Hero in the Landscape

Charlotte's first complete manuscript was *The Professor*, but it was *Jane Eyre* that was her first publication, and despite her reservations about Austen's works its hero bears a close resemblance to Darcy. When we look at Emily Brontë's first (and only) two-volume novel, *Wuthering Heights* (1847), we likewise witness the repetition of the troubled and difficult hero. Rochester and Heathcliff are on the continuum of this brooding brotherhood of fictional men. Charlotte and Emily used this archetype to great effect.

The Brontë sisters' fictional worlds were a combination of idealism, Romanticism, experience and environment. Charlotte was critical of Austen for not being of their world and therefore replicating her ideal of novelistic invention. If Austen represented a 'fenced' and 'highly cultivated' garden, then Charlotte and Emily evoked the mood of their rugged Yorkshire home. This is the popular perception of them: changeable and dramatic, like the weather. And these were the qualities possessed by the heroes in their landscape. Heathcliff's name echoes the very forms and geography of his location.

Charlotte took a passionate and personal line in her fiction. The tone in Austen's work that she objected to was partly due to the fact that Austen uses irony so frequently. This creates a sense of distance and detachment from the sentiments expressed and the feelings these might provoke. Cool and passionless disappointed our Charlotte. In contrast, her approach to fiction produced a more tormented, turbulent narrative. Where Darcy seeks to express his 'ardent' feelings after months of brooding, Edward Rochester lives his from day to day on a much more dramatic scale.

Rochester is perpetually haunted by the consequences and implications of his actions, so much so, in fact, that they dwell under his very roof at the suitably spiky-sounding Thornfield Hall. Adèle Varens is the reason that *Jane Eyre* enters his home. The little girl is Rochester's ward. It turns out that she is the child of his former mistress, Céline – a star of the Paris Opera. Rochester denies that she is his daughter, but he still allows the precocious little French girl to benefit from his wealth and protection. He feels some sort of duty to her, whilst denying his paternity of her.

Hidden away in an upstairs chamber is Antoinette, his wife. She is simultaneously the symbol of his passion and his shame. First, he tries to claim she is Bertha Mason, a crazed and distracted servant. He must, finally, own up to what he has done. By keeping secrets, trying to confine and compartmentalise them in his mansion – this only leads to big trouble for him. Family secrets, as Darcy discovered, have a habit of escaping.

The meeting of Rochester and Jane is dramatic and symbolic of their roles in the novel. His horse, a dark and muscular animal, slips on the ice, unseating Rochester because it shies to avoid Jane. She literally bowls him over. He is hurt. His hound, Pilot, bounds past her, and as Jane sees the dog the image of a supernatural 'Gytrash' leaps into her head. This is the animal spectre of Yorkshire folklore that is said to appear to travellers on the moor.

F H Townsend illustration, 1848

This imagery, threaded through the characters' interactions, shows us Charlotte's affinity for the Gothic. She introduces the suggestion of a diabolical hound, but then the fantasy dissolves and Jane is confronted with the mortal man, horse and hound.

Rochester is a man of substance, of the earth and rocks. Charlotte has *Jane Eyre* describe all in the first person:

> 'He had a dark face, with stern features and a heavy brow; his eyes and gathered eyebrows looked ireful and thwarted… I felt no fear of him and… but little shyness. Had he been a handsome, heroic-looking young gentleman, I should not have dared to stand thus questioning him against his will, and offering my services unasked.'
>
> Jane Eyre, Volume 1, Chapter 12

Rochester is an intimidating figure, like Darcy, but not one who can terrify Jane. Like Elizabeth Bennet, Jane can be bold. Rochester is not, to her, a typically handsome or 'heroic-looking' type. He is a frowning, moody, solid man. Jane's lack of worldly experience: 'I had hardly ever seen a handsome youth; never in my life spoken to one. I had a theoretical reverence and homage for beauty,' stands her in good stead when she and Rochester first clash. The worlds of 'elegance' and 'gallantry' are alien to her, and if she had encountered them in Rochester she 'should have shunned them as one would fire, lightning, anything else bright but antipathetic.' Jane Eyre always thinks about how she can shrink away from attention.

We are in emotional and spiritual territory here, rather than Austen's satiric world. Charlotte was deadly serious. This episode of her encounter with Rochester demonstrates how Jane has no self-esteem, she is one who believes that the bright, elegant or heroic will find no interest in her. Charlotte emphatically sets her heroine up as one who takes a lower place and lives in the shadow of others.

'If even this stranger had smiled and been good-humoured to me when I addressed him; if he had put off my offer of assistance gaily and with thanks, I should have gone on my way and not felt any vocation to renew enquiries: but the frown, the roughness of the traveller, set me at my ease.'

Jane Eyre, Volume 1, Chapter 12

Jane is so used to bad manners and gruffness that she is immediately at 'ease' with Rochester. She admits she prefers this type to a more elegant, gallant variety of man. They are made for each other. His gruffness is akin to that of Darcy. The elements of Darcy's character that so alienate him from Georgian society are deemed to be desirable qualities in Charlotte's Victorian hero. It is better that Rochester is not conventionally handsome or approachable.

We can see in this that Charlotte was taking a risk with Rochester. He is moodier and harsher than Darcy in his dismissal of others. He is a damaged man, and not just at this first encounter with Jane when he is unseated and injured. He fires short questions at her as she helps him, his rudeness putting her at 'ease'. She assists him back to his horse, and he remarks drily: 'aid Mahomet to go to the mountain.'

In the hoary moonlight, in which Jane experiences some deceptive imaginings, she and Rochester have clashed unexpectedly, and he must lean on little Jane for support. Her slight, delicate figure supports his craggy, powerful one. They are elemental beings: she is 'air' and he is 'rock'. He has power, status and money – but is knocked off his mount and helped up by the seemingly helpless woman. She destabilises him and then supports him.

Once determined to have her in his life, however, he resorts to desperate measures and deception.

> 'Like heath that, in the wilderness
> The wild wind whirls away.'
>
> Jane Eyre, Volume 1, Chapter 12

This quotation appears in the text when Rochester meets Jane, like an incantation(or prophecy of what is to come as he rides away from her. It is from the poem *Fallen is Thy Throne* (1824) by the Irish Romantic poet, Thomas Moore (1779–1852).

Charlotte referenced it at this point in Jane's story to invoke an elemental spirituality to her first meeting with Rochester. It suggests both devotion and passion bursting through from nature, a feature of the work of the Romantics. Moore was a close associate of Lord Byron, who entrusted his memoirs to Moore. Byron gave him instructions to publish them after his death, but Moore burnt the manuscripts at the behest of Byron's family, who were fearful of their frankness and potentially scandalous content. Austen's family was not the only one that sought to re-write the life of the writer.

Charlotte was unambiguous about how the Romantic symbolism surrounding Rochester and Jane should be read and how it carries events forward in the plot. He is mysterious, like the darkened landscape around him (which he owns, remember, it is after all his estate of Thornfield) and appears partly supernatural with his spectral hound. We find out very quickly that he is real, and all too human.

Nevertheless, Jane is lost. The human and the natural, and supernatural, coalesce around Rochester. This is the poetic and Byronic inspiration, suggested by Moore's words. Jane's life has now been changed for good by Rochester's presence in the world – he already haunts her:

' …I stopped a minute, looked round and listened, with an idea like a horse's hoofs might ring on the causeway again, and that a rider in a cloak, and Gytrash-like Newfoundland dog might be again apparent…'

Jane Eyre, Volume 1, Chapter 12

Rochester has a powerful physical effect on Jane, as Darcy has on Elizabeth. In both Charlotte and Austen's works dominant masculine types have their lives totally disrupted and destabilised by the arrival of modest, intelligent and unconventional young women. Austen allows the passions to burn bright, albeit subtly, for Darcy and Elizabeth at Pemberley (his natural abode):

> 'As they walked across the hall towards the river, Elizabeth turned back to look again; her aunt and uncle stopped also, and while the former was conjecturing as to the date of the building, the owner of it himself suddenly came forward from the road which led behind the stables.
>
> They were within twenty yards of each other, and so abrupt was his appearance, that it was impossible to avoid his sight. Their eyes instantly met, and the cheeks of both were overspread with the deepest blush.'
>
> *Pride and Prejudice*, Chapter 43 Vol III

Men of property, handsome, rich and influential, show their impact on the world around them especially within their domain. The Victorian dramatic scenario between Rochester and Jane witnesses her close proximity to him, supporting his imposing figure with her slight one. The Georgian 'no touching' social convention is not violated by Austen, and so

Elizabeth and Darcy each have a flush of emotion to indicate deep feelings without expressing them. These situations from Charlotte and Austen suggest a 'Beauty and the Beast' tale. The young woman intrudes into the enclosed world of the male estate, disrupts life and reveals secrets.

Dark and Light

We are aware of this passionate dynamic between Rochester and Jane, that echoes Austen's 'pride' and 'prejudice' and 'sense' and 'sensibility'. However, Rochester's dark secret – his imprisoned wife and the threat of 'madness' – is a devastating one. It leads to destruction at Thornfield. In fact, it sparks off an actual explosive conflagration. Darcy's secret is one he keeps for someone else, his sister, of her near elopement with Wickham. Both men gather their 'family pride' around them to hide what might be shameful or damaging truths.

For Charlotte, there was more narrative logic to the phases of Rochester's development of feeling than there was for Darcy's love story. For many Victorian readers, Darcy's shift from indifference to ardent lover was too abrupt and incredible in its arc. Charlotte established a successful fictional hero for her time, that possesses a consistent foundation for such a love.

Rochester, Jane finds, is 'changeful and abrupt' from the

start. Mrs Fairfax, the housekeeper, tells her that it is his 'nature' because he has experienced 'family troubles'. Darcy's nature is not on show nearly as much and does not reach the same level of intensity seen in the later Victorian heroes. Rochester outdoes Darcy with his adventurous and romantic past as well. He has been to Paris, for heaven's sake, and like William Wordsworth has a half-French illegitimate 'foster' daughter – because none of us are really fooled. We all know that Adèle is Rochester's child. He is not known for his up-front honesty, after all.

Conservative reviewers considered *Jane Eyre* a risk to society. Some critics were so concerned for the influence the novel might have on young women that it was banned in certain circles. The worry was that low-born and poor women in service, such as maids and governesses, might develop romantic feelings for their masters. They might think they could rise above their station by stirring up his feelings. Charlotte's favourite feature of her story – the passion – was the factor that elicited negative reaction from some quarters. Anything that put new, risky ideas into a young woman's head was treated as a threat to society.

Austen's ironic distance from such passions enabled her to satirise such things. Catherine Morland in *Northanger Abbey* is one such impressionable reader of novels. The fear that women might take the romance novel too seriously persisted well into the nineteenth century, and some would argue lasts to this day. Would they take it as real? Would they want life to imitate art and develop feelings for their employer, or another man well above their station? The Cinderella complex was feared.

And there was a very real fear that a young woman could become ill because she was disillusioned with real life. In Richard Sheridan's *The Rivals*, he gave us – and Austen – the prototype for such an avid female reader, in the character of Lydia Languish. Authors and playwrights recognised this giddy, obsessive female devotion to favourite stories. In the twenty-first century we refer to it as fan culture, and it is often (unfairly) disparaged in similar ways.

Charlotte Brontë, similarly, exploited this romantic dedication to the heroic ideal. Hers was not a tone of comic, satiric irony; Charlotte's imperative was a focus on the seriousness of the Romantic narrative. Jane Eyre, written in the first person and subtitled 'an autobiography', contains the personal coming-of-age sentiments of the bildungsroman, throughout. Jane's adventures are Charlotte's and our adventures. Jane learns and then she teaches Rochester. We live it with her and through her: 'Reader, I married him.'

Charlotte's version of the Byronic, tormented Romantic figure and Prince Charming archetype (combined with the Beast) was an endeavour to create an authentic, passionate, Victorian hero. She used a 'battling the monster' as well as a 'rags to riches' plot form. In order to create the credible bond between Rochester and Jane, he – like Darcy – must change.

The bildungsroman form applies to him as much as it does to her. It is why Jean Rhys was able to take the back story of Rochester and Antoinette for her novel, *Wide Sargasso Sea* (1966). There was so much for writers to explore in the life stories of Charlotte's characters, just as she gave us Jane's 'autobiography' in the original novel.

In Charlotte's novel the metamorphosis of Rochester is a brutal, physical one. The guilt of his actions, his attempt at bigamy and his unjust treatment of Antoinette, are finally enacted on his body. The harm and the injury he endured represent the ordeal he has to go through in order to be worthy of Jane. His monumental 'granite' form, as Charlotte describes it at one point, like the hills and rocks of his home county, is left cracked and broken. Jane appears at the end with her restorative powers, to begin the healing.

Somehow, Rochester must pay the price and learn the lesson for the treatment of his wife and his duplicity towards Jane. He atones for it by fire and suffering, as a sort of purge and redemption. His narrative is much more dramatic and hyperbolic than Austen's pathway for Darcy through her novel. He shows growth and change without anything like the physical trauma that Rochester suffers.

Now, however, in the early twenty-first century, the understated Georgian hero is more popular than his Victorian successor. This is because the Victorian period translates as a more directly censorious, moralistic time. It does not seem quite as sexy, perhaps. This has a lot to do with Andrew Davies, I feel, of whom more to come.

As appealing as the classic heroes of Victorian literature might be, they enjoy nothing like the universal appeal of Darcy. Rochester's narrative is not just one of growth and development towards true love. It is atonement and retribution, and the taming of a forceful nature. The power structure is reversed when Jane returns to him. From his pinnacle as master of Thornfield he is reduced to a shattered ruin disabled by injuries, and this requires Jane to be nurse and wife.

The Brooding Brotherhood

If we think of these heroes as lined up along the spectrum of the Byronic, Darcy-like archetype, then we can place Rochester at some point further towards the Gothic than Austen's subtler creation. The Gothic and the dramatic show us the direction in which characterisation moved in the Victorian period. Further along the spectrum, and marching across the Pennines and onto the moors, we move even closer to the darker side of male behaviour with *Emily* Brontë's creation, Heathcliff in *Wuthering Heights* (1847).

More brutal than Rochester and from the opposite end of

the social scale to both Rochester and Darcy, Heathcliff transgresses social and moral boundaries, going further than Charlotte's hero. Emily adopted a very interesting approach, in which she ramped up the tension and danger of the true outsider hero-villain. Heathcliff arrives at the end of the old century and on the threshold of the new, with this story set in 1797. He is a poor foundling wandering the streets of Liverpool, and we never discover his origins. He is a devastating, stormy interloper, a cuckoo in the nest who takes over. He ousts the occupants of both *Wuthering Heights* and Thrushcross Grange. Heathcliff's growth and coming of age entails taking everything from Hindley Earnshaw and Edgar Linton.

As troubled and tormented souls go, Heathcliff is the outright winner. Taciturn, objectionable and difficult heroes abounded, and then Emily took it further. Heathcliff is genuinely dangerous, and the sense of threat from his turbulent mind that emerges during childhood and adolescence, results in actual aggression and violence directed towards Hindley, his son Hareton and Isabella Linton. Isabella, the genteel, delicate girl who marries Heathcliff against all advice, could have been fashioned by Emily on Anne Isabella Milbanke and her fateful, disastrous marriage to Lord Byron. Lady Byron was mother of a daughter with him: Ada Lovelace, the famous mathematician. After their separation she accused her husband of insanity, of brutality towards her, acts of sodomy and of having an incestuous affair with his half-sister Augusta Leigh.

Some scholars speculate that Emily insinuates Heathcliff is the illegitimate son of old Mr Earnshaw, brought from Liverpool after the death of his mother. He arrives, sheltered in Earnshaw's cloak, on a wild and windy night on the moors. Before he even gets in the door, he has crushed Hindley's hopes. The foundling 'gypsy' boy has splintered the long-anticipated violin that Earnshaw had purchased for his eldest, legitimate son and heir.

The descriptions of Heathcliff's dark complexion and colouring have caused critics and directors to wonder if Emily meant him to be of mixed race, and this compounds his outsider status. Andrea Arnold, director of the 2011 film version of *Wuthering Heights*, cast Yorkshire-born James Howson as Heathcliff, the first time a black actor had played the role. However we might now try to interpret or explain his origins, Emily's point was made. In a remote, late-eighteenth-century rural moorland community in Yorkshire, he is known as a 'gypsy', the catch-all racial term for anyone dark or 'different'. The other characters' descriptions link him to darkness and devilish forces.

If Catherine Earnshaw and Heathcliff *are* half-brother and sister, then the suggestion of incest between them – for which there is no direct reference in the text, but is nevertheless heavily hinted at – indicates further influence from the Gothic and from the life of Lord Byron. It not only gives us an atmosphere of threat and violence, but also the moral danger of forbidden and risky passions.

Half-brothers and sisters are frequently connected in sexual intrigue in Gothic tales, and are punished for their illicit relationships, even if at the time they are innocent of the knowledge of their blood ties. In some versions of Norse and Germanic myths, including the stories contained in *The Ring Cycle* opera sequence by Richard Wagner (composed from 1848–1874), Siegmund fathers a child, Siegfried the dragon slayer, with his half-sister Sieglinde. So perhaps Cathy and Heathcliff are Emily's fictionalised Augusta Leigh and Lord Byron, or her version of a Germanic myth of forbidden love?

With its tempestuous moods and brooding, difficult lust, the relationship between Cathy and Heathcliff takes us into this Gothic, later Wagnerian, landscape at times. Heathcliff and Rochester (the potential bigamist) are men of pride, boundless emotion and sexual energy. Even though they contrast starkly with Darcy on moral grounds, especially because he demonstrates protection and concern for his sister, they are nevertheless linked.

If we take Darcy's masculine nature, pride and 'ardent' devotion, and magnify it through a Victorian lens with the addition of pathetic fallacy from a tempestuous landscape to create mood and tension, we are taken into the world of the Brontës' heroes. Plus, Rochester and Heathcliff constitute an actual threat to the women they meet – and marry. Heathcliff moves further across the threshold of the Gothic when he invokes the supernatural by calling out to Cathy's ghost to come and haunt him. He is as close to a devilish man-wolf as he can be, a predatory 'Gytrash' in human form – aggressive when wounded – symbolically crossing the boundaries of nature.

Laurence Olivier as Heathcliff, 1939

He crosses other boundaries too – social and domestic. He is violent and manipulative. Emily moved further into the shadow world of an anti-hero with Heathcliff. He dies with a tortured grimace on his face. He has been unambiguously blighted since birth. He lives out his potential for cruelty by deliberately conquering every shred of his better nature. As much as any fictional character can be, Heathcliff is a form of anti-Darcy.

"i Am Heathcliff!"

Heathcliff invades the Earnshaws' home and, without legitimacy, acquires all the property. He reinvents himself as a gentleman and turns the tables on those who had looked down upon him and abused him. He moves through the Heights and Thrushcross Grange communities as a force for both destruction and creation. Heathcliff is all passion and ardent feeling. In this way he harks back to the foundations of the archetype in the Germanic, Romantic heroes.

Emily had a great enthusiasm for Goethe and his *Sorrows of Young Werther* (1774), in the original German. In the *Brontë Studies* journal (2008), Paola Tonussi discussed the 'convergences' between *Werther* and *Wuthering Heights*. She examined how reading Goethe probably influenced Emily's composition, because the realms of the novels contain similar philosophical outlooks towards nature, God, death and the afterlife. They are kindred novels.

And, *Wuthering Heights* is a binary novel. It was published in two volumes and is concerned with the contrasting duality of light and dark, the Grange and the Heights, Heathcliff and Edgar Linton. These two men are oppositional moral, emotional and philosophical masculine forces. It is another Victorian novel of dramatic extremes and duality.

Cathy's connection to Heathcliff is intensely powerful and possibly sexual as they grow up together. Emily was, however, at pains to stress how much Young Cathy resembles Edgar Linton, so that there can be no doubt as to who her father is. She wanted to dispel the notion that Cathy and Heathcliff might have been lovers once Cathy married, but their connection nevertheless runs deep. Cathy explains to Nellie Dean, the housekeeper at the Heights, why she cannot marry Heathcliff: "I *am* Heathcliff,… whatever our souls are made of, his and mine are the same." This was relayed to Nellie first hand, and it is she who tells the story of the two families to Mr Lockwood, the tenant of the Grange. Cathy insisted on this deep, abiding Romantic connection between herself and Heathcliff. They are spiritual counterparts, on a different level to all other relationships.

Nobody else understands them. Nellie is bewildered by the two young people's complication of everything. She tries her best to help Heathcliff, suggesting he cut his hair and present a kinder face to the world. He struggles with his identity and feels tormented all his life. He does, however, clean up his act, but not in the way that Nellie had hoped. He returns from his travels a gentleman, having acquired wealth from… somewhere, we never find out. Destructive and abusive, he travels further along the continuum of the archetype than either Charlotte's or Austen's heroes. Involvement with him leads to terrible consequences.

Isabella Linton's reaction to Heathcliff is crucial to this understanding of him. The attraction she feels towards him is an act of rebellion on her part. Poor Isabella behaves in a naïve, petulant manner, as she observes Cathy and Heathcliff with jealousy and finds excuses to be in his company. Seduction, elopement and pregnancy soon follow and quickly change her mind about her romantic ideals. His abuse of her is very real. The notion of taming the difficult, brooding man and finding the true gentleman within does not belong in *Wuthering Heights*. Heathcliff's attitude towards Isabella is a particularly bleak, cynical and calculating one. He tells Nellie that the first thing he did on their elopement was to seize her dog, Fanny, and hang her up on a hook. He never, he claims proudly, demonstrated any 'deceitful softness,' he was always cruel, so, in his opinion she should have known what she was getting into.

Charlotte reforms Rochester with repentance and growth that echo Darcy's character change. *Wuthering Heights* depicts an altogether bleaker prospect, with the pathetic fallacy of the windswept, rugged surroundings that reflect the turmoil inside the walls of the Earnshaw home. A romantic resolution eludes the characters of the first generation. It takes Heathcliff's death for harmony to be restored at the Heights. For Young Cathy and her cousin, Hareton (no incest risk, but a close family connection), a brighter future awaits. The houses of the Grange and the Heights, and the two branches of the families: the Lintons and the Earnshaws, are united.

Celebrity, Melodrama and Gothic Desires

These hero-gentlemen and anti-hero-gentlemen of nineteenth-century fiction have their values challenged and their expectations shaken up. Drama and turbulence prevail, especially for the relationships in the Brontës' novels. The wild and melodramatic rhetoric is very persuasive.

As the nineteenth century progressed, the Victorian stage was a domain upon which vigorous action and passionate plots were acted out to great acclaim, and the dark, difficult, brooding heroic archetype thrived. Emerging from eighteenth-century melodrama, Gothic novels and romances, this tormented man appeared in different guises, thanks to the various depictions of roles by the great tragedians of the age. Foremost amongst these was the celebrated actor Sir Henry Irving (1838–1905).

To see Irving on stage as Hamlet, Macbeth or Mathias in the melodrama *The Bells*, was to be in the presence of an electric personality and a genius of performance. In 1876, Irving met a young Irishman who went on to become his assistant for the next twenty years. On first acquaintance, Irving invited the young man to dinner and gave an impromptu performance of *The Dream of Eugene Aram* (1831) by Thomas Hood, a poem about a school teacher who commits a brutal murder in order to steal an old man's gold. The young Irishman, named Bram Stoker (1847–1912), described the experience of this private performance years later:

'So great was the magnetism of his genius, so profound was the sense of his dominancy that I sat spellbound. Outwardly I was as of stone... The whole thing was new, re-created by a force of passion which was like a new power.'

Bram Stoker, *Personal Reminiscences of Henry Irving*, 1906

Irving was the magnetic master of the melodrama, the performance mode that used a system of gesture, movement and rhetoric to express feelings, mood and emotion, accompanied by music. Irving specialised in the tormented characters of the tragedy, and those – like Eugene Aram – with a dreadful secret to hide.

The memorabilia of his acting career include daguerreotypes and illustrations of Irving in character. His Shakespearean roles (Hamlet, Macbeth, Richard III) were rightly famous, and as the murderer Mathias he is shown in suitably tortured poses. In Leopold Lewis' melodrama *The Bells* (translated from Erckmann-Chatrian's *Le Juif Polonais*, 1833), Mathias is a figure fraught by greed, guilt and terror. The play opened at Irving's Lyceum Theatre in 1871 and it became his trademark production.

Mathias the innkeeper is haunted by past crimes, so much so that he enters a hallucinatory state in which he imagines that he is on trial for the murder he committed in his youth. The role called for extreme emotion and the pushing of the boundaries of characterisation. The vision Mathias has is so vivid that he collapses with a fear-induced heart attack. Throughout the play Mathias (and the audience) hear 'the bells'. These had hung on the harness of the victim's sleigh when he came to the inn where Mathias murdered him for his money and hid the body. Mathias' guilt tortures him, causes the visions and drives him steadily to his death.

This was a well-crafted tragic Gothic melodrama that showcased Irving's talents and contributed to his celebrity status. Irving's fine looks, his patrician profile and electrifying presence worked well on stage and were a powerful influence on popular culture. There are both anecdotal and authentic reports about the response of some female fans in the audiences at the Lyceum. He induced such an extreme reaction in some that they fainted. He was so charismatic in character as the popular rogue Robert Macaire (a French brigand and Robin Hood-style figure) in performance in 1883, that three women had to be carried from the auditorium. He certainly had the ability to induce a fan mania among Victorians.

Irving's success was a consequence of his wide range of work in regional and London theatre, and his determination to legitimise actor training. He was the great animator of the Victorian stage, bringing thought, spirit and fire to the discipline of the actor. It is difficult for us to ascertain from our twenty-first century perspective, however, the impact this had and its far-reaching effect. Nothing was captured on film or recorded at the moment of creation so therefore we can only work with anecdotal evidence, published reviews and recollections of those who knew him.

Edward Gordon Craig (1872–1966), the actor, scenographer and theatre innovator, was the son of Ellen Terry (1847–1928). Dame Ellen Terry was Irving's acting partner and sometime lover. Craig grew up with Irving as his friend and mentor. Irving helped to form in Craig's mind the theory of the perfect actor, the 'ubermarionette', about which he wrote for many years in essays and articles. The 'ubermarionette' could be distilled down to the 'actor plus fire, minus ego'. Craig wrote of Irving: 'Let me state at once, in clearest unmistakable terms, that I have never known of, or seen, or heard, a greater actor than was Irving.' (*Henry Irving*, by Edward Gordon Craig, 1899).

With theatrical performance it is certainly a case of 'you had to be there', and this applies to Victorian melodrama in particular. This style now has a very bad reputation. It is viewed as overblown and excessive and is easily mocked because the styles of acting changed so radically in the early part of the twentieth century, moving towards naturalism and psychological authenticity. It is difficult for us to imagine the thrill of the *melos* – the musical refrain – and the tension that arose as a figure such as Irving appeared on stage, lit by flickering gaslight. Physical presence in theatre is everything.

In the role of Mathias, he emerged from the shadows wearing a haunted expression that transmitted emotion to the whole of the auditorium. An audience that worked hard all week and sought entertainment largely from theatre and live performance, such as music hall, wanted broad brushstrokes, amusement, sentiment and thrills. In addition, they could call for repeated performances of their favourite scenes – to re-live the enjoyment. So, encores were common and encouraged by the theatre management; the nineteenth-century version of entertainment on demand.

A New Anti-Hero and A New Genre

Irving's air of mystery, his charisma and his stature on stage inspired his assistant Bram Stoker with his writing career. In 1897, Stoker published *Dracula*. As landmark novels go this is one of the most important, genre-defining works of all time. With *Dracula*, Stoker created a composite character of charm, torment and diabolical powers. The Count is an aristocratic outsider who moves across the supernatural boundary into the world of the undead. He is a distillation of pure Gothic fiendishness, and he was based on Henry Irving.

Stoker fused together the ancient and modern and invented a new kind of vampire for the turn of the century. On the brink of the new century he plundered existing Gothic culture and European folklore, and overlaid this on a tale of modern men and women struggling with issues of fidelity, sexuality, coming of age and being a success at the dawn of the twentieth century. The foundation of fear and threat comes from a deadly, foreign, ancient 'other' with dangerous anti-Christian ideas and a threatening sexuality. He seeks to seduce and deliberately corrupt the pure English women, Mina Harker and Lucy Westernra. Stoker's narrative explored and exploited a range of contemporary social anxiety.

What people feared, Stoker made into a physical threat in his novel. Dracula can mesmerise his victims and cause the women to manifest helpless, uncontrolled demonstrations of sexuality. They commit acts, the memory of which sicken and shame them in the light of day. Lucy and Mina are both drawn into the Count's web of death, destruction, lust and vampirism because he can invade their minds with his supernatural powers.

The novel has a composite structure with letters, diaries, newspaper reports and telegrams contributing to the narrative. Some of these, such as telegraphed messages, typewritten letters and transcripts of recorded speech on wax cylinder, are products of turn-of-the-century technology. This gives the reader multiple perspectives on the unfolding storyline, with different characters giving their point of view in the first person. We join them to embark on a supernatural detective trail and piece together the story elements behind the mystery: the strange behaviour of Lucy, the encounters that Jonathan Harker has in Transylvania and the creature that is preying on Mina. Dr Van Helsing is our guide through this diabolical minefield. As the fount of knowledge, he explains the history of the Count and the nature of vampirism with a scientific, academic authority.

Dracula has an intense connection with the violent history of his people and that of Eastern Europe, and is a man of 'family pride' who appears at the opposite end of the century to Darcy. The archetype grew steadily darker as the century progressed. The Count is both refined and barbaric, someone who wishes to defend his honour and violate and invade that of others. He is an actual blood-sucking aristocrat who has out-lived his usefulness but will not die. He has proved so effective as a character that he generated a whole new departure in fiction and popular culture for the twentieth century.

One of his most potent powers, like that of Irving, is the effect he had on women to lose their senses because of the passions that are aroused in them. Lucy, Dracula's first English victim, represents a steady moral corruption of purity as chronicled by Stoker. She is courted by a set of suitors: Arthur, the son of an English lord, Quincy, an American millionaire and Dr Seward, who is a modern professional psychiatrist. These young men are in contrast to Dracula, as examples of youthful gentility, modernity and success, and scientific thinking.

However, instead of settling down with one of them, Lucy begins to exhibit strange behaviour and startling and disturbing displays of sexuality. She 'acts out' in her trances as she is drained and infected by the Count on his nocturnal visits to her. Seward observes this ghastly process with horror and fascination, and secret desire:

'DR SEWARD'S DIARY
20th September
...And then insensibly there came the strange change which I had noticed in the night. Her breathing grew

stertorous, the mouth opened, and the pale gums, drawn back, made the teeth look longer and sharper than ever. In a sort of sleep-waking, vague, unconscious way she opened her eyes, which were now dull and hard at once, and said in a soft, voluptuous voice such as I had never heard from her lips,

"Arthur! Oh, my love, I am so glad you have come! Kiss me!"'

Dracula, Chapter 12

Once fully transformed into a vampire, Lucy stalks London at night. The local children she preys upon call her the 'Bloofer Lady' ('Beautiful Lady') who lures them away in the park. Later they are found wandering alone, confused and distressed, with small bite marks on their necks. Instead of becoming a wife and mother, Lucy's transformation means she abandons all decency and happiness and becomes a crazed seductive, blood-sucking monster. The newspapers dub her the 'Kensington horror'.

The foreign, Gothic, blood-sucking anti-hero succeeds in representing Stoker's point that the corruption of blood equates to the corruption of society. Dracula penetrates and perverts English society. Once finished with Lucy, he turns his attention to Mina, the wife of the man that he imprisoned in Castle Dracula. Jonathan knows of the Count's powers but can do nothing to protect his young wife. Dracula invades the Harkers' marital bedchamber:

'DR SEWARD'S DIARY
3rd October
On the bed beside the window lay Jonathan Harker... in a stupor. Kneeling on the near edge of the bed facing outwards was the white-clad figure of his wife. By her side stood a tall, thin man, clad in black... the instant we saw we all recognised the Count... With his left hand he held both Mrs Harker's hands... His right hand gripped her by the back of the neck, forcing her face down on his bosom. Her white night-dress was smeared with blood, and a thin stream trickled down the man's bare chest... The attitude of the two had a terrible resemblance of a child forcing a kitten's nose into a saucer of milk to compel it to drink... [The Count's] eyes flamed red with devilish passion. The great nostrils of the white aquiline nose opened wide... and the white sharp teeth... clamped together like those of a wild beast.'

Seward and Van Helsing witness this supernatural violation. The human/animal links empower the Count and defile Mina. Her shame becomes palpable.

'Mrs Harker... had drawn her breath and with it had given a scream so wild, so ear-piercing, so despairing... it will ring in my ears till my dying day... Her face was ghastly... the blood... smeared her lips and cheeks and chin. From her throat trickled a thin stream of blood. Her eyes were mad with terror. Then she put before her face her poor crushed hands, which bore... the red mark of the Count's terrible grip, and from behind them came a low desolate wail which made the terrible scream seem only the quick expression of an endless grief.'

Dracula, Chapter 21

Opportunistic, deadly and violent, Dracula is a symbol of decadent aristocracy. The ideals of honour and duty that once were so important to his line are now dead and decayed. His 'family pride' is in gathering his minions together and controlling his fiendish 'brides', seducing innocent English-women and running with the pack of wolves – his servants – as one of them.

High birth and a purity of blood do not guarantee a purity of action and high-minded ideals. Dracula has become cor-rupt and obsolete. It was not enough to be born into privilege. Writers remarked on how duty needed to be observed also. Darcy is emphatically described as 'the best master'. Elizabeth understands his character all the better after speaking to his housekeeper at Pemberley. His 'family pride' includes his responsibility to his workers as a landowner. Otherwise it is just empty rhetoric and superficial snobbery.

A Darcy of the Industrial Age

The duty to workers became more of a focus in the Victorian industrial age. New parameters for the urban labour force, harsh working conditions and the rapid growth of cities saw new responsibilities for employers. Concerns over safety, education, poverty, over-crowded housing and stressful work in factories had to be taken on. In literary terms, Elizabeth Gaskell tackled many of these issues in her novels that were concerned with the urban life of Manchester. *North and South* (1854–1855), her serial social novel, appeared first in *Household* Words edited by Charles Dickens.

In this story, John Thornton is a self-made businessman and factory owner who must deal with the responsibilities of leadership and employment of a large mass of workers. Margaret Hale has to leave her childhood home in the south of England and move to 'Milton' (the fictional Manchester) and into John's life. She must find a place in his world of densely populated streets and the smoggy, industrial atmosphere.

Gaskell was an admirer, and eventual biographer, of

Charlotte Brontë. John Thornton shares his name with the town of Thornton in West Yorkshire where Charlotte was born. Clearly, Margaret and Thornton's dynamic owes a great deal to Jane and Rochester. However, Thornton is an elevated, self-made man and possessor of a naturally kind, noble and generous disposition. Like Darcy, he takes some getting used to, as he can be difficult and dour on the outside. And like Darcy, he too has a formidable female relative – his mother, a working-class Lady Catherine.

Thornton is a really good guy and strives to assist Margaret and her family when they find themselves in trouble. The Hales attract trouble, a little like the Bennets. Margaret's brother, in this case, is the wayward one. Frederick is a naval mutineer who is on the run and must meet with his sister in secret. When Thornton sees her embracing Frederick, he mistakenly takes him for Margaret's lover. Thus, she is in danger of facing disgrace and losing Thornton's respect.

As with Darcy and Elizabeth, Gaskell gives Margaret and Thornton a difficult journey. Margaret, like Elizabeth, rejects his first proposal of marriage. He remains faithful and loyal to her, however, and like Darcy, works in the background to protect her and maintain even the slightest connection with her. Mrs Thornton, on the other hand, is highly disapproving and does not think that Margaret is worthy of her son's friendship, let alone love. Like Lady Catherine she makes her point of view very clearly and loudly. The relationship with her prospective mother-in-law gets off to a very rocky start for Margaret. Mrs Thornton, a plain-speaking, working-class Lancastrian, commands a room just as effectively as Lady Catherine.

The connection between Gaskell and Charlotte Brontë is well-known and enduring, thanks to the publication of the *Life of Charlotte Brontë* (1857). This was written after Gaskell had come to know Charlotte and then conducted substantial research after the novelist's death. The book forged and confirmed the reputation of the writing sisters and their unfortunate brother and helped create the Brontë 'myth' as investigated by Lucasta Miller in her so-called 2001 book. Gaskell's *Life* provided a sort of template for describing the literary life of the Victorian female novelist. In Charlotte's case, Gaskell presented this as a life of solitude, punctuated with tragedy and loss, followed by artistic triumph. It is as much a reflective narrative on Romantic, creative endeavour and self-scrutiny as any work of fiction from the period.

Gaskell, Charlotte and Austen had much in common. This includes the removal from a beloved family home and the loss of family members – not unusual features of nineteenth-century life. They, however, reflected this eloquently in their narratives. The atmosphere of loss and a certain domestic instability and disenfranchisement haunt the work of these writers. Gaskell articulated it by sending Margaret into the smoggy, crowded neighbourhoods of 'Milton'. This is a huge wrench for her, but it is the defining event in her life and means that she encounters Thornton.

Thornton educates Margaret in the real life of the urban industrial condition. Gaskell was very authentic in her descriptions, as she was a Unitarian minister's wife in Manchester and based her descriptions on what she encountered every day in the city. In the end, despite being removed from her adored home and having to adjust to a different life, Margaret not only finds the true love that she needs but also a social conscience and a new outlook. She, in her turn, helps Thornton to build a more harmonious relationship with the workers under him.

Thornton and Margaret's most dramatic scene, and the defining one of the novel, draws them together in mutual peril. This is when the riot takes place at Thornton's textile mill, when there is – literally – 'trouble at t'mill'. Thornton has used scab labour to break the strike and keep his factory operating. The workers' unioniser, Nicholas Higgins, the father of Margaret's consumptive friend, Bessie, leads the strike.

Margaret hates to see conflict and discord, and when trouble starts at the factory gates between the strikers and the scab workforce, she persuades Thornton to try and reason with Higgins and the workers directly. However, Thornton being the proud fellow he is only manages to stir things up further. When the fighting breaks out, the workers hurl their wooden clogs at him. On an impulse to protect the man she secretly loves, Margaret stands in the way of the missiles, and a sharp rock strikes her on the temple. She passes out, bleeding heavily. Thornton carries her to safety but cannot contain his feelings any longer, and he speaks what is in his heart as she lies insensible:

'He bore her into the dining-room, and laid her on the sofa there; laid her down softly, and looking on her pure white face, the sense of what she was to him came upon him so keenly that he spoke out in his pain:

"Oh, my Margaret – my Margaret! No one can tell what you are to me! Dead – cold as you lie there, you are the only woman I ever loved! Oh, Margaret – Margaret!"

Inarticulately as he spoke, kneeling by her, and rather moaning than saying the words, he started up, ashamed of himself, as his mother came in. She saw nothing, but her son a little paler, a little sterner than usual.'

North and South, Chapter 22

Thornton's declaration happens when he fears that Margaret might be dead, and like Darcy to Elizabeth, he must get his feelings out. Darcy's protestation of 'ardent' love and admiration finds its match in Thornton's passion, and then his embarrassment returns when his mother walks in and he appears 'stern' once more. Thornton's gentleness is in contrast to the anti-heroes Dracula and Heathcliff and their cruel manipulation of female victims, such as Mina Harker.

We can see this spectrum of heroes displayed across the century, from gentlemen to Gothic anti-heroes, to the downright diabolical undead aristocrats. The interest is in the possibilities that lie hidden in their personalities. This is why Darcy, at the beginning of the century, had so much power and potential and became the archetype he did. It is why the humbly-born, honourable and dedicated Thornton is such a natural successor to the robust Georgian hero. His honesty and goodness are not immediately apparent. We learn of his worth as Margaret does.

Heathcliff, Rochester and finally, Dracula take us down a darker pathway, punctuating the century alongside their more honourable fellows. Attraction for low-born, genteel and aristocratic heroes such as these is fraught with difficulty. They are complicated, cruel, Byronic or devilish – you have to agree to love a bad boy, for certain. Their attraction is undeniable, however, especially when it's against your will and driven by a supernatural force. They are passionate, dangerous and exude a very blatant sexuality. Their dark side presents actual threat, and to move in their orbit means drawing closer to the boundary of the Gothic, beyond which is the allure of the supernatural. To be Dracula's bride puts one's very soul at risk.

Thus, we can see how the Victorian age tempered, adjusted and exaggerated the Georgian/Darcy archetype. Different values and cultural influences came into play and new social roles had to be filled. The early twentieth century, however, saw a resurgence of the Georgian and Regency hero and the huge popularity of a new historical genre: Regency Romance.

Georgian and Regency values, manners, risks, dramas and fashions attracted readers and enthralled audiences of stage and film productions. The twentieth-century descendants of the Georgians, entering a *new* Georgian period in 1910 with the accession of King George V, wanted to go against the grain of their Victorian/Edwardian parents and enjoy the adventures of rakes, libertines, the 'Regency Buck' and a character who is – possibly – the first superhero: the Scarlet Pimpernel.

Chapter 4

Elegance, risk and revolution:
Darcy's descendants in the regency romance

'They seek him here, they seek him there,
Those Frenchies seeks him everywhere.
Is he in heaven, or is he in hell?
That damn'd elusive Pimpernel.'

The Scarlet Pimpernel, Chapter 12

Baroness Emma Orczy (1865–1947) launched onto the world in 1905 the man who could be called the first modern superhero, the Scarlet Pimpernel.

The Pimpernel has all the attributes of the superhero: a secret identity, faithful sidekicks, honour, duty, strength and the love of a beautiful woman who does not know of his alter ego. He also has many features that can be tracked back to Austen's work.

The English Mi'lord

Sir Percy Blakeney is the foppish 'English mi'lord' by day and the 'elusive', daring Scarlet Pimpernel by night. He is a bridge from the brooding, troubled modern nineteenth-century hero to the mobile, innovative world of the twentieth-century popular hero, who nonetheless harbours dark secrets. To create such a figure, Orczy skipped the immediate predecessors of the Victorian age and harked back to the late eighteenth century and the 'Terror' that followed the French Revolution.

Lord Antony, one of the Pimpernel's men, explains to a rescued French aristocrat once she is safe on English soil, the specific reason why they follow their leader and owe him such loyalty:

> "Sport, Madame la Comtesse, sport," asserted Lord Antony… "We are a nation of sportsmen, you know, and just now it is the fashion to pull the hare from between the teeth of the hound… I vow, I love the game, for this is the finest sport I have yet encountered – Hair-breath [sic]

escapes... the devil's own risks! Tally-ho! – and away we go!"

The Scarlet Pimpernel, Chapter 4

Love of the challenge, the chase and the championing of the underdog drive the group on. The elderly French Comtesse, on the receiving end of this explanation is, understandably, rather bewildered – considering everything she has just been through. It probably did not feel much like 'sport' to her. 'Tally-ho!' indeed.

Sir Percy, the Pimpernel, is Orczy's masterpiece of witty characterisation. He hides in plain sight with his persona of the foppish idiot. She used the late-eighteenth-century character, the ridiculous figure of the fop, as the perfect veiled identity for her hero. For who would suspect that a perfumed fool could possibly be the masculine, bold and dynamic Pimpernel?

Disguise, guile, trickery and dissembling, mixed with secret pain, make him an intriguing figure. He has a title, popularity, immense wealth and Marguerite – his beautiful wife – but he cannot trust her with his secret identity. These are all the characteristics of a superhero. He is Bruce Wayne or Clark Kent.

Marguerite Blakeney longs to know the real man. She does not understand her foolish, strange husband. He is her spouse but at the same time an enigmatic, distant figure to her. The Pimpernel predicts many of the character tropes that distinguish the later twentieth-century superhero archetype from comic books, popular culture and film. The outsider heroes, such as Clark Kent and Peter Parker, share the same loneliness and also possess the same moral fortitude as Sir Percy. With great power comes great responsibility.

In common with Batman, however, the Pimpernel does not possess superhuman or supernatural powers. He seems to spirit French aristocrats from under the very noses of the Public Prosecutor and the Minister of Justice during the Reign of Terror in Paris in a magical fashion, but to do this he relies on his wit, ingenuity, cunning, strength, money and the bravery of his faithful companions.

In the first chapter, Orczy sets the scene with the daring rescue of the Comtesse, her son and her daughter. We launch straight into an adventure rather like the opening of a James Bond film. The Pimpernel is disguised as an old woman and drives his cart right through the checks and roadblocks surrounding Paris. The French authorities are looking for a tall Englishman with some escaping aristocrats. They expect their quarry to be foolish and decadent. The Pimpernel uses their prejudices against them. Like Batman, he deceives his enemies in the fight against an undoubtedly corrupt and cruel regime.

However, he also shares with Batman the questionable practice of vigilantism and does not waste too much time on soul-searching. He is not excessively violent, but he lays his cards very definitely on the table when it comes to his belief in maintaining an ordered society built along the lines of class division. In his mind, the nobility is noble by reason of their birth, and this must be preserved.

Like Darcy, Sir Percy's public character is gradually stripped away by the woman he loves. He is at the centre of both an adventure story and romantic plot with his estranged wife. He thinks she is loyal to the Revolutionary forces of her native France and has betrayed prisoners to the authorities in Paris. In fact, she was only trying to save her brother's life.

The conflict and lack of trust between Sir Percy and Marguerite do not diminish their attraction for each other. He endures a fraught period of unrequited love. It is especially difficult for him and Marguerite because they see each other all the time, and yet he believes this astonishing and beautiful woman, former star of the Paris Opera, has worked against him in his mission to rescue the people he sees as innocent.

So, Percy and Marguerite, for the first half of the novel, play out the charade of their fashionable marriage. She is bewildered and hurt by his distance, and he plays the heavy-lidded, bored fop. Percy's façade is not one of family and social pride, but of jaded foolishness. His physical characteristics, however, contradict this demeanour because he embodies the qualities of Georgian English manhood: height, bearing, strength, athleticism and perfectly-tailored clothes. We are reunited with the 'Beau' and Mr Darcy.

'[A] pleasant though distinctly inane laugh, was heard from outside, and the next moment an unusually tall and very richly dressed figure appeared in the doorway.'

The Scarlet Pimpernel, Chapter 5

What was Emma Orczy's agenda in creating this intriguing, distinctive character and his exploits? He is 'Tall, above the average, even for an Englishman, broad-shouldered and massively built…', and when he first met his wife she recalls: 'He seemed to worship me with a curious intensity of concentrated passion, which went straight to my heart…'. And as for his followers, the Pimpernel's faithful band, they worship him. The beautiful Suzanne, daughter of Madame la Comtesse, wants to know more.

What is the Scarlet Pimpernel?

" …Why! What a droll name! What is the Scarlet Pimpernel, Monsieur?"

She looked at Sir Andrew with eager curiosity. The young man's face had become almost transfigured. His eyes shone with enthusiasm; hero-worship, love, admiration for his leader seemed literally to glow upon his face.

"The Scarlet Pimpernel, Mademoiselle," he said at

last, "is the name of a humble English wayside flower; but it is also the name chosen to hide the identity of the best and bravest man in all the world…"'

The Scarlet Pimpernel, Chapter 4

Orczy rhapsodises upon the qualities of the English gentleman of that period.

Emma Orczy; or the Baroness Emma Magdolna Rozalia Maria Jozefa Borbála Orczy de Orci, the Hungarian-born daughter of composer Baron Felix Orczy and the Countess Emma Wass de Szentegyed et Cege, had a life that could be straight out of one of her own storybook adventures. She was a truly cosmopolitan, internationally educated European aristocrat. All the breeding and culture were hers, without the fortune and the security, unfortunately.

Dispossessed because of the fear of revolution in Hungary, her family moved from Budapest to Paris, then to London where Emma studied art and became a well-known and pro-lific writer, playwright, artist and translator. She had the full émigré experience of genteel poverty, good education and the resurgence of success and true love.

Key to this success was her happy marriage of nearly fifty years to illustrator, Montagu Barstow, whom she married in 1894. In 1903, after the birth of their only child, a son John, Orczy and her husband co-wrote the script for *The Scarlet*

Pimpernel. Before it became a novel, it was a successful London play for four years.

The beginning of the twentieth century marked the start of Orczy's dedication of her writing career to the 'Pimpernel' s eries of novels. The market for historical fiction in print grew more receptive to her work, as audiences' taste for her stage plays had grown. Orczy became an eminent novelist with more than a dozen titles about her famed creation. She also punctuated her writing career with contributions to different genres in the popular fiction market. She became so wealthy from her writing that she was able to afford an estate near Monte Carlo. In many ways, her anti-revolutionary, pro-aristocratic hero helped to restore the wealth and status of the Orczy family.

Orczy's politics can certainly be described as conservative, pro-aristocracy and monarchist. She embraced the British establishment and imperialism. She presented in her novels an inherent superiority of the well-bred British nobleman. This is shown in the Pimpernel's triumphs over his French adversaries. Her depiction of the adored Sir Percy in contrast to the loath-some Chauvelin is presented in melodramatic terms. There is a passion from Orczy for the sanctuary that England repre-sented for émigrés: 'The Comtesse looked round at the quaint old-fashioned English inn, the peace of this land of civil and religious liberty…'. Orczy likes to make these comparisons, emphasising the moral superiority and security of England. Sir Percy Blakeney is an 'eagle', and Chauvelin a 'weasel'.

Sir Andrew Ffoukes and Lord Antony, with their 'native British wrath' in the face of injustice and bad manners, stand up to the insolent, revolutionary French on their missions across the Channel. Marguerite Blakeney has to remind Sir Andrew to curtail his 'British-born instinct' of clenched fists and the desire to strike the surly French innkeeper Brogard. She tells him ' …you are in France, and that… is the temper of the people.' Revolution has made them thuggish, lazy and rude.

As Orczy formulated her tale of derring-do in Revolutionary France, she (a dispossessed Hungarian noblewoman) helped to establish and reinforce some of the most unshakeable national stereotypes of Britishness. These persisted long into the twentieth century, and populated literary, theatrical, film and eventually TV culture. She contributed to the popular dramatic vocabulary in the form of a character that was played on screen by a string of notable actors: Leslie Howard (1934), David Niven (1950), Anthony Andrews (1982), and Richard E Grant (1999–2000), all of them known for their portrayal of English gentlemanliness.

Where Darcy is a thorough gentleman, Sir Percy is equally so – but more political. However, they are both out to help others and have no thought of gain for themselves. Sir Percy, too, is a fascinating leading man and the opposite of

Chauvelin, just as Darcy and Wickham are opposites. Orczy contrasts the English gentleman with the French blackguard along obvious physical lines. Percy, blond and blue-eyed, might have a different colouring from the perception we have of Darcy, but they are both examples of the same masculine archetype. Percy is the English gentleman hero versus the sneaky, vulpine, swarthy Chauvelin. The physical characterisation fitted some of the prevailing stereotypes of the time, particularly as seen on stage, that fed into widely-held prejudices about nationality and identity at the time.

Orczy maintains her equilibrium of politics and morality. Marguerite and Percy's relationship is reborn as an affirmation of their virtue. When Sir Andrew escorts Marguerite on her mission into France to warn Percy of Chauvelin's trap, Orczy is at pains to explain that Sir Andrew is the perfect gentleman whilst posing as her 'lackey'. Decorum and propriety reign supreme.

Marguerite puts herself in danger in order to help the man she loves. Once she discovers her husband is the Pimpernel, the world changes. With her heart pounding, she hides behind the tattered curtain in the tavern, Le Chat Gris, at Calais and witnesses Percy confronting his enemy: 'She looked… across at the handsome face of her husband, in whose lazy blue eyes, and behind whose inane smile, she could now see the strength, energy, and resourcefulness which caused the Scarlet Pimpernel to be reverenced and trusted by his followers.'

From behind the curtain, the veil is lifted, and the true character of her husband is revealed. Percy is the Pimpernel; that is the real man behind the 'lazy' and 'inane' disguise. Previously, Sir Andrew had admitted that he too was one of the Pimpernel's men, and: "There are nineteen of us ready to lay down our lives for your husband, Lady Blakeney."

Marguerite then decides to join their number. Off she goes in order to protect Percy from Chauvelin. Like Elizabeth Bennet at Pemberley, she must venture into the hero's territory, and there she discovers the real man behind the mask:

' ...the whole aspect of the man, of indomitable energy, hiding behind a perfectly acted comedy, his almost superhuman strength of will and marvellous ingenuity, she understood the fascination which he exercised over his followers, for had he not also cast his spells over her heart and her imagination?'

The Scarlet Pimpernel, Chapter 25

Sir Percy the fop is the masked man with the 'superhuman' resources and initiative as the Pimpernel. This enables him to take a stand and protect those he sees as innocent victims of the vile, radical Revolutionaries. He is the heroic Georgian, a proper gentleman who can ride, fight, outwit and hoodwink his enemies with his powers of disguise. He slips in and out of

France on his rescue missions, always one or two steps ahead, thanks to superior skills, intellect and honour.

Regency Risk

Georgian and Regency heroes grew in popularity thanks to this dramatic potential on stage, in print and then on screen into the twentieth century. They were a contrast to the Victorian world, a throwback to a more risqué, flamboyant and permissive age. The Regency, with its sense of risk, extravagance and passion, was a fruitful period from which to draw fictional adventurers and prototype superheroes.

Orczy published an early collection of short stories called *The Man in Grey* (1918) set in post-Revolutionary France. Her 'Man in Grey' is a mysterious government agent known only by the name of 'Fernand', and his series of stories bear such titles as: 'The Emeralds of Mademoiselle Phillipa' and 'The League of Knaves.' Mysterious, sinister and dangerous, these heroes had secret lives and identities. The 'grey' suited men and the 'Scarlet Pimpernel' portrayed this archetype in entertaining historical pastiches that could offer thrills and suggestiveness. The life of disguise, secrecy and duplicity was an attractive one. Characters presented one face to the world and kept their inner lives a secret. The appeal of the drama of this lies in steady revelation. What do we find when we peel back the layers?

For the Pimpernel, it is his struggle to find a way to be reunited with his beautiful wife. His biggest challenge is in resisting her whilst thinking that she might have betrayed him. The sexual attraction between Percy and Marguerite puts them both in danger. The 'honesty' of it would mean risk for her. He might disclose something to her or be blackmailed, so their love must be unrequited which leads to great tension and drama:

> 'The dim, grey light of early dawn seemed to make his tall form look taller and more rigid. The lazy, good-natured face looked strangely altered… the eyes were no longer languid, the mouth no longer good-humoured and inane. A curious look of intense passion seemed to glow from beneath his drooping lids, the mouth was tightly closed, the lips compressed, as if the will alone held that surging passion in check.'
>
> *The Scarlet Pimpernel*, Chapter 16

Sometimes, the mask slips and hidden depths are revealed. Percy, like Darcy, is a man who hides his feelings. Marguerite sets out to discover the real man under the surface. To do this she pursues him and witnesses him in action. Elizabeth discovers the real man at his home in Pemberley, away from socially awkward situations.

Marguerite goes behind the veil and into her husband's study, which he uses as HQ for his activities. In this private space she discovers who he is and the mission he has taken on:

'The door was ajar, and she could not see anything within. She pushed it open tentatively; there was no sound... and she walked boldly in.

At once she was struck by the severe simplicity of everything around her: the dark and heavy hangings, the massive oak furniture, the one of two maps on the wall, in no way recalled to her mind the lazy man about town, the lover of race-courses, fashion, that was the outward representation of Sir Percy Blakeney.'

The Scarlet Pimpernel, Chapter 18

In this 'inner sanctum' – his Batcave – Marguerite gets to know the real character of her husband. Like Lois Lane with Superman, his identity has been under her nose the whole time. She had not, for example, 'found it worthwhile to inquire – as to how Sir Percy, whom all the world has credited with a total lack of brains, administered the vast fortune which his father has left him.' She just assumed things, based on appearances, and that has been Sir Percy's best defence

– relying on society's superficiality. What Austen uses for humour and irony, Orczy can put to good use in order for her hero to lead a double life. In the final scenes, Percy plays up to the prejudices and entrenched anti-Semitism prevalent amongst Chauvelin and his men. Disguised as 'Benjamin Rosenbaum', a Jewish man, he hides once more in plain sight and actually escorts his enemy to where Chauvelin thinks he will trap the Pimpernel. His audacity in carrying out his missions knows no limits.

Percy uses their weakness against them, as they spurn him: 'that dirty, cowardly Jew'. Chauvelin's limitations make him stupid, while the Georgian Englishman trounces their forces with his greater cunning and sense of justice, and escapes undetected as the Pimpernel.

As Marguerite watches from her hiding place she does not for one moment suspect that the hunched figure of Benjamin, beaten, kicked then left tied and gagged by Chauvelin's men, is the elusive Pimpernel. Exhausted and overwhelmed with anguish about her husband's fate, 'the Queen of London society' remains Chauvelin's prisoner. She is angry at her passivity in the face of danger: 'She could not give that signal' to warn her husband of Chauvelin's approach, ' …for she was weak, and she was a woman.'

Percy is the man of action in Orczy's world, and Marguerite the damsel in distress. Traditional roles largely prevail in this series. Although Marguerite takes some risks, she resorts to type and this allows the couple to be reunited as husband and wife. There are no more divided loyalties, they prove their love once more. Family and marital ties, social standing and honour are crucial to the way that characters behave.

The Regency Buck

Georgette Heyer (1902–1974) came along in the twentieth century and followed Orczy as an author of hugely successful historical novels, most famously her Regency Romances that really helped to redefine the romantic fiction genre. *Regency Buck* (1935) is a tightly-constructed and dramatic novel in which her heroine, heiress Judith Taverner, must come of age amidst the challenges of London and Brighton society – ruled by the Regent and George 'Beau' Brummell. 'The Regency Buck' of the title is Judith's guardian, Lord Worth.

When first up from the country she is received into society and appraised by another 'dandy' Mr Mills. He is known as the 'Mosaic Dancy' thanks to his colourful attire, and is a rival to 'Beau' Brummell's dominance. Mills pays a morning call on Judith at her new address in Brook Street, and in order to emphasise her blowsy, rural simplicity he dubs her the 'Milk Maid'. Heyer exhibits the town and country divide of the eighteenth and early nineteenth century. This is the divide that Miss Bingley tries to exploit at Elizabeth's expense in *Pride and Prejudice*. Heyer's work has this ring of authenticity thanks to her thorough historical research, which enabled her novels to sound credible and convincing of the period.

Heyer was an Edwardian girl, born in the early twentieth century, with its legacy of the recent Victorian past. She spent some years in Africa with her husband Ronald Rougier, an engineer. On her return to England in 1929 she began her writing career in earnest, after successfully producing stories to entertain family members. Her settings of Georgian society with all of its thrills, risks, gossip and drama means that she effectively invented the Regency Romance genre, with twenty-four Regency novels and eight Georgian novels to her credit.

Regency Buck prepared the way for many of the romance novels that came later. Heyer created in this work a distilled version of the intrigues, sensation and hidden desires of a set of young Regency socialites. She dug deep into the world of the 'ton', the Georgian fashionable elite.

Judith Taverner is the ingénue, a young orphaned heiress. So, right from the outset she is at risk from fortune hunters and predatory men seeking to seduce her, marry her or attempt to abduct her and force marriage on her. This was a very real, prevalent danger for young, innocent, unprotected women in that age. She must therefore navigate merciless London society and establish an unassailable place in the 'ton' under the reluctant guardianship of Lord Worth.

There is a frisson attached to the relationship between Judith and Worth from the moment they meet, and their identities are known to one another. This power/trust relationship is between the feisty, outspoken but innocent young woman and the older, aristocratic, influential man. This sounds very familiar. Wealthy, older man and young innocent woman – these are our archetypes worked out from Richardson, to Austen and on to Charlotte Brontë – which then became the staple formula for much of twentieth-century popular romance. We have this dynamic happening over and over again, based upon Austen's contemporary Regency satires: Elizabeth and Darcy, Emma and Knightley, Colonel Brandon and Marianne Dashwood, followed by Jane and Rochester in the Victorian age.

As the innocent abroad, in many ways Judith represents a return to Catherine Morland in *Northanger Abbey*, and to Burney and Richardson's eighteenth-century novels. She is the beautiful, determined virgin beset by difficulties. Sexual threats and tension from the men towards the women are an ever-present element in *Regency Buck*. Lord Worth is both forward and impertinent. He does not wait to be introduced to Judith formally. Instead, he retrieves her fallen shoe and places it back on her foot – a real Cinderella moment – or as he calls her, 'Clorinda'. She is given different names by different men:

'Clorinda' and the 'Milk Maid'. She protests passionately at Worth's advances towards her and even attempts to strike him. He seizes this chance to kiss her, a classic manoeuvre in historical romance: the stolen kiss, the crossing of a line. This boundary is crossed even before she knows he has guardianship over her and her money for the next year, until she comes of age. In a moment the power-trust guardian/ward relationship is immediately compromised because he is instantly attracted to her.

Heyer's romance is also a sumptuous exploration of Regency fashions and apparel of women and men. She lingered on the descriptions of garments and finely-coiffed hair. Austen rarely dealt with such detail in her novels, although she was more forthcoming about the detail and cost of things like textiles in her letters. What Austen did was use a more general descriptive style to show, for example, the contrast between the modest attire of the Bennet sisters and the 'decided air of fashion' possessed by Miss Bingley and Mrs Hurst.

Heyer offered a great deal of detail: carefully arched brows, handsome profiles and firm, strong hands on reins. Her focus was more on the physical qualities of her characters that only thinly veiled their sexuality. Austen hid these aspects of sexuality and desire deep within her narratives, behind propriety and satire. Heyer could be bolder. With the distance of history her novels are well-crafted historical romances rather than contemporary social satire. Her work is not *of* the Regency period like

Austen's, it casts a perspective *on* it, and is not considered to be of the same quality as Austen's. However, Heyer helped to open up different fictional avenues for many writers of the twentieth and twenty-first centuries.

She did this by directing her readers to the intimate lives of the Georgians via psychology and sensuality. These elements are influences from later nineteenth-century novelists, such as Gustave Flaubert (1821–1880). He introduced readers to the controversial and tragic Emma Bovary in 1856. Throughout the complex and disturbing narrative of *Madame Bovary*, Flaubert is preoccupied with his heroine's body. He dwells on her skin, the turn of her ankle peeping out from below her hem and the tiny buttons on the wrist of her glove. Flaubert constructed his perfect sentences to minutely and ruthlessly undress his characters. Along with this physical appeal, Heyer also employed the domestic intrigue and social frustrations of Charlotte Brontë's characters.

Risqué Behaviour and Social Change

This adds up to a sense of the risqué Regency period and gives the readers the excitement they crave, that of modern values set amid a rigidly mannered society. *Regency Buck* transposes twentieth-century behaviour and values of social ambition and independence for women (soon after partial female suffrage) onto the life of a Georgian heiress. Money gives Judith a degree of independence, but she is still trapped by society's expectations and restrictions. She decides to rebel, in small ways, and drives her own phaeton unescorted, around the park and on the Row, and starts to imbibe snuff. 'Beau' Brummell becomes a welcome ally for her, and Heyer gives a charming, sympathetic portrait of the man. He is above the competition and rivalry, part-jesting and part-jaded. He is conflicted about the very society he has helped to construct. Being at the head of the 'ton' is not, perhaps, so much fun as trying to gain entry to it.

Brummell advises Judith on ways to fascinate the fashionable crowd whilst simultaneously finding her own identity. Interestingly, independence is repeatedly stressed. This is early-nineteenth-century society, full of dandies, sportsmen, prize fighters, cockpits, adventurers, carriage-racing and duels. The dukes and princes have their morganatic marriages with mistresses dotted around London and Brighton. The Duke of Clarence, the Regent's brother, earnestly wants Judith to join their ranks as he is so besotted by her. She has to repeatedly turn him down. She is surrounded on all sides by threats to her fortune and her sexual innocence.

In order to assert her identity and defeat the gossips and the fortune hunters, Judith decides to seek out thrills of her own. She challenges her brother, Peregrine, to a carriage race along the London to Brighton road, accompanied only by her groom. She rejects the stuffy social gatherings and the amorous advances of the Regent himself.

The Prince's preposterous fantasia of a building, the Brighton Pavilion, stuffy and pungent with tobacco, is a sparkling, garish prison for Judith. Her impressions of, and disappointment with, the outlandish décor of the interior is a masterpiece of satiric understatement on the part of Heyer. Her witty balance is here and there worthy of Austen. When the Prince invites her into his cosy and informal drawing-room:

'Miss Taverner could not help reflecting that 'cosy' was not the adjective she would have used to describe the Yellow Drawing-Room. Hot it certainly was, and extremely airless, but a room more than fifty feet long and over thirty feet wide, with a ceiling supported by white and gold pillars, enwreathed by serpents, and spreading into the umbrella capitals hung with bells, hardly seemed to her an apartment designed for informal use... The chairs and sofas were upholstered in blue and yellow satin, and the cabinet-maker who had the tasteful and original idea of placing a Chinese figure with a bell in either hand on the back of each one.'

Regency Buck, Chapter 20

Heyer reflected her society of the 1920s and 30s in *Regency Buck*, offering depictions of female identity and independence put to the test. Activities that increased women's mobility and visibility were a characteristic of Heyer's time. So, Judith's exploits mirror the lifestyle of the modern 'flapper' with carriage driving and snuff-taking akin to driving automobiles and smoking. Greater public interaction, employment, education, outspokenness, representation and participation emerged for women in Heyer's early life, and she investigated this in her historical romances, informed by contemporary readers' expectations.

Lord Worth, the 'Regency Buck' himself, restates the position of men, however. He has the greater power and can thus put the 'rags-to-riches' plot into operation; despite Judith's own personal wealth, she does not have control over her fortune because she is his ward. He makes all the decisions for her and her brother Peregrine. She tries to retaliate against this and attempts to rebel. The balance is tipped in Worth's favour, but from the start he appreciates Judith's spirit, drive and intelligence, and is infatuated with her.

In one of Heyer's novels written towards the end of her career, in the 1960s, she introduced another Regency heroine *Frederica* (1965). This young woman takes charge of her family's future in an even more independent fashion than Judith. She does this to secure their place in society after both parents die. The movements of independence and change that characterised the 1960s can also be represented in the Regency period, with the masculine-sounding heroine Frederica bypassing convention and deciding on her own future.

This brings us to the concept of 'Regency Risk' as entertainment. This was defined by Kathryn Sutherland in 'Jane Austen on Screen', her chapter in *The Cambridge Companion to Jane Austen* (second edition, 2012). She viewed Regency period tropes in cinema and romantic fiction as arising from the reputation the historical period had as one full of license, freedom and libertinism, compared to the later more censorious Victorian period. The Regency could, therefore, become a shorthand in film and literature, Sutherland tells us, for sexual suggestiveness. Heyer pushed her stories into this kind of territory. Frederica, for example, places power over her family in the hands of a patron, Lord Alverstoke, a distant cousin, who is rich and devastatingly handsome. He is a bored, jaded, hard-to-reach aristocrat in the mode of 'Beau' Brummell, but Frederica makes him question his principles and idea of honour. She is a fresh female influence and bursts his bubble of boredom, presenting an alluring possibility. Frederica is the perfect match for him because she is not impressed or intimidated by social reputation and only looks out for her family. She is unaware of her attractiveness and Alverstoke, of course, falls for he as she tames his bad-boy ways.

In or Out? The 'Ton'

Heyer specialised in the portrayal of the Georgian social ruling elite, the 'ton'. They were the 'bon ton' – literally 'good tone', with their equivalent in France being the 'beau monde'. This was the select group to which, it could be said, a man of Darcy's rank belonged. Certainly, Heyer's Lord Worth and Lord Alverstoke belong to this set. To be part of the 'ton' you had to wear the right clothes, as prescribed by 'Beau' Brummell at times, belong to the right London club and engage in the correct sports and pastimes.

Bingley's whole enterprise, for example, in taking a country house (to fish and shoot) and a house in town (to entertain), under Darcy's guidance, is to see if he has what it takes to become part of the 'ton'. Entry required patronage and means. Darcy, with his well-established connections and old money, offered a guarantee of introduction. He is there to lead Bingley along the right path, which is one reason why he persuades his friend away from courting Jane.

Heyer used the 'ton' as integral to her plots. It was a way of generating tension, to be 'in' or 'out', select or 'cut'. Peregrine Taverner, Judith's brother, is dazzled, distracted and positively besotted by the new society he finds himself in as he comes of age. He spends his days being fitted for boots at Hoby's, hats at Lock's. He chooses his watch fobs and jewellery in Wells

Street and inspects carriages at Long Acre, then horseflesh at Tattersall's. Being 'in' with Regency society shapes Perry's experience. He is willing to enter dangerous situations, lured by his social-climbing, greedy cousin. This cousin makes repeated attempts on Perry's life in order to inherit the Taverner fortune. Thankfully, Worth manages to stay one step ahead and to save him by out-thinking the fortune-hunting villain. Darcy-like, he has to problem-solve and save face for his naïve wards.

Judith's cousin also tries to court her and when that fails, he resorts to desperate measures. He abducts her and holds her at a secluded inn overnight to attempt a forced marriage. He tries to compromise her reputation by keeping her alone with him, therefore trying to compel her to marry and thus avoid scandal. Luckily, Lord Worth comes to her aid.

Judith, and soon Lord Worth with her, become tired of the over-exaggerated importance of 'society' in the form of the 'ton' and the restrictive mannered attitudes.

Ideas of fashion in the eighteenth century were first ruled by Richard 'Beau' Nash (1674–1761) the 'King' of Bath and Tunbridge Wells, the fashionable spa centres. Synonymous with mannered Georgian society, he commanded entry to the right places as master of ceremonies at the Bath Assembly Rooms, setting the tone for all the fashionable entertainments. Unimpressive as a lawyer, Nash instead took to gaming and socialising. He wore a black wig, rather than the regular white powdered wig, and was a pioneer of fashion.

Brummell, later, had entry to and dominance over the 'ton' thanks to his connections and style of dress, but he, like Nash, died in debt. Judith hears the name of 'Beau' Brummell at every turn, just one week into her first London season:

'Mr Brummell had invented the starched neck-cloth; Mr Brummell had started the fashion of white tops to riding-boots; Mr Brummell had laid it down that no gentleman would be seen driving in a hackney carriage; Mr Brummell has his own sedan chair, lined and cushioned with white satin; Mr Brummell has abandoned a military career because his regiment had been ordered to Manchester; Mr Brummell has decreed none of the Bow-Window set at White's [Club, St James'] would acknowledge salutations from acquaintances in the street if they were seated in the club window. And Mr Brummell, said Mrs Scattergood, would give one of his stinging set-downs if she offended his notions of propriety.'

Regency Buck, Chapter 5

This was an exhausting and complex set to be part of, as it appears here. Hard to keep up with the required behaviour, it was the correct form in Georgian society for a time to filter things past Brummell for his judgment and approval. Heyer based the mood of her novel on those historical times, and so she did not need to invent anything preposterous or extraordinary. The Georgians could do that – right enough – themselves. Judith and Brummell do become allies, however. He sees her sincerity and wishes to help her. So, she cultivates a dramatic and defiant persona under his guidance, embracing her identity as the 'Milk Maid'. She takes an insult and turns it into an attribute.

Peregrine, especially, wants to gain the approval of the 'Beau', and so he indulges in a prolonged toilette in order to make his outfits acceptable. He turns to his sister, proudly, to see if she likes it:

> 'There was a laugh in her eye, but she assured him he was quite the thing. In any other man she would have ruthlessly condemned so absurdly waisted a coat, so monstrous a cravat, such skin-tight pantaloons, but Peregrine was very much her darling, and must be allowed to dress himself up in any dandified way he pleased.'
>
> *Regency Buck*, Chapter 5

Heyer arrived at a point where her characters ask: what is important? Faced with the choice of extreme and ridiculous outfits and preserving dignity by not falling victim to fashion, Peregrine chooses fashion. Judith chooses loyalty to *him*. She does not ridicule and allows him the chance to be himself, find his own expression. Kindness and family concern come first for her, as they do for Frederica. Both these women teach the heroes what matters. Darcy is similarly witness to that sense of family devotion from Elizabeth, the devotion he prizes so highly.

It took a bold choice to go for independence and autonomy against fashion and not follow the dictates of the 'season'. Even the wealthiest of the upper classes could not comfortably avoid the requirements placed on them to be part of the right set at the right time of year. The London season ran from late January until early July based around the Parliamentary term. Before and since the Regency period, there has always been this formation of an elite group, attached to the monarchy and politics, that moves in court, social and Parliamentary circles.

Almack's Club in London, unusually, was ruled by a female social set. Influential women of the 'ton' could secure membership for newcomers. Judith, in Heyer's world, is able to join. Brook's Coffee House was another important place to be seen, where the consumption of tea and coffee was all the rage. Regency London was fuelled on caffeine, and Regency society at large has become emblematic in the modern popular imagination as a divided, competitive, elegant and romantic world.

Heyer's Frederica Merriville is a young woman on a mission. Rather like Mrs Bennet, she possesses a socially-oriented zeal on behalf of her family. Frederica's situation is complicated because she has a beautiful sister, Charis, who is the object of many a lustful male gaze. Frederica tries to secure her family's future and protect her sister from seduction or forced marriage. Being a beauty, like Charis or Jane Bennet, was both an advantage in the marriage market, and a disadvantage on the social scene.

Heyer creates a lovely conceit for her heroine. Frederica, with her manly name, strikes up an alliance with Lord Alverstoke to be patron to her family and take the Merriville orphans under his wing. The project appeals to the bored dandy, and he engages in the social game, whilst falling head over heels for the determined Frederica. Like Darcy, Alverstoke and Worth are used to things working for them, and they can move through society with supreme ease, untouched by rejection. These men do not have to marry, or they have the leisure to choose whatever heiress suits them. When confronted with these unconventional heroines they have to examine their feelings and step into the role of a more active, gallant hero.

Chapter 5

The flames rise higher: danger, sex and regret with the twentieth-century hero

With more overt sexual tension than Austen, both Orczy and Heyer created ideal and idealistic Georgian and Regency heroes, who could function as new developments of the Darcy archetype. They fit the bill for historical romance as men of action and prototypical superheroes. These men have to have unquestionable princ iples, and their popularity resides in the fact that they are unlike real-life debt-ridden dandies and randy princes from the Regency.

Stemming from this, the mostly female readership of romantic fiction is often accused of trying to fulfil some kind of wish or fantasy by reading the genre. They do not have a grip on reality and think that the fantasy notion of an ideal love will come to them. In fact, the distance of history and a Happy

Ever After resolution create a sense of safety and comfort. This follows the jeopardy and misunderstanding contained in the plot. These stories, therefore, offer harmony and reassurance, and the *temporary* escapism that these readers crave. They are not a substitute for real life.

Real Readers of Romance

It is important to recognise that the fascination for, and repeated reading of, romantic fiction is not necessarily down to a deficiency in the lives of fans. They are not missing something in their experience; they simply want to make the addition of some escapist entertainment. Twentieth-century readers of romantic fiction wanted to engage with a plot that answered some elements of wish fulfilment, but one which also satisfied their enthusiasm for balance, harmony and structure in a story. Theirs was a pursuit that comprised the reading and re-reading of familiar plots that fit their expectations, offered reassurance and reiterated favourite story elements for repeated emotional enjoyment.

American professor Janice Radway made a significant study of romance fans' reading in the USA in the late twentieth century, years before the proliferation of e-texts and online material. *Reading the Romance*, which was first published in 1984 offered a social and commercial study of the fans of romance up to that point. The decades of the 1960s, 1970s and early 1980s were very important to the growth of the romance genre and the mass production of printed paperback books. Radway's study also offers a template as to how fan communities have grown in the internet era, from the mid-1990s onwards.

It is also interesting to see that *Reading the Romance* studied audiences up to the decade before the impact of the BBC's 1995 *Pride and Prejudice*. That adaptation responded to the tropes established at the end of the twentieth century in romantic fiction and drama, and further contributed to the growth of Austen-inspired works. The proliferation of romantic fiction occurred in the UK as well as the USA, with works by writers such as Jean Plaidy (aka Eleanor Hibbert, 1906–1993) with her 200 novels in the historical romance genre. She took readers into fictionalised accounts of history, from the Borgias to the Tudor court to the Regency.

No mention of twentieth-century romantic fiction would be complete without Dame Barbara Cartland (1901–2000), the *grande dame* of romance. She was a titan of the form and one of the most prolific novelists of all time, with 723 titles to her name. This genre usually demands the proliferation of many versions of favourite plots containing favourite archetypes. The readers rule the market.

The staggering success of such authors as Heyer, Plaidy and Cartland indicates the power and importance of the form, and reinforces Radway's findings that readers of the twentieth century loved the familiar and the predictable based on the reproduction of different archetypes and the repetition of popular tropes. Radway asked: what are the features and factors in certain women's lives, as the principal consumers of romantic fiction then and now, that prepare them to see romance as relevant to their lives and offer a route to pleasure? She wanted to know: what *makes* a romance reader, and causes them to find the act of reading desirable and *necessary*?

It is helpful to look at some of the information about the Romance genre publishing of the second half of the twentieth century alongside the data Radway collected from her interviews with American readers from the 1970s and early 1980s. Her research pre-dates the confluence of the BBC *Pride and Prejudice*, Colin Firth and the internet of the late 1990s. So, how did readers access and respond to their favourite titles before the online revolution?

They relied upon mail order subscriptions from publishing houses and the new point of sale in the supermarket, as well as traditional outlets like newsstands and bookshops. Of these, the chance to browse a romance title at the supermarket checkout probably made one of the biggest commercial and cultural impacts of the time. Displaying novels as impulse-buy items, alongside snacks and groceries, was a new and successful marketing strategy.

Romance readers told Radway why they enjoyed the depiction of the heroes in the genre. They were very clear that they liked a hero with sexual magnetism and strength, but he also must possess tenderness and sincerity. Consumers of romance fiction find satisfaction in the formulaic approach to the plot that authors employ. The familiar territory is reassuring and entertaining as a form of escapism. Are readers simply on a search for satisfaction and wish fulfilment? Or is there something else at work? Radway reported that some readers also felt a sense of defiance when reading their romance titles, as though asserting an identity separate from work life, domestic chores and family commitments was tied up with their reading interests and the activity of reading alone. Reading romance functions as a relaxing past-time and a way of rediscovering the female reader's sense of identity.

By-Gone Times and the Distance of History

Before the internet and the proliferation of fan fiction and e-texts, the romantic fiction genre was already undergoing fragmentation and development. This was a reflection of the readership's demands. Consumer habits were moving towards more variety and diverse forms of story. A constant remained, however, and that was the use of the archetypal hero that dated from Austen's inception of Darcy at the start of the nineteenth century.

To illustrate this diversity, different historical romance sub-genres grew to become the most popular and widespread forms. Radway's reader surveys, and publishing figures, demonstrate this. It did not mean, however, that the genre was stuck in the past. She found that romance writers were helping to revolutionise and change the form to introduce new ways of thinking about female characters. So, that meant, for example, that heroines did not require marriage to affirm their identity. Instead, authors began to focus on desire and sexuality in women. The heroine became her own free agent, rather than an object of the hero's desire.

Romance with a 'bygone-times' context, in which firm social boundaries and rules of etiquette and manners apply, has universal appeal. The Regency period is one such, in which an author is at liberty to break rules, rebel and play around with the historical context. As with Heyer, and the cinema and stage melodramas of the nineteenth and twentieth centuries, the risqué possibilities allow female characters at last to be rule breakers and rebels.

Elizabeth Bennet is an inspiration for this, and the possibilities of fashioning rebellious, unconventional heroines has turned many readers of romance into writers. Radway found that reading romance encouraged some women to become writers themselves and speak more openly about their interests. She observed that the activities of writing and reading romance encouraged exchanges between authors and fans, and she tried to foresee the exciting results of such community interaction about a favourite genre. This is now a good model for thinking about the interfaces online between writers, readers, writers of fan fiction, reviewers and commenters across different publishing platforms. Radway's thoughts, published in the early 1980s, aptly predicted some of the uncertainty that now shapes the forms and the fluidity of online material in the new millennium. Change and unpredictability seem to be the bywords. Interaction is not limited to the reader experience.

The 'interaction' is an event, on a personal and commercial level, affected and partially controlled by the material conditions of book publishing. So, we need to think about the marketing, distribution channels, availability and how the product and the author are pitched to the market. These were important features for the late-twentieth-century romance market, and the online twenty-first-century culture has only supported and expanded this, as well as witnessing the explosion in Jane Austen and Regency-inspired fiction. The conditions in which Jane Austen fan fiction takes shape and reaches its readers will be explored in a further chapter.

The Commercial Romantic Revolution

A range of different publishing formats and social movements, such as the rise in public literacy, powered the mass production of paperback books and the romance market's growth over the twentieth century. Romance fiction was at the leading edge of the market. In the UK this included Heyer, Plaidy – and Cartland of course – and Agatha Christie (under the pen-name of Mary Westmacott). These authors were part of the pre- and post-WWII publishing boom.

In the USA, books were distributed through the same channels as newspapers and magazines, as well as via mail order subscription. After WWII, paperbacks became everyday purchases, so along with magazines consumers could buy paperbacks at the grocery store. The UK market followed suit. Publishers, therefore, sought to minimise risk in order to achieve bestseller status with as many titles as possible. So, they introduced more category and genre fiction titles and started to rely upon and then encourage readers' brand loyalty.

This sums up the modern commercial publishing formula. Predictability and reliability became key, and romantic fiction was one of the most effective and brand-loyal forms. Daphne du Maurier's *Rebecca* (1938) for example, was an inspiration for publishers of popular, cheap fiction in America from the early 1960s.

Based on Jane Eyre, *Rebecca* had been consistently in print from 1938–1960 and remains so today. Daphne du Maurier inspired other authors and their publishers to use this type of plot as a template for new series of novels. The modern rags-to-riches derivation of *Pride and Prejudice* and *Jane Eyre* involved added mystery, further suggestions of the Gothic and, at the centre of the story, the young narrator – the enigmatic, innocent, un-named 'second Mrs De Winter.'

Imitations of this novel that became hugely successful in the 'gothic' line included Phyllis Whitney's *Thunder Heights* (1960). Whitney and Victoria Holt (aka Jean Plaidy, aka Eleanor Hibberd) were represented by agent Phyllis Myrer. Myrer had noticed that in the 1950s mysteries had suffered a sales dip, because women readers had come to dominate the market and they wanted romance, not crime or horror. She encouraged her authors like Holt to tap into this change. Holt's *Mistress of Mellyn* (1960) sold over a million copies in its first edition and stays very close to the plot of both *Rebecca* and *Jane Eyre*. To Mr Darcy, Mr Rochester and Heathcliff, can be added Maxim de Winter from the 1930s and Holt's Connan Tremellyn from the 1960s. The archetype persisted throughout the most popular romantic novels, with class boundaries crossed and adaptations fitting a variety of settings. Romantic fiction survived the middle years of the century and emerged triumphant into the post-war period to enjoy new phases of popularity.

Some of these phases, particularly from Holt and Cartland are fondly remembered, others are more controversial. Radway reminds us that in the 1960s and 1970s in the USA readers were faithful consumers of their favourite authors' novels. They were subscribers to historical and romantic fiction magazines, journals and paperback publishers. It was a short step for publishers to expand their lists in the 1960s to offer more and more derivations of *Rebecca*, *Jane Eyre* and *Pride and Prejudice*.

And at this time romantic fiction came up against the women's movement. One of the overriding questions was, how could traditional and modern values co-exist in such a genre? Attempts had already been made to transcend class boundaries and tackle questions of social injustice and oppression. A solution, Radway noted, was to make heroines feisty, or in the American vernacular, 'spunky', and pit them against strong, wealthy men whom they could tame.

So far, so balanced: a traditional love story, with a woman in the mode of Elizabeth Bennet, and less of the wallflower Jane Eyre.

The Birth of the Bodice-Ripper

The Flame and The Flower (1972) by Kathleen E Woodiwiss, however, took that formula and changed the landscape of mainstream romantic, historical fiction in the new decade. This novel is a Regency blockbuster – but only in the sense that it loosely corresponds to Anglo/American history. It was published first in paperback, a significant departure from the commercial model. It is a real epic, running to 600 pages. The vast length of the book would typically justify a hardback publication. However, it appeared in the cheaper, readily available paperback form.

What else was different about this story? The heroine, Heather Simmons, has more to combat than most. She is forced into a vulnerable position from the outset of the narrative and is, like previous Regency heroines, threatened with, but then subjected to, sexual violence. This, at the hands of the novel's hero, Captain Brandon Birmingham.

Brandon is handsome, wealthy and overwhelmingly masculine. We notice that behind Heather's fear of him she acknowledges his attractiveness. She is innocent of all sexual experience and completely intimidated by him, however. He is tall, powerful and hard, and wears tight (*very* tight) breeches and an open-neck ruffled white shirt.

This is the fantasy romantic hero, and a sea captain. Andrew Davies' 1995, and Joe Wright's 2005, versions of Darcy were based on, and channelled, this physical archetype. Dark and brooding (Firth had to dye his hair black to be Darcy), moody and sardonic and extremely butch, Brandon is a devilish pirate. He is a throwback to Lord Byron and his 'Corsair' and 'Turkish Tales'. On first meeting Heather, however, Brandon mistakes her for a prostitute, and in what are now controversially eroticised scenes, he rapes her repeatedly.

Obviously, here is where the difficulty lies. The dark, brooding hero in this context moves way beyond the threat of aggression and deviates from the sense of honour and decorum possessed by Darcy, Rochester or even Maxim de Winter. Brandon goes further even than Heathcliff. The playful suggestiveness of the 'bodice-ripper' nickname given to this genre hides a darker aspect to the fiction. The Flame and The Flower starts with a problematic and repellent set-up to the romantic plot. Once clear that Heather is not a prostitute, Brandon realises he has raped her – but still keeps her prisoner on board his ship. He decides instead he will install her as his mistress.

Woodiwiss leapfrogged back in time to the situations presented by the precursors of Jane Austen. Richardson in *Clarissa* and John Cleland with *Fanny Hill* (1748): both used contentious and conflicted story devices that involved acts of rape. These eighteenth-century authors had a satirical, as well as a prurient, agenda in depicting these acts: they were writing about exploitation in their contemporary society. Woodiwiss, however, with her historic, romantic fiction had no such satire in mind. She portrayed a masculine, dominant hero in whose eyes a protesting, desperate, sobbing woman is eroticised.

Captain Brandon is convinced she will fall for him and eventually engage willingly as his mistress. In the meantime, he rapes her. This is a world away from Darcy, or Austen's Colonel Brandon in *Sense and Sensibility*.

And yet, these bodice-rippers by Woodiwiss and others, such as Rosemary Rodgers' *Sweet Savage Love* (1974), despite being referred to as 'rape sagas' by interviewees of Radway, were incredibly popular and sold by the million. They present immense difficulties with their plots around taming, including abduction and coercive, aggressive sexual acts. The eventual passion between the couple, resulting in true love, perhaps functions as a redemptive storyline for the hero. This, after the initial trauma and violation of the heroine, is a hollow act, however, and remains disturbing for readers to this day.

Once Heather in *The Flame and The Flower* finds out that she is pregnant from the rape, she is forced into marriage with Brandon. Here is the escapist resort into fantasy. Reservations and repulsion at such a plot, that contains the conditioning of and cruelty towards a woman, have to be temporarily put aside for this to be of any entertainment value – possibly. Instead, it is read as a dramatic, tense scenario in which the heroine is trapped in an intimate relationship with a rich, handsome, passionate man who finds her truly irresistible. It is necessary to jump through some fantastical fictional hoops in order to work through the problems with the story. One of the characteristics of these 'bonk'-buster novels is the borderline pornography they employ.

Woodiwiss intersected the characters such as Heathcliff and Margaret Mitchell's Rhett Butler from *Gone with the Wind* (1936) to create the devastating, piratical figure of Brandon Birmingham. He, like Butler, is a seafarer, plantation owner and trader from Charleston, South Carolina. Unfortunately, with Brandon, Woodiwiss presented a slave-owning rapist as the hero. This book does not travel or age well, and we have to keep on reminding ourselves this is fantasy.

To give Woodiwiss due credit, however, more than twenty years on she revisited the Birmingham family saga with co-authored collections and sequels. In *The Elusive Flame* (1998) and *A Season Beyond A Kiss* (2000), the successors to Brandon Birmingham's legacy, Beauregard and Jeff, reinstate the ideal of passionate gentlemen who behave with nobility and honour. Woodiwiss, it seems, regretted the misstep of including a rape scene at the beginning of her first novel.

The Return to Innocence

For many twenty-first century readers of romance and now Jane Austen fan fiction, these sweet, savage romance novels of the 1970s and 1980s are anything but sweet, even with

Darcy-esque heroes. They move too far off track from moral and romantic ideals for them to be an engaging read. It is easy to see why, and also why, Woodiwiss felt the need to address this. A return to Austen for inspiration and character-isation is a refreshing, intelligent and restorative act after such fictional forays.

Rodgers' *Sweet Savage Love*, that followed Woodiwiss (and was also published by Avon Books), is a tale of powerful men and damsels in distress in nineteenth-century America. Steve Morgan, the hero, is a selfish and sexually immature man who uses coercive and forceful tactics to have sex with as many women as possible, including Ginny Brandon, the heroine. (That name, Brandon, again). In the hands of some authors this difficult hero archetype can turn into a dangerous, cruel and sexually aggressive character.

In mainstream, popular romance of the new millennium these heroes are still causing problems. In *The Marriage Miracle* by Liz Fielding (2005, Mills & Boon), for example, the hero Sebastian Wolseley is very rude on first meeting the heroine, Matilda, at a party. Insensitive is an understatement when he asks Matilda – in her wheelchair – if she is the cabaret act. He thinks of it as sarcasm, but it just comes across as nasty. When authors seek to emulate Austen's version of a brooding, socially awkward hero they sometimes get stuck in the mire of inves-tigating the anguished male psyche tinged with bitterness and aggression. This shows that the employment of this archetype is more complex than it first appears. The shadows of Shakespeare, Goethe and Byron are long and loom large and dark across the centuries. Is the hero troubled, or just plain nasty? That is up to the author and the balance they strike.

Yet, authors return to the type again and again. What is the draw? Probably, the versatility. They can be difficult or docile, threatening or tender, savage or sweet. This is the trajectory of their narrative that draws readers in.

The *Twilight* novel series by Stephenie Meyer, for example, has this attraction. Published from 2005–2008, their origins lie in *Jane Eyre*, *Wuthering Heights*, *Dracula*, *Romeo and Juliet* and Jane Austen's *Pride and Prejudice*. The series attracted millions of readers, from teens upwards. Meyer is an English graduate, avid literary fiction and romance fan and a member of the Church of Latter-Day Saints (LDS), or Mormon faith, community in Utah, USA. She cites Shannon Hale (a fellow LDS author) as one of her favourite writers. Hale penned *Austenland* (2007), which was the first of a series of fan-based adventures. In an interview, Meyer has said she adores it and it's the perfect book for 'Austen-obsessed freaks (like me)'.

In *Austenland*, Hale's light-hearted take on an American woman's crazed obsession with Austen (and Colin Firth in particular) is infused with a sense of romance and humour that supports the notion of faithful, married love. Happiness is a result of a legitimate union based on mutual love and respect.

'Austen-obsessed' Meyer's vampire-teen-romance novels are also essentially very moral. Meyer's Edward Cullen is a 100-year-old vampire and still a virgin, like the mortal heroine, Bella Swan.

Edward and Bella have a mystical and chemical attraction, based on his vampire instincts and her power of fidelity, purity and protection. Their relationship begins as high school angst, but quickly turns Gothic. Edward begins as standoffish and confusing for Bella, who gradually breaks down his barriers. He modifies his blood-sucking desires and resorts to hunting wild animals rather than preying on humans.

Meyer's handling of the characters tames the violent and diabolical nature of vampires. They become noble, nurturing and even divine. The effect of sunlight is not to render these vampires into dust. When hit by the sun they sparkle and glow. Initiation into this vampire 'family' is an allegory for conversion into the LDS religious community – a sort of re-birth and baptism. Edward is educated, clean-living, prosperous and pure – an ideal boyfriend to introduce to Bella's father, and perfect potential marriage material. This version of the dark, brooding hero appeals to the moral and deeply conservative tastes of the readers in the Mormon and Evangelical Christian communities in the USA and beyond. There are still, however, some problematic characteristics about Edward. He watches Bella whilst she sleeps, for example, and some detractors of the novels consider this obsessive behaviour in the relationship to be unhealthy.

Naughty and Nice

What started out as a fan fiction tribute to the *Twilight* series, by British writer E L James, exploded into a publishing phenomenon across the online, ebook and print markets and then into cinemas. *Fifty Shades of Grey* (2011) was the first in a three-part saga that started life as an eroticised version of the *Twilight* stories.

James handles the features of innocence and seduction, taming and transformation via sexual awakening, very differently from Meyer. The same plot and archetypes, again, result in extremes of tone, depending on the author. James resorted to the more graphic, explicit formula employed by earlier writers of the 1700s and 1970s, resulting in an intense and sometimes pornographic novel.

Again, the hero is problematic, rich and extraordinary. James' contribution to the lineage of the archetype is Christian Grey. He is young, attractive and a billionaire. He dresses in fabulously well-tailored suits but has an unruly, dark and very difficult personality. Anastasia Steele (Ana) contemplates the events around her meeting with Christian in the first person; she is present for this and wants us to be also. Christian is a Darcy equivalent of the early twenty-first century: a driven, determined, young, super-rich capitalist. He also has a highly sexualised lifestyle and initiates Ana into his bondage/dominance/sado-masochistic (BDSM) practices.

Fifty Shades of Grey features sexual danger and explicit acts like those of *The Flame and The Flower* and *Sweet Savage Love*, but all consensual. It is a blockbuster style of saga that fully explores and describes the sexual awakening of the two protagonists. Where Heyer, du Maurier, Cartland and Meyer only suggest such aspects, James employs that angle as the focus of the narrative. In fact, the physical and sexual journey that Ana and Christian embark on is the foundation of their love story. This type of narrative references other innocence-to-experience tales and coming-of-age stories found in famous pornographic novels such as Cleland's *Fanny Hill* and *The Story of O* by Anne Declos (1954).

With Christian Grey some of the danger is realised, but Ana actually discovers a power in herself with which she can confront him about his past and help to heal him. This leads to his true love for her. These powerful men come in many guises, and Grey, like Brandon Birmingham, forces a problematic sexual initiative on an innocent partner. Selfishness and exploitation on their part does not mean that they cannot finally arrive at true love, however. Even some villains can be redeemed. Grey, after working out his issues with jealousy and control, is finally saved by Ana and by fatherhood in the third of the series, *Fifty Shades Freed* (2012). Heathcliff and Dracula are another matter, as examples of this archetype that fail to attain freedom or redemption. However, in some of the film versions of Dracula's story, the Count is rendered more sympathetically, such as the Francis Ford Coppola-directed *Bram Stoker's Dracula* (1992). Count Dracula (Gary Oldman) is finally saved by Mina (Wynona Ryder) at the point of death, thanks to her love for him. Heroines that show an inner core of strength can battle most of a hero's flaws, and even save them from the fiery pit of hell.

E L James is considered something of a pioneer in popular fiction. Just as Woodiwiss broke the mould with the epic (600-page) blockbuster paperback, so James replicated this with the astonishing success of first the online fan fiction version, and then the ebook format, of Fifty Shades. From web publishing on a fan fiction site, to download, to print version, to movie, this novel established a new route in modern publishing.

An early draft of *Fifty Shades* started life as part of the proliferation of online works whereby fans become authors. Chatrooms, blogs and fan sites in various forms are as old as the internet. They are established, develop, combine and grow thanks to a supportive, like-minded community. There is always someone out there who shares your passions. *Fifty Shades, Twilight, Rebecca, Regency Buck* all generated their own huge fanbase. The fan culture that is stimulated with certain novels continues unabated, after which fan fiction investigates every corner and every possibility of every storyline.

The other key ingredients that influence such fruitful and long-lasting invention around the character of Darcy and the Darcy archetype are the on-screen depictions. The role of Darcy as played by Colin Firth in the 1995 adaptation marked a massive shift in the narrative emphasis, bringing the hero level with the heroine.

More and more spin-offs followed that broadcast. These increasingly feature Darcy as the central protagonist, and the new figurehead of romance and passion. And like the history of the Darcy archetype in print, there is a substantial history of the portrayal on screen. The role of Darcy is now one that distinguishes an actor's career and may blight or bless their future.

Chapter 6

Darcy on screen: Colin Firth and beyond

In an interview with the *Radio Times* magazine in 1981, scriptwriter and novelist Fay Weldon described how in *Pride and Prejudice* Elizabeth Bennet gets her man thanks to her unconventional attitude and audacious manners. This was in reference to Weldon's dramatisation of Austen's novel for the BBC. It was one in a long line of adaptations – but who got it right? Who did it best? Opinions are divided. It's a generational thing. If fans grew up with a particular version of Darcy-on-screen, then that actor's performance tends to be imprinted on their minds, thanks in part to new portable media. This was first in the form of VHS, then DVD, box sets, and now online media and streaming. These media mean that fans can access their hero anytime, anywhere in one of his various on-screen manifestations. Where once the Austen obsessive had to keep the novel to hand to fuel their passion for Darcy, now they can see him in the flesh on their phone, tablet or social media page. Darcy-in-my-pocket. Touchscreen Darcy.

Playing the role of Darcy on screen has taken on different meanings over the decades. In this chapter the focus will be on the four major screen versions, two on television and two in cinema. The 1940 MGM screen adaptation of *Pride and Prejudice* was followed by other versions, but none so prominent as the 1980 BBC TV version adapted by Fay Weldon. The 1995 BBC version, adapted by Andrew Davies and directed by Simon Langton, starred Colin Firth and Jennifer Ehle and is looked upon as a landmark adaptation that changed television culture and the approach to costume drama. Joe Wright directed the 2005 cinema version of *Pride and Prejudice* with a script by Deborah Moggach and Emma Thompson. Matthew Macfadyen was the fortunate actor who starred opposite Keira Knightley as Elizabeth.

A range of other screen versions exist, featuring characters in different guises and contexts, and these will be looked at regarding spin-offs, sequels, derivative storylines and alternative narratives. Darcy comes in many forms. He emerges from the storyline in dramatised versions in all sorts of different ways.

Morale-Boosting Darcy

In the beginning there was Olivier, as far as fame and popularity goes. He was a man of many faces. His Darcy in 1940 shows warmth and humour. If he seems a little uncomfortable in the role, however, that's because he was. He did not like the adaptation and felt that he and Greer Garson (Elizabeth) were not suited to their roles. A serious and serious-minded actor, Olivier spent his downtime on set planning a large-scale stage production of *Romeo and Juliet*, in which he was to star with his wife Vivien Leigh. So, the movie was a useful and lucrative vehicle for him to be able to pursue other projects. Also, starring in feel-good, romantic, morale-boosting, thoroughly English comedies was an excellent contribution to the war effort.

What do we make of his performance now, and how is it received? As well as feeling uncomfortable in the role, Olivier lamented the fact that so much of the original material from the novel had been lost. 'Dissatisfying' is probably the verdict that most fans come to about this movie. Opportunities were missed and anachronism abounds.

Whilst not fuelling a specific Darcymania at the time, this version nonetheless was very popular and formed part of a surge in a more general Austenmania in the 1940s wartime period. Austen helped to boost morale and had wide political and cultural resonance, as Kathryn Sutherland accounts in 'Austen on Screen' (*The Cambridge Companion to Jane Austen*). Olivier as Darcy at one point recites Byron's *She Walks in Beauty Like the Night* to Elizabeth. While this might hint, as Sutherland suggests, at risqué Regency suggestiveness and satire, the adaptation is overwhelmingly a rendition of Merry Olde England with a purpose. It helped to popularise the British plight in 1940, just before America entered the Second World War. Regency risk was deemed unsuitable for mid-century American audiences, so had to be toned down with a domesticated, highly idealised version.

Greer Garson and Laurence Olivier from the 1940 film poster
for Pride and Prejudice

The American movie industry's proscriptive Hays Code (introduced in 1930) operated as a decency filter for audiences. It stated: 'No picture shall be produced [in the USA] that will lower the moral standard of those who see it. Hence the sympathy of the audience should never be thrown to the side of crime, wrong-doing, evil or sin.' Fear about the effect of new media on audiences was something American society became alert to in the 1920s, just as the novel, as new media, had been flagged as a potential danger in the eighteenth and nineteenth centuries.

This rigidity of permitted content that Hollywood filmmakers faced meant that *Pride and Prejudice* on screen was 'Victorianised', from the fashions (crinolines replaced the sexier Empire line dresses) to the idealised chocolate box settings instead of the English country house. There is no hint of risqué behaviour such as that surrounding Lydia's elopement with Wickham.

Olivier and Garson were associated with other morale-boosting entertainments of the period. Garson starred in *Mrs Miniver* (1942), a movie that highlighted the situation for ordinary people on England's home front. Such dramas depicted both nostalgic and dramatic scenarios of English life. Olivier went on to make the 1944 *Henry V*, evoking Shakespeare and medieval victories in battle to coincide with the progress towards the end of the war. Sutherland points out that the casting of Olivier and Garson was an attempt to reinforce the link between Britain and America, and show the importance of

Austen as an example of the culture that was at stake.

Contemporary with this toned-down version of the Regency and in sharp contrast, British cinema's Gainsborough Pictures, without the same restrictions as Hollywood, handled historical drama very differently. There was risk on display. Actor James Mason made a specialty out of playing sinister, sexual, anti-heroes in a string of Gainsborough melodramas. In *The Man in Grey* (directed by Leslie Arliss in 1943), which was based on Lady Eleanor Smith's 1941 novel, he plays the evil Lord Rohan. He is attractive, arrogant and dangerous. Hesther (Margaret Lockwood) is a penniless actress who gets drawn into his web of desire, schemes and sexual intrigue.

Gainsborough Studios did not shy away from stories that showed off raw passion in escapist, historical dramas. Rohan is an eighteenth-century amoral rake in the style of Lovelace in Samuel Richardson's *Clarissa*, who rapes Clarissa as part of a cruel, manipulative and destructive game. While Regency risk was shown on screen for British audiences of the mid-twentieth century, in Hays-controlled Hollywood there was a different agenda, and Austen worked as effective escapism even with the absence of such risk.

Austen was marshalled for the war effort, and although the 1940 adaptation of *Pride and Prejudice* does not sit comfortably with viewers today – Austen's satirical edge is totally removed, for example – it does show that the confluence of popular sentiment and nostalgia in her work can stand on its own.

Despite the shortcomings, there are elements of the MGM version that suggest a theatrical strength in the modification of the story. Helen Jerome's 1935 stage version of the novel had already been a hit on Broadway and in the West End. The screenplay was based on Jerome's script and, whilst it is easy to disparage it, we need to bear in mind that it had already proved its worth as popular entertainment. The deficiencies include the loss of Austen's satire, and without the authorial voice the ironic and humorous tone is lost, but by the time it reached the screen the imperative was to present cinematic flow and narrative logic.

The way in which the script condenses the novel is an object lesson in dramatisation and effective summarisation of the essential story elements. Darcy and Elizabeth hold our attention as their relationship builds in a short space of time. For example, the action of the Meryton Assembly and the Netherfield Ball is condensed into one 'act' in the film. Darcy's attraction for Garson's Elizabeth leads him on to a sequence of interactions with her that do not occur in the novel.

So, at one point, an eager Mr Collins (Melville Cooper) pursues Elizabeth through the shrubbery at the Netherfield 'garden party'. This scene was invented specifically for the film by co-writers Aldous Huxley (yes, *the* Aldous Huxley) and Jane Murfin. The Bingleys throw this gala to announce their arrival in society, and Elizabeth has to evade Collins with help from a suddenly amused, charming and conspiratorial Darcy.

It is hard to imagine the character from the novel in this mood – it is quite a shift in characterisation. Olivier has to switch between cold disapproval and whimsy. Also, in the rapid run of final scenes towards the conclusion, Lady Catherine (Edna May Oliver) invades Longbourn as the Bennet family makes their plans for a move to Margate in the wake of the scandal with Lydia.

Events are telescoped together as they cascade to a happy resolution. It turns out that Darcy has recruited his aunt in order to test Elizabeth's devotion. Lady Catherine wanted him to be matched with a strong woman who will stand up to him. She has had her eye on Elizabeth and declares her approval: '(She is) good for you, Darcy!' This is another example of the satirical edge of the novel being lost in the film. Even Lady Catherine's claws are sheathed!

Of all the aspects that might be wrong, what does feel right is Olivier's physicality in the role. He moves and behaves like a gentleman and a 'dandy'. This is a performance conscious of the men of fashion from the early 1800s, like Brummell. Olivier expresses the breeding and status of Darcy in his well-cut, expensive clothes. Even though his costume is an amalgamation of Regency and early Victorian dress, he presents a fine figure. He knew how to bear his head in a neckcloth and high collar that restrict movement and still portray a convincing character. His posture and clipped speech patterns denote Darcy's class.

Feminist Darcy

Discomfort and aloofness are also the characteristics that we associate with the next prominent screen Darcy, David Rintoul, in Fay Weldon's 1980 adaptation of *Pride and Prejudice* for the BBC. There were other versions in the intervening years from 1940, including one in 1952 on the BBC starring Peter Cushing, the master of mystery and horror, as Darcy. None of these have had quite the same effect on fans, largely because recordings have not survived, and it is likely that the 1952 version was a live studio broadcast.

Rintoul, like Olivier, is one of those professional actors often characterised as 'classically trained'. This is a label popular with American critics and audiences that denotes quality in performance. As well as the career development of RADA, followed by the Royal Shakespeare Company, Rintoul also has the best Regency period 'look' and bearing of any Darcy. He appears as someone who would have been considered a handsome man of fashion of the time. He, like Olivier, is at ease in the clothes; he looks as though he wears a high neckcloth every day. Rintoul definitely has a look of Beau Brummell about him.

The initial clipped, dismissive tone that Rintoul employs is contrasted beautifully by the softening that happens to the character as he falls in love with Elizabeth (Elizabeth Garvie). Because he is very conventional and secure in his manner, the change in him is all the more affecting. His way of showing this is probably best demonstrated when he responds to Elizabeth's acceptance of him and expression of her love. In the novel:

> 'The happiness which this reply produced, was such as he has probably never felt before; and he expressed himself on one occasion as sensibly and as warmly as a man violently in love can be supposed to do. Had Elizabeth been able to encounter his eye, she might have seen how well the expression of heartfelt delight, diffused over his face, became him…'
>
> *Pride and Prejudice* Volume 3, Chapter 16

When Darcy smiles. That is Austen's point here. Passion and joy diffuse across his face in an uninhibited way for the first time. Rintoul is very effective as a proud, stilted and embarrassed Darcy who learns how to relax and bask in the happiness of his union with Elizabeth once all is resolved.

Weldon's 1980 adaptation was a ground-breaker in a number of ways. It was extremely faithful to the novel and followed the pace and action of each volume quite closely. Weldon did not dispense with some of the peripheral characters, such as the Hursts, but used them for excellent dramatic effect. Weldon was, by this time, well-known for her television writing credits. She wrote the first episode of the long-running period drama *Upstairs, Downstairs* (beginning in 1971) and the screenplay for *Life of Christine* (1980) based on a true story of a teenage girl's incarceration. With *Pride and Prejudice* she adopted as much of a feminist tone as possible with an early-nineteenth-century text, without too much alteration of story or character.

The first character we see, and the first of the Bennet sisters to appear on screen, is Mary (Tessa Peake-Jones) – the 'forgotten' daughter. She is an emblem of the minor intellectual role permitted to women of her class during the period. She has some access to books thanks to their father's library and spends her time in practising the piano and engaged in extensive reading. Therefore, she partly fits the mould of 'accomplishment', about which there is of course much discussion in the novel between Darcy, Miss Bingley, Elizabeth and Mr Bingley. Mary is 'plain', however, and is typically portrayed as bespectacled and quiet, until she feels compelled to pronounce upon others' folly or perform on the piano at a gathering.

Weldon's adaptation foregrounds the women's intelligence and feelings and also isolates a moment for Elizabeth to make mention of Mary Wollstonecraft's *A Vindication of the Rights of Women: With Strictures on Political and Moral Subjects* (1792).

This is Weldon's declaration to the viewer, that the Bennet girls to a greater or lesser degree, and at the very least Elizabeth, have been exposed to Wollstonecraft's new proto-feminist political philosophy. Elizabeth's unfolding personality in this drama is represented by her reading and approach to new independent (revolutionary) thinking.

The speculation that the novelist, too, had read *A Vindication* has been subject to robust and vigorous debates in academic circles for many years. Marilyn Butler brought a new focus to Austen with *Jane Austen and the War of Ideas* (1975), and this continued with Claudia Johnson's *Jane Austen: Women, Politics, and the Novel* (1988).

In the light of Weldon's adaptation, Austen can be connected both to radical proto-feminist ideas and more conservative thinking on marriage and social order. Liberal or reactionary, Austen still provokes debate. Miriam Ascarelli has offered an overview of the discussion around the 'Feminist Connection' for *Persuasions Online* (Winter 2004) . Whichever side of the argument you might come down on, there is no denying Weldon's striking observations and contribution to the debate in her adaptation.

This version was part of a new approach to costume drama on television. Editing style, location filming, strong musical score and authentic costume detail all help to make the 1980 version a visual landmark that departed from the style of, for example, Hugh Thomson's illustrations for Austen's novels of the 1890s. For most of the twentieth century, Thomson offered the 'look' that dramatists and stage and screen designers relied upon for Austen adaptations.

Hugh Thomson illustration, 1894

Thomson's illustrations of Austen were set in an idealised, non-industrial nineteenth-century world without grimness or deprivation. This effect is now light-heartedly known as the 'Cranfordisation' of Austen. This is in reference to the 2007 BBC adaptation of Mrs Gaskell's collection of social sketches *Cranford* (published from 1851–1853) that depict the idyllic community of Cranford in Cheshire. Based on Gaskell's childhood, it was a hugely popular series on the BBC running from 2007–

2011. Set in the 1840s – the decade in the nineteenth century known as 'the hungry forties' due to nationwide famine – the Cranford stories from the BBC contain none of that realism. They are comic and gentle with Christmas-card Victoriana as a backdrop to the tight-knit group of, mostly female, characters. Amongst the cast was Julia Sawalha (as Jessie Brown), after she had come to prominence as Lydia Bennet in 1995.

As Thomson showed with his illustrations, and the BBC reinforced, there is a desire amongst readers and viewers to have an idealised, escapist nineteenth-century idyll. Thomson's images are still highly popular today, with the 1890s editions highly collectible. Television Darcy began to overtake this idealised imagery with Rintoul's Regency looks going some way to change it. He is more than just handsome and snobbish. He is given the opportunity to smoulder, with his sharp cheekbones, dark colouring and fashionably kiss-curled hair. Garvie's Elizabeth is a clear challenge and, as future mistress of Pemberley, is destined to bring something exciting to the position. Will, as Weldon speculates, her reading of Wollstonecraft cause revolution on the estate?

Weldon went on to write controversial works such as her 1983 novel *The Life and Loves of a She-Devil* that was adapted for television in 1986 by the BBC. It won the BAFTA for best drama series. Her 'macabre' and 'cautionary' tale, as the *Times* called it, about modern marriage and adultery, has a rich and beautiful woman Mary Fisher (Patricia Hodge) victorious in love over the plain and frumpy Ruth (Julie T Wallace), or so it would seem. Ruth, with her large, awkward body and hairy facial moles, decides to exact revenge.

This satire on the risks of adultery and the competitiveness of love and marriage echoes some of Austen's plotlines, showing Weldon to be a successor in this mode of story-telling and a suitable adaptor of Austen's beloved novel to the screen. It is because Austen's novel and her hero are not simple or simply idealised that the drama and variety in them needs to be drawn out for the screen.

Weldon went on to adopt Austen's archetypes in a distinctly unorthodox fashion with *Darcy's Utopia* (1990). In this modern morality tale about marriage, society and money, Professor Julian Darcy is the figure behind the action because the plot circulates around his charismatic wife, Eleanor Darcy, and her social revolution of 'Darcynomics'. She bases her philosophy on idealised romantic love. But more on this unconventional interpretation of the world of Darcy in chapter eight.

The Creature from The Lyme Park Lake

And so, we come to what some call the definitive adaptation. In 1995, Simon Langton directed Andrew Davies' imaginative yet faithful adaptation of the novel. Elizabeth (Jennifer Ehle) gazed upon Darcy (Colin Firth) and he smouldered back at her, and television history was made. It was a refreshing and energetic version, no doubt. Carl Davis' opening title music set the tone as the camera panned across the scattered, charming debris of embroidery and bonnet-trimming clearly left over from a Bennet sisters' shopping expedition in Meryton: an idyllic afternoon of female pursuits at Longbourn. This is a good example of the development of the dramatic world of the novel and the attention to detail rendered by Langton's direction.

This time it is Elizabeth who greets us at the beginning of the first episode. She strides across the countryside and observes the gentlemen galloping across the fields. Darcy's black hunter is seen outrunning Bingley's white horse. Darcy appears, without speaking, as immediately more dangerous and daring than his friend. This was part of Langton's visual vocabulary for us to get to know the characters. Darcy is faster, ahead, and owns better horseflesh because he is richer. Bingley is not so competitive or advantaged. Elizabeth looks on from her vantage point as she takes her regular walk, relishing the solitude. What is also interesting is the contrast that Langton introduced part way through the series. Darcy switches to a white horse, to be the dashing hero on the white charger, once he falls in love with Elizabeth. And that is how he sets out to rescue Lydia.

Firth was not the first choice for the role, or, to begin with, Davies and Langton's ideal choice in terms of looks and manner. In a 2015 celebration of the twentieth anniversary of the BBC broadcast at the Chawton House Library, Hampshire, Langton addressed an audience about the background to the production. He described how Firth had to slim down and become more of a sportsman to portray Darcy, as well as have his quite light ginger hair dyed black; all this to suit the archetype. So, from a not too promising start, Firth metamorphosed into the beloved hero and embodied the role so well – with his respectful and literate approach to Austen's material – that he succeeded in fleshing out the character from the novel. Davies, Langton and Firth brought into being a Georgian male that resulted in a landmark performance.

Davies' script used the foundation of the novel to build the particular Regency world of the Bennets, Longbourn, Meryton, Pemberley and the Rosings/Hunsford set. Elizabeth and Darcy move amongst them and show their dynamic as heroine and hero. It is an energetic drama. Ehle and Firth were having an off-screen romance at the time of shooting, and Langton put some of their on-screen chemistry down to that.

During the discussions conducted at the Chawton *Pride and Prejudice* anniversary event the cast members who were present recalled the shoot with great fondness. They talked about the 'family' feel to the production, and the knowledge that the series is still just as popular as ever was very gratifying for them. Friendships were forged. Polly Maberley (Kitty) was in her first major role, and at seventeen she was the right age for her character. She found herself growing up on set surrounded by great colleagues, many of who remain close. Crispin Bonham-Carter (Bingley) retired from directing and acting and went into teaching. He works as a secondary school English teacher in London. He, Joanna David (Aunt Gardiner) and Susannah Harker (Jane) reiterated the satisfaction they felt at being cast in such finely drawn literary roles, and remain friends off-screen.

The choreographer for the dance sequences in the series, Jane Gibson, put the actors through their paces for the outstanding set-pieces of the Netherfield Ball and the Meryton Assembly. These were shot on location at historic houses, and the actors had to learn the pace, form and steps of the dance along with their lines. This stylisation created the intimacy of the scenes between Elizabeth and Darcy and highlighted the strengths and weaknesses of the different characters. Behaviour on the dance floor exemplified social graces and social standing, from Lydia's wayward flirtatiousness, to Collins' (David Bamber) comedic clumsiness and faux pas.

This is another exercise in the fleshing out of the Georgian scenarios and characters undertaken by Andrew Davies. Davies has returned to this process in interviews and reflections upon the 1995 series on a number of occasions. His challenge, in particular, was to establish Austen's male characters as fully realised roles, when Austen is widely known for her omission of exclusively male exchanges in her novels. So, Davies sought to redress that imbalance – if it can be called that – somewhat. He augmented her material for dramatic purposes in order to include a more emphatic male perspective in places. He invented some scenes that Austen never wrote.

Some of these include the flashbacks as Darcy is writing his letter, overnight, to Elizabeth, explaining his difficulties with Wickham. Alongside Firth's voiceover, as he narrates the letter's contents, we are shown scenes acted out to demonstrate Wickham's (Adrian Lukis) bad behaviour, actualising what Darcy is disclosing to Elizabeth. In their university days, for example, Darcy discovers his fellow student in a compromising situation with a young woman. Langton's method for this scene was the development of non-verbal exchanges. No words exist from Austen for this context, and no words, in Langton and Davies' televisual version, were needed. Darcy bursts in on the son of his estate steward 'in the act'.

Wickham possesses a crumpled, rakish demeanour, and Darcy's disgust is clear. Firth perfected the hard-set jaw and glowering expression of disapproval. He could show Darcy's moral and upright personality without words, and his uncompromising stance on breeding and 'family pride' is shown with the briefest of expressions, stern but still attractive.

Again, wordless reactions are used in the scenes in which Darcy pursues Wickham, first to Ramsgate to prevent Georgiana's elopement. He then hunts Wickham down in the back-streets, stinking courtyards and cheap lodgings of Regency London. Darcy is resourceful and determined and knows his way around. He is ready to go into the hellish stew of London for the rescue of the innocent and the misguided.

This is where this dramatisation demonstrates what the novel implies, and what other adaptations struggled to do, which is to offer a full sense of Wickham and Darcy as enemies and show just how much damage Wickham did. It is not a light-hearted, charming matter, and any showdown between the two men could turn serious. Darcy is there at every turn to thwart Wickham's devious plans to carry off young women to their disgrace, either for seduction or, if she is rich enough like Georgiana, forced marriage. Jane, optimistically, tries to see the good side to Lydia and Wickham's folly in her first, hurried letter to Elizabeth at Lambton: ' …I am willing to hope the best, and that his character has been misunderstood. Thoughtless and indiscreet I can easily believe him, but this step (and let us rejoice over it) marks nothing bad at heart. His choice is disinterested at least, for he must know my father can give her nothing.' Darcy and Elizabeth know, immediately, that this is not the case. In full knowledge that Lydia has no inheritance, Wickham's intentions are far from honourable.

The shared background and the bond that Darcy and Wickham had from boyhood is also shown in the drama, thus developing the on-screen tension between the two men. This adds further enjoyment to the story, and repeated viewings allow fans to fully embed this backstory of the characters. Davies' additional material augments Austen's narrative and has subsequently contributed to the increase in interest surrounding her work and the ever-growing fan culture.

The elegant, poised Jennifer Ehle gave a low-key interview to the *Daily Telegraph* in 2015 to mark the twentieth anniversary of the series. She was asked about relationships, family and *Pride and Prejudice* but could not be drawn out on any of it. Ehle is from an acting and arts background and grew up between Britain and America. She has won awards and appeared on screen and stage regularly over the past twenty years, but never with the same fuss and exposure that her early television roles received. She is happy to do the job she loves and spend time with her family in their country retreat in up-state New York. It was Ehle who originally featured as the 'star' of *Pride and Prejudice*.

In 1992–93 she appeared in the television adaptation of Mary Wesley's 1984 novel *The Camomile Lawn*. This was a landmark television event, as it rode the wave of Wesley's popularity and was directed by Sir Peter Hall. Felicity Kendall and Claire Bloom also starred, but it was the twenty-one-year-old Ehle who made headlines as Calypso. Ehle recalled how the nude scenes shook her confidence, made her sick with nerves and gave her cause for concern: to be known as a 'sex symbol' at such a young age. Reassured by her mother, the veteran actress Rosemary Harris, she happily took on the role of Elizabeth Bennet the following year.

As Calypso, the 1930s peroxide blonde reminiscent of Veronica Lake, she had gained a certain label and notoriety that she was not comfortable with. The tabloid newspapers took delight in dubbing the series 'The Camomile Porn'. So, a total shift was welcome, and Ehle found it with Elizabeth Bennet. She described *Pride and Prejudice* not as a period drama but as a 'romantic comedy' that happened to be costumed in Regency dress. All the publicity and all the popularity have only left her with fondness for the role and no fear of typecasting, which her acting career since then has shown.

Ehle as Elizabeth was the original 'hook' for the series, appearing on the cover of the *Radio Times*. So, it is further testimony to Davies' great skill as a scriptwriter and to the fact that the role of Darcy delivered so much that Firth became co-star with Ehle. Davies playfully worked with the notion that viewers sitting down after Sunday dinner wanted entertainment that included sex, romance and intrigue. Dramas in this early evening slot came to be called 'Sex on a Sunday'. Weldon's *Pride and Prejudice*, Dennis Potter's *The Singing Detective* (1986), Alan Bleasdale's *The Monocled Mutineer* (1986) and *The Camomile Lawn* all fitted that demand. Quality literature, great storylines and direction, and star names generated quite an output from the BBC across the late 1980s and early 1990s, forming big budget productions that included some titillation as well.

Davies pushed the limits of the storyline to include as much sex as Austen could allow. He included his now notorious directions in the script for the encounter between Darcy and Elizabeth after his dip in the lake. When he sees her: 'Mr Darcy gets an erection.' Simon Langton confirmed that this is what Davies added to the script to give the actors the 'sense' – and the sensation – that had to accompany that scene. The lake scene, now known as the 'wet shirt' scene, was first written as a Mr Darcy nude scene. So, to follow in the footsteps of Ehle's Calypso, her co-star of *Pride and Prejudice* was expected to strip off. Davies is an equal opportunities writer.

As if to reinforce the double standards in male/female portrayals in the media, the decision was eventually made to keep Mr Darcy clothed. This resulted in the now iconic image that offers as much as the viewers' imaginations might wish. Firth-as-Darcy stripped off, partially, and then a stuntman dives into the lake, at Lyme Park in Cheshire (doubling for Pemberley).

We next see Firth swimming underwater, filmed in an indoor tank. Langton recalled the heart-stopping moment when Firth surfaced from his swim during the shoot and smacked his face against the edge of the pool cover. He immediately felt concerned for the actor, as well as worried about the shooting schedule, the insurance and, he admitted, 'is it too late to re-cast the role?' immediately came to mind. The show must go on. Fortunately, Firth was only slightly injured and able to continue, and so television history was born.

Firth as Darcy wearing 'The Wet Shirt', BBC, 1995

What the viewers don't see is Firth himself (the shot is of the stuntman) diving in or climbing out of the lake. Where other, later, examples of Darcy (such as Eliot Cowan in *Lost in Austen*) have waded out and emerged, dripping, Firth is next seen striding across his grounds leading his horse and wearing the wet shirt. He has tried to cool off after his ride from town and from his 'ardent' desire for Elizabeth – the latter without success, of course. It will take more than a quick dip in his lake to dampen *that* particular ardour. This is how Davies created what became this famous sexy scene, the impact of which surprised him.

The script kept indicating this heat, passion and energy. Darcy's fleshed out scenes include one that has him engaged in a vigorous fencing bout, to expend his pent-up energies, stating, "I *will* conquer this!" in reference to his feelings for Elizabeth.

After trying a swim, he is joined by one of his grooms on the walk back to the house. When Darcy hands his horse over to the fellow there is a brief master/servant exchange that demonstrates his affinity with his estate workers. This just happened naturally on the day of the shoot, as Langton recalls. The groom was played by one of the stunt riding team and he and Firth interacted for a moment. This also worked as a device to show that the horse was not to be left unattended by the lake. Langton admitted that he was well aware of the vigilance of viewers and that he would not get away with the horse appearing to be left hot, un-groomed and un-stabled in the open. He would, he said, 'get letters.' So, this fortunate inclusion of the groom in the scene enables us to see Darcy in a friendly light and ensure the horse is looked after. No animals were harmed in the filming.

A brief, casual exchange with an unnamed character gave visual reinforcement to Darcy's good nature and his kindness as a master. When he is able to appear natural and unaffected in his home environment of Pemberley, he is a gentle and courteous host and a considerate and generous brother. The 1995 series sought to bear out these qualities from the novel and animate them into dramatic form. In addition, his sister Georgiana (Emilia Fox) and his housekeeper, Mrs Reynolds (Bridget Turner) are portrayed as contented and exhibit love and genuine loyalty to their brother and master.

The power of these scenes, those direct from the novel and those 'fleshed out' additions, include charming nuances that enable viewers and now Jane Austen fan fiction writers to enjoy the expansion, begun by Davies, of the characters. In an interview with the Actors' Studio (New York) in 2011, Colin Firth commented perceptively that the gloss and interpretation put on the 'wet shirt' scene and the enduring sexiness of his portrayal of Darcy were down to the viewers' imaginations more than his portrayal. People love to fill in the blanks and build on developments to Austen's original narrative.

The cooled-off Darcy soon overheats again. The next scene gave Davies another chance to elaborate in a suggestive, sexualised direction. Elizabeth and Darcy's eyes lock and he is aroused. Here begins their renewed romance against the backdrop of Pemberley. Firth's shyness and astonishment on encountering her is endearing, and immediately he rushes off to make himself presentable before her Aunt and Uncle. He races to complete his toilette – far from making it a Brummellesque, lingering five-hour affair – and pelts downstairs in time to say farewell at the door and proffer a further invitation.

Charming, boyish, and eager – in the ensuing scenes Darcy wins over Elizabeth, Aunt and Uncle Gardiner, and the viewers. Here is where Firth also put his stamp on the role as we move into the next phase of the action because he shows his range. He echoes the warmth that Olivier brought to the character, in love with his 'dearest, loveliest Elizabeth', as the brusque, proud man gives way. He becomes the sincere, credible lover for an intelligent, wounded woman like Elizabeth. She is not stupid. She does not surrender like an eighteenth-century ingénue or fall prey to a libertine. Therefore, his transformation in her eyes must be genuine.

This transformation began after he was rejected at Hunsford. Instead of the clipped, brief process employed for Rintoul in the 1980 version, in which he just hands the letter to Elizabeth with a small bow and walks away as she reads it; Firth has a fully developed, dramatised composition scene through the night. It is this part of the novel: Darcy's upbringing, family life and dealings with Wickham as described in the letter, that gives us deeper insight into his character. By working them in as acted, non-verbal scenes, Davies and Langton helped to humanise Darcy.

From the text and the 'performance' of the letter we clearly appreciate Darcy's anguish as he puts his history down on paper and tries to explain his justified outrage based on his experiences. He also apologises for misinterpreting Jane's character, and for the first time in his life reveals secrets from his family's past. His pain for Georgiana is clear, the gradual dissolving of his pride into honesty is both touching and intimate. He still maintains sincerity, depth and sex appeal. Voiceover and repetition in the filming were used to reinforce the passion, regret and remorse felt by both characters over this misunderstanding. Darcy is growing and learning.

One of the features Langton enjoyed about making this series was that in Andrew Davies he had a writer who was abundantly confident and upfront about his material. He was not impeded by an over-reverence for Austen's work, which he felt had great depths of desire – hidden and denied. He had no reservations about making the series sexy and giving viewers something to get excited about. This can be discerned in the tone of the scenes. When Darcy gazes at Elizabeth as she sings and plays the piano, the atmosphere in the room contains that 'electricity' that Faulkland was so suspicious of in *The Rivals*. These incidents create a great build-up of sexual chemistry. For much of the action Elizabeth is subject to Darcy's gaze, from the moment of his prejudgment that she is 'tolerable'.

Women in the Georgian period were expected to be pleasing to the eye and pleased to attract and accept the male gaze. It was an age of great portraiture and the pose plastique (highly stylised, statuesque posing), made famous by the beautiful Emma Hamilton, mistress of Lord Nelson, in the 1780s and 1790s. Women were required to be alluring but respond with modesty and charm at the attention they received. So, Emma, Lady Hamilton, was both admired and vilified. Davies turned the tables in the drama. Not only does he even up the balance between male and female characters, with Elizabeth allowed to delight in Darcy's appearance as much as he does in hers, he affords her the chance to wallow in his handsomeness uninterrupted by introducing a full-scale portrait into the gallery at Pemberley, rather than just showing a miniature.

Langton also described the process of creating Darcy's 'point of view' shots in the series. They start from a high angle in the early episodes, looking down upon Elizabeth. This gave him an air of superiority over her and, as reviewers of the time pointed out, allowed us to delight in Ehle's impressive cleavage. However, as the action progresses and their relationship develops, the shots even up and the points of view come level. This coded language adds further dimension to the equality of the dramatised relationship.

By 1995, Andrew Davies had already achieved great success with, amongst his many works, the adaptation of *Middlemarch* (1994) for the BBC, political satire in *To Play the King* (1993) and acclaimed feature film *Circle of Friends* (1995). He is the dynamo of literary adaptation for TV and film across the past few decades, having also tackled the monumental task of Tolstoy's *War and Peace* for television in 2016. His literate, intimate, sexy, sometimes irreverent, always confident approach to 'classic' literature has remained consistent and consistently popular. He seems to be able to tap into the psyche of the modern television audience as well as channel the key elements of a given author's tone and distinctiveness.

To the pantheon of Austen heroes on screen can now be added Sidney Parker of the unfinished novel *Sanditon*, played by Theo James. Davies' adaptation appeared in 2019 for ITV and, working with the scant eleven chapters from Austen's surviving manuscript, he once again 'fleshed out' this modern Georgian hero. Parker is stern, aloof, even rude to heroine Charlotte Heywood (Rose Williams). There is an element of 'Darcyfication' about the role, perhaps in an attempt to repeat the success of 1995. This remains to be seen.

Davies' fame, and that of Alison Steadman (Mrs Bennet), Julia Sawalha and Jennifer Ehle were the original star power draws for the series run of *Pride and Prejudice*. Steadman was already considered a great actor and a bit of a national comedy treasure after her superb portrayal of the immortal 'Bev' in Mike Leigh's Play for Today: *Abigail's Party* (1977). Sawalha was the teen star from children's series *Press Gang* (1989-1993) who had gone on to star as the long-suffering Saffron in comedy *Absolutely Fabulous* (first broadcast in 1992), the daughter of the appalling Edina Monsoon (Jennifer Saunders) a mother who makes Mrs Bennet look restrained and saintly.

It is all the more admirable and creditable therefore that the abiding and most affecting memory of the series is that of Firth-as-Darcy, with his disapproving glower that melts into 'ardent' passion and then true, unchanging devotion. It is a credit to the writing, Firth's performance, Simon Langton's direction and the unique efforts of the cast and crew that a new mania for Austen and specifically for the character of Darcy formed. It is only growing more and more widespread as the twenty-first century progresses.

This is a crucial, defining factor that turned Austen from a popular, beloved and highly regarded novelist of wit and invention into an international icon of romance, feminism, politics, conservative family values, literature and global writing culture. She is now commandeered for all sorts of movements and beliefs, from conservative Christians and Mormons to outlandish, trolling 'alt-right' voices online. Her face has adorned the £10 note since mid-2017, the first female writer to be thus honoured on British currency.

The now superstar status of her most beloved male creation has succeeded in drawing more and more attention to her skill and originality. In November 2015, in celebration of the 200th anniversary of *Emma*, for example, John Mullan in conversation with Melvyn Bragg on BBC Radio 4's *In Our Time* stated that Austen 'invented' free indirect narrative style for the modern novel, and that this is the 'default' style for modern, European fiction. Authors must first make a conscious effort to *distance* their voice from Austen's style in the effort to work in a different form because hers has become so universal.

Austen mediated the thoughts and passions of *her* characters to us, so we feel close to her as we read and listen to or view them on screen. It is one of the reasons why fans feel such a *personal* affection for the author. To insert new conversations, therefore, and embellish her action takes audacity and confidence. So, after the explosion of popularity for the 1995 adaptation, where were writers and directors to go?

Dressed-down Darcy

The answer came a decade later, in 2005. Ten years seemed like a suitable gap for Joe Wright to develop and direct his film adaptation of *Pride and Prejudice* with a script, principally by Deborah Moggach. Critic and poet Tom Paulin had called the

1995 version the 'Crabtree & Evelyn' Jane Austen, after the purveyor of supposedly thoroughly English herbal and floral bath, beauty and home products. The atmosphere of lace and lavender (think of the opening titles) and the impression of a marketed Englishness makes this seem like an accurate assessment. That aesthetic might be widely popular, but it can pall after time. Joe Wright's adaptation modified that and was dubbed the 'muddy hems' *Pride and Prejudice*, after Joanna Briscoe's review of the film in *The Telegraph* in 2005.

Still picturesque (shot in the Cotswolds) but rustic and threadbare, the Longbourn of 2005 is a different ideal from the 'Crabtree & Evelyn' Austen that inspired thousands of visits to National Trust properties. It is an embodiment of shabby, genteel chic. The Bennets, led by matriarch Brenda Blethyn and patriarch Donald Sutherland, are the offspring of gentleman farmers, fallen on hard times and with the real threat of eviction hanging over them. Their existence in the house is decidedly precarious, and this is discernible in Mrs Bennet's attitude and appearance. She is attired in older fashions, late-eighteenth-century bodice and panniers from her girlhood – the remnants of when she was a renowned 'beauty'. Her hair escapes in wisps around her face and she is ruddy and flushed by housework and fatigue; she carries an air of desperation. You can sense the relief she feels when Jane (Rosamund Pike) and Elizabeth (Keira Knightley) make their brilliant matches.

The Bennet girls are very hands-on with chores. They move about, sleeves rolled up, plucking birds and clattering dishes, often bonnet-less and with shabby lace, unkempt hair, aprons and those muddy hems. The family pig runs through the house. Mealtimes are especially noisy, as they pass dishes across the table and clink cups and butter knives. There is not, Wright indicates, a servant to wait on them at table for informal meals; this is a luxury reserved for formal dinner parties when guests like Mr Collins attend.

In this atmosphere of rusticity with genteel habits, Mr Bennet is a composite of late-eighteenth- century learned gentlemen. We can imagine him as an embodiment of Austen's own father, the Reverend George Austen, in amongst his books, and the Hampshire parson and naturalist, Gilbert White of Selborne. White's 1789 work *The Natural History and Antiquities of Selborne* chronicled his scientific fascination with his local parish, which is a near-neighbour to Austen's childhood home of Steventon, and Chawton where she eventually settled. White's *Natural History* has been in print since 1789. Donald Sutherland's Mr Bennet is a devoted and loving father but easily distracted by his hobbies, lost in his library and collection of curiosities, specimens and taxidermy.

Knightley as Elizabeth is elegant, bookish and independent with a ready wit. She communicates more of a rebellious contempt for social conventions than the other Lizzys, Ehle or Garson, did. She sniggers, grins broadly and conducts herself with a casual, informal air. Dressed practically and more often than not without a bonnet when outdoors, she is pretty shocking for a young, Georgian lady. She is very provocative and stands up to Darcy (Matthew Macfadyen) face-to-face and almost nose-to-nose (considering his height) when he makes his first proposal to her. They linger just that little bit too long when she refuses him for her contempt to be devoid of lust. They are an exciting and tempestuous couple with a love/hate dynamic.

What of Macfadyen's millennial Darcy, then? For some fans he is their Darcy of course, a Darcy for their time, when they first encountered the novel and its dramatisation. This Darcy, too, spends a lot of his screen time in casual dress. This is a dressed down *Pride and Prejudice.* His open-neck shirt, minus neckcloth, and his gown flapping in the dewy morning as he strides across the fields, were an attempt to challenge and even out-do the supremacy of the wet shirt.

For many fans this was a success. Macfadyen has slowly stolen the mantle of Darcy for some viewers, but with nothing like the cultural impact of Firth. A reason for this is that the 2005 version is a feature film, the structure of which means that the action is condensed into a limited timescale and there is little room for manoeuvre. Much like Olivier's uncomfortable studio-bound Darcy, Macfadyen's scenes are telescoped into a series of vignettes. He, unlike Firth's Darcy, does not have the scope to develop over six episodes. There are fewer scenes and fewer characters to play off. The Hursts, for example, are cut entirely.

However, despite the missing characters and condensed action the dramatic licence is remarkably effective. Like the 1995 version, the broad use of outdoor locations and historic properties add extra dimension to the scenes. The use of pathetic fallacy creates interest, where brevity and the changes to the language might have caused the action to suffer.

For example, the use of the neo-classical folly at Stourhead, the National Trust gardens in Wiltshire, has become a landmark scene. For Darcy's proposal he pursues the nymph-like Elizabeth to the miniature temple, which is dedicated to love, in the landscaped park that represents Rosings very convincingly. In the lashing downpour their hair and clothes are drenched, and they have an angry and passionate confrontation. Instead of a wet shirt clinging just to Darcy's body, both of them are soaked to the skin.

This Darcy and Elizabeth is an outdoor couple. Most of their key scenes take place in nature. Loose and informal clothing is their signature style, and they abjure the confinement of rooms, indoor spaces and company for the solitude and freedom of the outdoors. Even in a crowded ballroom the camera tracks around them and suddenly they are alone. They dance and gaze into each other's eyes in an empty space. And when Elizabeth accidentally stumbles upon Darcy and Georgiana (Tamzin Merchant) at Pemberley and eavesdrops on their happy reunion, she flees from the house and onto the terrace (in this case the location is Chatsworth House, Derbyshire), again pursued by Darcy.

Throughout the film the countryside idyll as it surrounds the couple plays a huge part. The opening titles show us the environs of Longbourn with the morning mist drifting across meadows. For their final scene, Elizabeth and Darcy meet in the meadow at dawn in an echo of the opening. "Your hands are cold," she says, kissing them. This is a bold reversal of the social convention – for a woman to kiss a man's hand! We have come full circle, from one dawn to another, a new day with a bright future ahead of them.

There is an even, dramatic balance about the pace of the film and a true poetic and romantic core. Elizabeth is thoughtful and strong-minded and Macfadyen-as-Darcy is stern and awkward, and melts readily to reveal a sensitive, inner self in affecting ways. The two scenes in which this happens most memorably were inventions for the purposes of cinema and are beautifully achieved as part of the film's styling and visual language.

In one of these, Elizabeth is exploring Pemberley when first her ear is caught by music, and then her eye is caught by the display of affection between the Darcy siblings in the privacy of their home. Georgiana ceases her (accomplished) playing and delightedly hugs her brother. Elizabeth is embarrassed and flustered – caught in the act of spying. Darcy's easy and relaxed manner dramatically shifts when he sees the fine eyes of his beloved peering through the crack in the door. Each has seen the other at their best and most unaffected – he at Pemberley and she when caring for her sister at Netherfield – and they know for sure in the film's narrative trajectory that they are in love. The recognition of their feelings in this scene really suits the emotional logic of how the characters are portrayed, and it is one of the many strengths of the adaptation. Moggach's, with Thompson's input, use of dramatic license in the script is faithful to the complexity of characterisation in the novel.

Another scene in which the invention and the cinematic license have a great effect is the final scene in which Darcy and Elizabeth meet again in the dawn mist. Knightley's Lizzy is in her natural environment, like a heroine from the Romantic or Pre-Raphaelite Movement. With loose hair and informal garments, she is waiting. And then *he* appears – open-neck shirt and loose gown, his informality mirroring hers. They have the 'just got out of bed' ruffled look. Their ease, sexuality and intimacy are immediately evident. They will be an inseparable, demonstrative, unconventional and thoroughly loving married couple.

The sunrise is the backdrop as their love opens up. The

writers interpreted Austen to offer a mediated, modernised and naturalistic rendition of the scene with dialogue based on Austen's original that connects with the twenty-first century audience. Darcy's gentleness and informal, 'ardent' declaration of love: "You have bewitched me, body and soul, and I love – I love – I love you," even includes a slightly shy, faltering tone. Fans that comment online, via blogs and social media, describe how much they love this endearing, hesitant quality in Macfadyen's speech, and how it shows Darcy's struggle, vulnerability and devotion.

It can either be heard as a line that shows his ardent feelings, or is a poor dilution of Austen's original dialogue. Opinions are divided on this way of re-fashioning the language for a twenty-first-century audience, especially after Weldon's and Davies' fidelity to the text for the television versions. Both feature films, 1940 and 2005, have less time to deal with the novel's action and must take such short-cuts. It is all part of the compromise in producing these literary adaptations on screen and choosing the most effective ways of communicating meaning to the audience.

Knightley, in an interview for *Premier Magazine* in 2005 at around the time of the film's release, offered a perceptive summary based on her film career at the time. She contrasted Macfadyen-as-Darcy with the other leading men she had starred with to date, such as Johnny Depp and Orlando Bloom in the *Pirates of the Caribbean* franchise. These actors she thought of as beautiful men, but Macfadyen was more ruggedly handsome in her view. He could also play vulnerable, however, which made him doubly appealing. Macfadyen's portrayal is a return to masculinity. This archetype speaks to a universal appeal and contributed to further interest in Austen's character. A new Darcy for a new audience.

Soon after the release of this film version, Guy Andrews created a fantasy adaptation of *Pride and Prejudice* for television, *Lost in Austen* (2008). This too gave us a strong yet vulnerable 'big man' with Eliot Cowan as Darcy. At 6'2" Cowan fits the type, like the 6'3" Macfadyen. Darcy's vulnerability and awkwardness are compounded in *Lost in Austen* when he is transported to modern-day London. His stable, fictional world in which he is powerful and in control is fragmented, and this wacky post-modern device leaves him a fish out of water, wet shirt and all.

In 1869, with Edward Austen-Leigh's *A Memoir of Jane Austen*, Austen's novels were positioned within the sphere of Christian, sentimental and romantic traditions. As a family-endorsed memoir it sought to place her within the spectrum of respectable novelists in the 'golden age' of nineteenth-century publishing. The memoir had a function: to encourage readers to respect and appreciate 'dear Aunt Jane' as a model of simple domesticity who nonetheless wrote superbly but as a part-time occupation.

Austen-Leigh, as his aunt's biographer, was caught in the paradox of the Victorian age. Whilst great artistic and intellectual capabilities could be acknowledged in women, simultaneously they must not be seen to be employed in such efforts that might act as a distraction from their domestic duties. By the 1860s a woman could be a novelist and write under her own name, but it was still deemed to be somewhat inelegant and unseemly.

Austen's nephew, therefore, reinvented her 'character' for the Victorian age. As Kathryn Sutherland remarked in her introduction to the *Memoir* (Oxford University Press, 2002), Austen had to be all things to all middle-class people. Her reputation was mediated by her sister, Cassandra, who censored their correspondence and filtered Jane's opinions and comments after she died in order to maintain respectability.

In a similar way, those that adapt her work and prime it for television and cinema audiences also filter Austen. They develop an 'Austen' for their time, informed by the popular fiction and culture that prevails. Faithful to the text and able to explore the story over six hours of television, minus any commercial breaks, Andrew Davies and Fay Weldon could explore Austen's language and retain the novelist's authorial voice via the characters' scripted dialogue.

On the other hand, Wright and Moggach had to engage in a project to curtail and condense the speech and action whilst retaining, like Cassandra, a feeling of reverence for the work. In this way, they made use of the dramatic and stylistic precedents of the past 200 years and how Austen has been received and modified, or how she has worked as an influence on other writers. So whatever gloss might be placed over her work, the novels have held up. A Victorianised (Cranford) filter, a Romantic or stylised Gothic filter; whatever feel there is to a production it does not mean that the satirical edge must suffer.

In 2005, the Romantic sensibilities of Elizabeth and Darcy and their passionate scenes reminiscent of a Brontë novel, are contrasted with the late-eighteenth-century fashions, as worn by Mr and Mrs Bennet and Lady Catherine (Judi Dench). This aesthetic underlines the clear generational differences between parents and children which make their remarks, advice and attempts at control appear all the more dated and out of place in the face of early-nineteenth-century social pressures. Lady Catherine's insistence on 'accomplishments' and suitably qualified governesses from her bewigged and corseted gloomy perch speaks volumes about how out of touch she is. Her captive parrot that shrieks at visitors is a warning claxon to stay away from Rosings. Likewise, Mr Bennet's remoteness and declarations that he wishes to be left alone in his private museum-like study full of books, fossils and stuffed birds suggests his wish to preserve something that has already been lost or declared extinct.

Darcy is different. He hugs his sister with genuine affection and joy. He demonstrates all the passion for life that is lacking with older relatives and more cynical suitors, once Elizabeth has managed to penetrate his outer shell. When she walks into the sculpture gallery of Pemberley (in reality the plaster court of the British Museum) she meets him face-to-face in the form of his marble portrait bust. Not only does the 2005 film allow Lizzy to eavesdrop and spy on Darcy in his unguarded and private moments, the three-dimensional depiction of him allows her to circle him and spend a long time contemplating his looks with her female gaze.

Elizabeth could not so brazenly stare at the flesh-and-blood version of the man, so this statue permits her to focus on his form and consider him. Where some women of the Regency period might be caught in the pose plastiques, so that men could gaze upon partially nude women in classical postures and attire, the same chance for a woman of Elizabeth's class to look upon a man was nigh-on impossible. The sense of endearment, attraction and even love she shows to the statue comes across in this scene. The Greeks had a word for it: 'agalmatophilia', or 'statue-love'. The Victorians called it 'Pygmalionism' thanks to the Greek myth of the king who moulds the perfect woman, Galatea.

Macfadyen, in the form of this resin Darcy prop bust, is the ideal for some fans. He certainly fits the bill for some that visited Chatsworth House, where the bust was eventually housed for the 'Georgian Summer' exhibition in 2013, because they kept kissing it. Nick Dutton sculpted the prop for the film in 2004, and it has been considered such a good likeness of the actor that fans could not help themselves. The residual lipstick marks constituted a health hazard, so it was put away. Author and Austen fan Cassandra Grafton started a campaign in 2014 to have it reinstated. Her appeal worked and it was once again put on display, but with the condition: 'please do not kiss the statue'! Janeites can be incorrigible.

'Please do not kiss': The Matthew Macfadyen bust at Chatsworth House

A Pride of Darcys

A world of Darcy on screen has supplied everyone from avid fans to casual viewers with a repetition of the archetype that satisfies in a variety of ways. Sometimes the character has possessed a dangerous, Gothic style. At other times he is a figure of Georgian excellence and vigorous, youthful, patrician gentility. He is given an innate sense of justice and duty. His gentlemanly (and gentle, manly) behaviour is very modern and at the same time chivalrous, traditional and self-sacrificing. Writers and directors have produced a series of Darcys from the foundation in the novel that offer viewers an interesting set of choices.

Olivier-as-Darcy is a man of charm and wit, although he is overshadowed by the early-Victorian anachronistic settings and costumes. However, forsaking authenticity created a feel-good, morale-boosting, star-powered vehicle at a time of global crisis. Amidst this moves the dignified figure of Darcy. He expresses himself with eloquence and passion at the right moments, and even indulges in game-playing and conspiracy with Elizabeth and Lady Catherine. The 1940 MGM film is a fantasy with fairy-tale settings of country cottages and garden parties. It is a respectful, dramatically efficient version that sought to evoke a sense of affection and loyalty towards 'Merry Olde England'.

Rintoul-as-Darcy emerged in a landscape of late-1970s feminist-influenced culture. It took Weldon four years to finalise the script. The process for her was one of retaining detail and evidence of nineteenth-century influences. The adaptation she chose was informed by literary and academic trends that re-evaluated the role of women in culture and society. Weldon referenced Mary Wollstonecraft and slanted the action towards the need for women to assert and educate themselves (as no-one else would do it for them) with strength and audacity rather than compliance. She gave Elizabeth her chances to speak out and also allocated a share of screen time to Mary. Poor, forgotten Mary.

Weldon importantly regarded it as a great romantic tale, suitable for weekend tea-time viewing. Darcy chimed with this as the prototype of the modern romantic hero. It also constituted a plot that had great suspense as to when and how Elizabeth will 'get her man'. Rintoul embodies the looks and poise of the fashionable Regency gentleman with time-less nobility in Weldon's faithful and detailed representation of the novel.

With this helpful legacy, Davies could tackle the novel afresh. Firth-as-Darcy has been the most far-reaching, influential and popular. Davies has exploited this popularity for the depiction of Sidney Parker in *Sanditon*. Firth, and the 1995 adaptation, still regularly top popularity polls online for 'favourite Darcy' and favourite version of *Pride and Prejudice* as well as favourite all-time television drama. His scenes responded to the popular demand for some 'sex on a Sunday' and drew on romantic and historical costume drama. He is a popular culture reference point now and has generated many, many imitations.

Threaded through the work of Helen Fielding is the admiration for Austen, Darcy and Firth-as-Darcy. He is re-imagined as the human rights lawyer, Mark Darcy, in the *Bridget Jones* series: still very much the good guy. The latest, early-twenty-first-century mania for Austen is centred upon Darcy and the possibilities that might arise from the heroic persona and archetype. From Andrew Davies' sexier version, writers and fans have taken plot and character into many different directions. Alternative Darcys abound, most with their origin in Firth-as-Darcy.

Macfadyen-as-Darcy took off from where Firth had finished and evolved into a distinctive character in his own right. Again, informed by themes in popular culture and costume drama to that point, the 2005 *Pride and Prejudice* marked out a new departure. We are shown the Bennet girls with their hands dirty, loose hair trailing and muddy hems. Moggach and Thompson's script delivers a freer more modern speech: from Charlotte's "Don't you dare judge me!" to Elizabeth's un-Austen-like "You can't make me!" over marriage to Mr Collins. Macfadyen is widely approved of, whether the aesthetic and overall style have an appeal or not. His Darcy has an informal, devastatingly romantic manner.

When he seeks out Lizzy to give her the letter explaining his actions, he appears at the Hunsford parsonage in the early hours of the morning. His Darcy is associated, in a very effective way, with the early dawn: the romantic junction between sleeping and waking, night and day. There is an other-worldly quality to these scenes, and when he is in Elizabeth's presence in this atmosphere there are hints as to their intimate future life together. They will have a sort of spiritual bond. It is a more discreet, perhaps Victorian, depiction in this adaptation, in contrast to the 'Regency implications' of Davies' more suggestive 1995 script variations and directions.

So, what are the routes down which Darcy has travelled since 1995 and 2005? And what drives the popularity amongst fans? He has appeared in print now on countless occasions in the different Jane Austen fan fiction forms. He is on screen in a number of spin-off stories for television and film and has been appropriated into a number of different genres to represent the male archetype in various settings and cultural contexts.

Now that we have established who *the* Darcy might be – in print and in the direct adaptations of the novel – we can move to what *a* Darcy might be in a variation, spin-off, sequel, etcetera of *Pride and Prejudice*. Who is creating them? Who is reading about him? The variation, sequel market and the energy and invention of Jane Austen fan fiction are up next.

Chapter 7

'What if?': the master of Pemberley and the mania of sequel and fan fiction

Jane Austen fan fiction (often referred to as JAFF) is a personal and passionate world. Writers and readers are heavily invested in it. Jane Austen fan fiction is a performance. The authors regularly ask: "what if?" and plunge into the characters' new scenarios. The overall motivation for authors of sequels, spin-offs, prequels and variations in fan fiction, and the wider publishing world, is to see the characters live – and love – on.

For the first time, Jane Austen fan fiction will be put under the microscope here and evaluated as to its effectiveness and how writers approach it and readers enjoy it, or not. Long considered an ineffectual and derivative approach to writing, the fan fiction story is nonetheless hugely significant in popular culture, the evolution of publishing and online access to new publications.

For instance, the Republic of Pemberley website (https://pemberley.com) is a long-standing fan community, many of whom claim to be the first organisation of Austen devotees on the web. They discuss Austen-related topics and compose variations of the stories. Founded in response to the fan mania created by the 1995 adaptation, the intense enthusiasm displayed concentrates largely upon the adaptations, other spin-offs and romance and historical fiction, not just Austen's novels alone. In the composition of fan fiction, members adopt narratives that appeal to them, trying out their voice as authors in the tradition of romantic adaptations, and simplifications, of Jane Austen.

The Origins and Functions of Jane Austen Fan Fiction

Some might say: 'How dare they?' These fans-turned-authors. Who do they think they are – trying to write like Austen, using her characters and trying to imitate her style?

It is an interesting conundrum. Should potential authors avoid the risk of referencing their admired favourite? After all, Austen herself made use of Richardson and Sheridan, and *Northanger Abbey* is peppered with influences from Ann Radcliffe. Could that be categorised as fan fiction? Maybe, but Austen did not go so far as re-imagining Radcliffe's actual characters by name. She did re-fashion them according to archetype, however.

The Republic of Pemberley fan fiction writers focus their compositions on *Pride and Prejudice*. That seems to have been the springboard for the fan fiction. That novel, and Darcy and Elizabeth, are by far the most common subject matter for Jane Austen fan fiction. *Pride and Prejudice* fan fiction would be a more appropriate term in most cases. Elizabeth's blossoming relationship with Darcy is their inspiration and endlessly fascinating. If you explore the site and dip into the short stories, some interesting trends emerge.

In one anonymous story, *The Branches of Denial*, Elizabeth is caught out expressing her love for Darcy when (and here the author draws directly from the 2005 film) she kisses Darcy's statue in the Pemberley gallery. Her display of agalmatophilia (statue worship) mirrors how the presence of the prop bust of Matthew Macfadyen was treated when on show at Chatsworth House in Derbyshire and the housekeeping department had to resort to a direct appeal to visitors not to kiss it.

A Slip of the Tongue is another anonymous 'what if?' storyline. Instead of simply asking Elizabeth to dance at the Netherfield Ball, Darcy makes a Freudian slip and reveals his true feelings by asking her to marry him. In the middle of a crowded ballroom, witnessed by dozens of people, Lizzy, expecting a request for a dance, perfunctorily responds with an acceptance. This places them in quite a pickle – witnessed by the gathering – they have decided to get married!

A trend emerges here that involves the protagonists tripping over their words or having unguarded moments, their attraction for each other is so strong. They are drawn into embarrassing and compromising situations because they cannot help their feelings emerging. They are prone to unintentional utterances and Freudian slips. This is a common feature for budding writers as they experience and experiment with romantic vignettes for fellow fans. It is a useful device: create a pivotal moment based on an inadvertent revelation of true feelings and see how it plays out. They regularly reflect the style and tone of dialogue from the screen adaptations in the romantic declarations. The origins of Jane Austen fan fiction lie in this 'what if?' questioning of the narratives and the adaptations.

The fans on the Republic of Pemberley site that both read and compose these stories, post mainly favourable critiques and comments. That is a characteristic of the Jane Austen worldwide fan communities; they are mostly a supportive, friendly and welcoming bunch. Complimentary comments and constructive criticism are usually the order of the day. They do, however, express their feelings with passion, from behind their keyboards, when it comes to feeling displeased over the perceived breaking of the unspoken 'rules' of Jane

Austen fan fiction and alternative universe (alt or AU) fiction. The seriousness with which fans treat it is best revealed when things irk them.

In response to an alt-fiction storyline from one Jane Austen fan fiction writer, in which Elizabeth gives birth to Darcy's illegitimate child, one commentator vociferously disapproved. The storylines in Jane Austen fan fiction must be sympathetic and honest, and this reviewer passionately disagreed with how the characters were made to change to fit this one. You cannot turn a hero into a villain. Jane Austen fan fiction stories can be a pastiche or a faithful, affectionate homage to the author containing the key recognisable features of the original. They should not be something that abandons the tone of the original. Other fans prefer the short and immediate gratification of the curtailed plot; they enjoy quick episodic tales and vignettes putting their favourite characters in different scenarios.

There are, it seems, rules that both fans and writers follow, and they perceive the breaking of these rules to be a personal affront. This is a subjective world, and readers of romantic and fan fiction are often to be found on the defensive. As much fun as it is, and as supportive and charming as the community might be, many can feel attacked by critics and other sectors of fan culture. The reading of any kind of romantic fiction is often met with derision, and derivative fiction inspired by Austen can be met with both cultural and critical snobbery.

The 'Problem' with Romantic Fiction

'Society does not approve of the reading of romance novels,' asserted Jayne Ann Krentz in *Dangerous Men and Adventurous Women* (1992), a study by romance authors of their genre. The labels are judgmental, sexist, hurtful and, she argued, the books are often called 'trash' and the readers branded 'unintelligent, uneducated, unsophisticated or neurotic.' As we saw earlier, the reading of romance fiction is sometimes seen as indicative of deficiencies and frustrations in the readers' lives. So, whilst being vastly popular it is simultaneously an outsider activity. The authorship of such books is also often derided as unremarkable, formulaic or simplistic.

In the 1990s, Krentz and a group of fellow romantic novelists compiled this collection of essays to provide a robust counter argument. She, like Janice Radway, described the act of reading the romance as a brave one in the face of 'relentless hostility'. From the eighteenth century onwards, the romantic novel and its readers were looked down upon and disparaged. So, in the years just prior to the 1995 *Pride and Prejudice*, the group of writers in *Dangerous Men and Adventurous Women* provided a useful set of reflections on a range of romance writing that still speak to the problems faced by romance and fan fiction authors online today.

There is much justification and defence of the genre, which

sadly was deemed necessary on the part of the authors and editors, all of them successful writers. Krentz remarked upon the fact that negative criticism targets this predominantly female genre and, unlike the criticism aimed at, say, horror or sci-fi, it includes personal attacks upon fans and writers. As if there is no differentiation between the creator and the medium, and the reader and their taste in fiction.

Simplistic, clumsy criticism often makes this conflation. You are what you read – or write. They are derided for their lack of intellect and inability to discern real-life from fiction or fantasy. As Krentz strenuously points out: if a person reads a murder mystery or horror novel, it does not lead them to expect corpses or monsters around every corner. Instead, the contributors to and consumers of the romance genre agree that they are involved in an exciting exchange that includes a degree of fantasy, excitement and wish-fulfilment combined with re-laxation: 'Like all other genres, romance is based on fantasies and readers know it.'

In addition, Krentz stressed, 'The fantasies in the books have nothing to do with a woman's politics.' So, for example, where marriage and childbirth might be exalted in a narrative, the book can be read and enjoyed by a single, pro-choice wom-an. When put like that it is clear and unremarkable, of course. The case for the reader's imagination should be the same for every genre. Also, the responses can be manifold, including the reinforcement of traditional values, exciting wish-fulfilment, and the exercising of independence and identity.

Krentz and fellow author Linda Barlow reflected on the important elements that *Pride and Prejudice* bequeathed to the genre. In their chapter, 'Beneath the Surface', they remind us that 'Elizabeth's fine eyes' and 'ready wit' attract Darcy. The characters of hero and heroine in modern romantic fiction never miss the opportunity to 'engage in verbal sparring.' Krentz and Barlow point out that 'it is far more likely to be her words than her beauty that win her the love she most desires.'

Romantic heroes, as descendants of Darcy, 'eschew the company of beautiful but insipid women who would rather fawn than fight'. The 'duel of wits' is the true route to romantic fulfilment. It is Austen's characters' mental and intellectual compatibility that inspires the relationship. Krentz and Barlow maintained that often the hero is shown listening to the heroine, taking her words to heart and then changing in response to 'her stated criticisms'. Here is the clear legacy from Darcy: 'Elizabeth's scathing refusal of his marriage proposal... forces Darcy to revaluate his own behaviour and relinquish the worst aspects of his pride...'

The challenge and the charm of such scenarios are part of the winning formula used by romance authors and now also by authors of Jane Austen fan fiction. Characters that possess witty, thoughtful qualities are shown to win out. Therein lies the fantasy.

'Pemberley': The Honeymoon is over

Fan fiction and the Romance market might seem marginal and niche, however large they are. The enduring popularity of the characters in *Pride and Prejudice* has not gone unnoticed by mainstream publishers, and they have attempted over the years, with varying degrees of critical and commercial success, to capitalise on the legacy of Austen.

Pemberley (1993) by Emma Tennant (1937–2017) was the first major, widely publicised sequel to *Pride and Prejudice* and came out in the period prior to the 1995 adaptation. The romantic fiction publishing world of the early 1990s had a clear interest in Austen, Austen-inspired works and sequels of famous titles. Susan Hill (author of *The Woman in Black*, 1983) wrote *Mrs de Winter* (1993) to continue the narrative of Maxim and his young wife from *Rebecca*. Jean Rhys could be said to have started this off with *Wide Sargasso Sea* (1966), her post-colonial prequel to *Jane Eyre*. The urge to tell expansive, further stories of famous characters is very strong.

The desire to prolong and extend the narrative lives of such characters as Edward Rochester, Elizabeth Bennet, Darcy and du Maurier's unnamed narrator from *Rebecca* is now commonly found in literary fiction. Dickens' convict character Abel *Magwitch* from *Great Expectations* (1861) featured in his own prequel, *Magwitch* (1983) by Michael Noonan, and former poet laureate Andrew Motion wrote *Silver: Return to Treasure Island* (2012) to explore the continuing adventures of Robert Louis Stevenson's notorious one-legged ship's cook from *Treasure Island* (1883).

Tennant, then, was part of this pursuit of the winning formula of *Pride and Prejudice* and the literary effectiveness of *Wide Sargasso Sea*. She was commissioned to develop a historically well-researched sequel. *Pemberley; or Pride and Prejudice Continued* was a bold and risky move any way you look at it. Risky, in that it could alienate readers and outrage critics. Tennant might have few defenders. She was brave enough to be the first to dip a toe in the *Pride and Prejudice* sequel waters as a high profile author. Whilst she has not been universally derided online since the digital revolution and the mania following the 1995 *Pride and Prejudice*, she could certainly not have foreseen the passion of the feedback from the internet when she was writing the novel.

Sadly, Tennant is not a popular figure among the Austen fan community. Her anomalous plot points annoy some readers, who know the novel well but also conflate it with the 1995 adaptation. Sometimes bloggers and fans of Jane Austen fan fiction are very vocal in their defence of favourite titles but neglect to remember the fantasy element when it comes to examples they do not enjoy. The criticism forthcoming from those who purport to be fans and claim ownership of some sort of Austen 'legacy' quickly becomes personal towards a well-respected historian and author.

Tennant wrote a further sequel in 1994: *An Unequal Marriage; or Pride and Prejudice Twenty Years Later*, which if it were possible provoked even more derision from Austen fans. There is dislike and legitimate criticism of a book, and then there is trolling and nastiness. It is a sad reality that writers must contend with on the internet. This is from an, unsurprisingly, anonymous reviewer on Amazon: '[Tennant] is a disgrace to the proffesion [sic] of being a [sic] author. She should be publically [sic] disgraced.' (from: 'A Customer', September 1999.)

This goes too far. It qualifies as trolling, the activity of emerging online to insult or call for harm (anonymously) and then creeping back into your hiding place. It offers a flavour of the lengths to which keyboard warriors will go, in order to try and put other readers off their hated titles.

At the time of writing *Pemberley*, Tennant, already a renowned author, editor and historian and Fellow of the Royal Society of Literature, did not have to take Janeite bloggers and Jane Austen fan fiction into account. In her introduction to the novel she reflected upon how the character had lived on in the author's mind after the original novel was finished. This is indicated in Austen's surviving letters; when she imagined a future for Darcy and Elizabeth, 'Mr D's' feelings for Lizzy had only grown and thrived in her mind. They built a life together, according to Austen that is a 'mixture of love, pride and delicacy.' There, is the story-teller's urge to ask: 'What happened next?' Many Jane Austen fan fiction authors now use that as their prompt for writing continuations and alternative storylines. Austen, as Tennant reminds us, had already imagined in her letters a future for the Darcys.

In Tennant's handling of the characters, Elizabeth's ambition for a happy life is set up well enough. She had hoped to soften Darcy and make him a more approachable, welcoming soul. However, their peaceful beginning does not last long as the action intensifies at the prospect of a family Christmas at Pemberley. That means both sides of the family: the widowed Mrs Bennet with her unmarried daughters, the Bingleys and their young daughter, the Wickhams and their four children, Miss Bingley, Mrs Hurst, Lady Catherine and Anne de Bourgh all under one roof for the festive season!

When looked at in this way we can only stand back and consider the sheer insanity of Darcy and Elizabeth agreeing to this, and then we remember – it's a story. So, naturally, Tennant created the perfect storm. The prospect for this Christmas at Pemberley is hardly a celebratory or relaxing one. In any case, there is no sense of relaxation at Pemberley – ever – for Elizabeth. Mrs Bennet is on typical form and does not disappoint when she provides Lizzy with some excruciating moments. Tennant pushes the action into some very un-Austen-like territory by allowing characters to comment on such things as intimate 'vinegar douches' in order to promote conception of a male heir to Pemberley.

Tennant manipulates the action extremely well to put Elizabeth through further ordeals in what *should* be the perfect marriage. She is anguished over how much Darcy has done for her family. He has bought Meryton Lodge for Mrs Bennet, Kitty and Mary to live in. Elizabeth is a devoted wife but does not feel comfortable in or convinced about her role as mistress of Pemberley. She is still, after a year of marriage, passionately in love with Darcy. That, fortunately, is the bedrock of their relationship. Darcy, however, still adopts the haughty, grave aspect familiar from *Pride and Prejudice*, and only Elizabeth can soften this hard exterior. Tennant embraced the Happily-Ever-After of *Pride and Prejudice*, but then set out to dismantle it for her new plot.

The fairy-tale existence turns out to be more complicated and fraught than Elizabeth could have anticipated. She finds herself in the situation of a low-born Frances Burney or Samuel Richardson heroine. The differences between the Darcy and Bennet families cannot dissolve overnight. Pemberley and its people intimidate Elizabeth. The house and its master are her challenge. She feels – hopes – that motherhood will be her salvation. If she can only provide the estate with an heir… but that requires her husband to share her bed.

Pemberley is an unwelcoming place, too long the domain of a bachelor to encourage a sense of home in a young bride. The brooding, difficult hero – now husband – has reverted to what we recall from Bingley's account of him when bored on a Sunday evening. Elizabeth's mission is to feel part of this world. The contrast between Darcy and Bingley persists in Tennant's novel. Bingley sunny and optimistic and Mr Darcy unable to avoid the dark clouds that cross his countenance. Inevitable as the sunrise are Darcy's melancholic moods. In Tennant's book, Darcy and Bingley remind us of Heathcliff and Edgar Linton – the dark and the light. Elizabeth is the buffer and shield for Darcy from the worst irritations of her family. She wants to try to prove that she is good enough for him, despite his reassurances that all he wants is to be happy with her.

This narrative also questions Darcy's commitment to parenthood. The reader, along with Elizabeth, is taken through this difficult and emotionally draining experience. Will Darcy be able to display the tenderness and interest that Bingley, for example, shows to his daughter, Emily? Darcy does display boundless kindness in support of Elizabeth's improvements for the estate workers. It turns out she is a social reformer in the mode of George Eliot's Dorothea Casaubon in *Middlemarch* (1871), infused perhaps with some of Fay Weldon's reference to Mary Wollstonecraft.

What is appealing about Tennant's version of the Darcys' life is how she shows the complexity, doubts and everyday messiness of the newly-married couple's world. They are conflicted, with moods and disagreements as well as passion and devotion. Mr Darcy's dark moods return to him when they consider the empty nursery on the house's upper floor, and this is at the centre of any sadness they feel. Tennant's Darcy is supremely happy with Elizabeth, but she is often thrown into confusion because he still cannot fully express this. The Byronic type is never far from the surface. How does he, then, function as a husband? How does he adjust to this life? Not much is forthcoming on that score from Tennant. He is still a closed book in many ways, as we follow Elizabeth and her concerns over family, propriety and expectations. Some things never change.

There are no doubts about Elizabeth and Darcy's mutual respect and attraction. Tennant is careful about affirming these feelings – and yet. There is still the reserve between them, an inevitable consequence of being attached to the archetype. So, rather like Orczy's formula for Percy and Marguerite, the Darcys need to rediscover one another in marriage. Elizabeth looks at Jane's relationship and sadly questions whether she can have the affection and openness that her sister and Bingley enjoy.

Elizabeth and Darcy do not talk very much in *Pemberley*. There is a lot of guessing and silence between them, so that she does not know his true feelings on, say, their lack of children. She can only try and use her intuition about his concerns over not having a son. The same imperative hangs over Elizabeth that plagued her parents' marriage. She needs to have a son to be a successful wife. She saw Mr and Mrs Bennet's relationship deteriorate as the years went on with no male issue, and the frustration of this threatened the family's future.

The embarrassment and pressure hang over Elizabeth – the woman always had to take the blame for failure to conceive. Tennant's Lizzy is a subdued character, much to the displeasure of many of the readers and fans of spin-offs and sequels. She is a diminutive 'Eliza', constantly worried about social etiquette and her unworthiness as mistress of Pemberley. And when she retires for the night and her husband does not visit her, her heart sinks and she sleeps alone.

With the death of Mr Bennet, Darcy assumed more of a patriarchal role for his wife's family, over and above Bingley. It seems natural that he, rather than the eldest daughter's husband, would do so. Mrs Bennet loves to brag about her daughter's status. Darcy has power and influence – more than anyone else – and he does help everyone in Tennant's narrative, including the Collinses and even the Wickhams, of all the most difficult and obnoxious relatives. Every day that passes with no news of a pregnancy, however, causes Elizabeth greater anxiety and makes her situation more precarious.

Elizabeth must try to reach out to her husband, and to do this she has to decode his behaviour, still with his bluntness and intimidation. She modifies her behaviour in order to avoid his irritation. She has to learn to speak up for herself and assert her identity, according to Tennant, which strikes some readers as inconsistent with the original novel and the naturally outspoken heroine. Darcy and Elizabeth do reunite eventually, thanks to their shared dislike of Caroline Bingley, Mrs Hurst and Mr Wickham.

Tennant also introduced the influence of the late Mr Darcy Snr. His influence upon his son and kindness towards the young George Wickham are clear when Georgiana explains that her father believed that children needed nurture and generosity. All that is positive about Darcy is thanks to the kindness of his father. In memory of their fathers, and especially the bibliophile Mr Bennet, Darcy arranges the cataloguing of the Pemberley library. He includes an engraved plaque in Mr Bennet's honour: *There is always something going on at Pemberley...* Having seen Elizabeth's grief at losing him, Darcy grows in sympathy and delicately, tenderly embarks on a mission to give her beloved parent a place in the history of Pemberley. Elizabeth is deeply moved by this gesture. This is the 'delicacy' that Tennant manages to include, as ascribed by Austen to 'Mr D' in her letter.

The narrative continues with more conflict for Elizabeth, because whenever she thinks she has reached a resolution and understanding of her husband she finds out something else that he has failed to disclose to her. Just when she thinks she has reached him he backs away again. He is still the difficult and troubled man. It is not easy being married to Darcy, so Elizabeth, typically, takes to the fields to walk off her frustration and fear. However, Darcy is thrown into turmoil when Elizabeth fails to return from her walk one evening. He searches for hours, calling her name until, hoarse and exhausted, he finds her asleep in the ornamental gypsy caravan in the grounds of the estate. We feel the passion and affection in their reunion when he cradles her in his arms in the back of the wagon, and takes her home to Pemberley.

Here, Tennant offered a return to the 'ardent' Darcy beneath the surface. She manages to tap into this dual aspect of his character at this point in the story. He calls her by the informal contraction of her name 'Eliza'. How Miss Bingley would seethe with jealousy to witness this touching reconciliation.

Tennant's Pemberley has been a cold and imposing place, stately and intimidating; a reflection of its master. Elizabeth confides her fears to Jane and knows that the vultures are circling, awaiting her downfall. Darcy's Cousin Roper, Lady Catherine and Miss Bingley all have reasons to wish her downfall. Darcy has to take a stand against them when they are under his roof and show his true love for his wife.

The rudeness shown by Lady Catherine and Miss Bingley

sometimes borders on the comically villainous. Tennant's depiction of them does not have the same satirical flair as Austen. Where Austen had a light touch, Tennant tends to labour the point, with Miss Bingley and her sister showing a level of intrusiveness that stretches credibility. For example, when Mrs Hurst tries to burst into Darcy's bedchamber, or when Lady Catherine and Miss Bingley, within earshot of Elizabeth, suggest Darcy has discussed his desire for children with them. Mrs Bennet also talks fertility and vinegar douches – the best way to conceive a boy in her opinion. She should have listened to her own advice.

Characters overstep the mark, show themselves up and make one another uncomfortable. Tennant is good at revealing the embarrassing truth and raising the social tension. We are introduced to the dubious 'Colonel' Kitchiner, Mrs Bennet's wooden-legged suitor, and things take a decidedly comic turn. Mr Roper chips in with pseudo-scientific remarks and attempts at learned musings which become quite heavy-handed, compared to Austen's light ironic touch with Mr Collins, for example.

While Tennant reflects Austen's storyline and characters, the imitation of the satiric and ironic style is absent in this replica. This is largely down to the fact that Austen was writing a contemporary social novel. Tennant was writing an historical domestic drama in the style of Austen. Her follow-up novel *An Unequal Marriage: Pride and Prejudice Continued* is set twenty years on when the marriage is under yet further strain. Social convention and prejudice have continued to chip away at their relationship and go on to affect their children, Miranda and Edward.

The son of Darcy, in Tennant's narrative, has not grown up to be like his father. He is a bit of a disappointment and lacks the family self-discipline. Miranda, on the other hand, has inherited her parents' best qualities but sadly cannot inherit the estate. In this continued telling of the Darcy story he still has to cope with the problems of his extended family and the injustice of social and legal conventions that do not reward the deserving characters. This third instalment reads more like '*Pride and Prejudice* and Difficult Teenagers', and it is not hard to see why it has not made it onto Jane Austen fan fiction readers' 'favourites' lists.

Cousin Roper is still waiting in the wings, the eager heir but wholly unsuitable. The strains on the Darcy marriage place the couple in danger of estrangement. These narrative decisions for the plot, putting so much trouble in the Darcys' future, has displeased a string of readers and Jane Austen fan fiction bloggers even more than the misunderstandings in *Pemberley*. The idea that Darcy could be less than successful as a husband and father and that he and Elizabeth do not gain their happy-ever-after – and might even separate – upset so many on Goodreads.com that one and two-star reviews abound. The disappointment is clear from 'VC': 'Emma Tennant is too depressing for me... I believe Elizabeth is smarter than this and that Mr Darcy would share a bit more with the love of his life.'

From most of the reviewers the consensus is that Jane Austen fan fiction sites and collections contain, on average, more engaging and entertaining reads than either of Tennant's sequels. The difficulty fans have with these books is that they are pessimistic, bleak and lacking in romance throughout.

'Different as Angels': Alternative Narratives and Variations on Darcy

So, what *does* a writer do with Darcy in a *Pride and Prejudice* variation, continuation or sequel?

In 2013, a different take on the *Pride and Prejudice* narrative came from historical novelist Jo Baker. *Longbourn* is told from the perspective of the servants, and meticulously so. Sarah is the maid with responsibility for Miss Elizabeth and the other Bennet sisters: dressing, laundry, ablutions and hair. Baker offers a unique tone, different from other historical novelists and variants in Jane Austen fan fiction. In the AU of *Longbourn* the tone is sardonic, bathetic, weary and naturalistic, told from the underclass and servants' perspective. She takes the story of the muddy petticoats, for example, and flips it:

> 'If Elizabeth Bennet had the washing of her own petticoats,' Sarah thought, 'She would be more careful not to tramp through muddy fields.'
>
> *Longbourn*, Chapter 1

In this reorganisation of the narrative, Elizabeth's demonstration of independence is set in contrast to the fact that Sarah has three days' worth of work to bring the linens back to life, involving a harsh lye soak. In the context of this novel Darcy is, for once, a marginal figure.

Sarah, appointed as Elizabeth's personal maid, travels with her on her journey into Kent to see Charlotte at Hunsford. On this trip she must make herself useful and fit into the structure of the household at the parsonage. When she has to methodically sweep up some scattered tea leaves from behind the door and there is a knock, Sarah risks a reprimand if she does the common-sense thing of opening it, because she is not the house-servant. But she need not have worried; Darcy and Colonel Fitzwilliam in their finely tailored garments sweep past her without a glance.

Sarah does not exist for them. Baker masterfully develops a huge gulf between the classes, in physical as well as social terms.

For Sarah, the 'gentlemen' are a different breed, as different from her as 'angels' must be. As Elizabeth confides in her maid about Darcy's repeated visits to the parsonage, the perceptive Sarah shares Charlotte's and Mrs Gardiner's observation: "You do not suppose he could be partial to you at all do you, miss?" This suggestion is met with: "Don't be such a silly, Sarah."

The next day, as Elizabeth nurses her headache, Sarah notices 'his big glossy self' Mr Darcy paying another visit. As the proposal scene takes place indoors, Sarah takes the chance to sit and rest outside. She composes a letter to her sweetheart, James (who is the illegitimate son of Mr Bennet and thus Elizabeth's half-brother). She has to do this in her head, because she has no pen and paper, in contrast to the lavish stationery enjoyed by the upper classes. 'I would,' Sarah thinks, 'write to you… about Mr Fitzwilliam Darcy, who is such a polished meaty thing that he makes me slip for a moment, out of this world entirely, and I become a ghost-girl who can make things move but cannot herself be seen.'

Sarah witnesses him leave after he has been refused. 'She got up off the step and stood aside just in time, or he would have walked straight through her;' as she says: 'a ghost-girl'. 'Mr Darcy strode past her shadow, and marched down the path. He left the gate swinging. When he was out of sight, she slipped down the path after him, and latched the gate shut.' There is nothing ideal or heroic about this perspective on Darcy.

Sarah hears Elizabeth crying in the parlour. She does not go in but leaves her to it. There is more satire in *Longbourn* than other sequels or variations. Baker is presenting another 'what if?' scenario but with a distinct reformulation that deals with the contemporary issue of the material world and class-consciousness. If we were to travel back to the Georgian period, without privilege, then we too would probably inhabit the 'ghost' world of the servant. When Austen fans dress up as their favourite characters and in period costume for promenades at festivals, it is rarely as one of the lower classes. If we were to have privilege like Elizabeth and Darcy would we notice the 'ghost' population? *Longbourn* confronts us with questions and challenges our perceptions of contemporary society.

For all the romantic drive in *Pride and Prejudice* of a high-born man smitten with a lower-born woman, there are some boundaries that are never crossed. Richardson might have chosen to depict this in *Pamela*, in which novel a master sets out to seduce a servant and later marries her, but Baker makes it very clear that such miracles rarely happen in an alt-fiction Austen world.

Marriage across the social boundaries might be a rarity, but seduction is another issue. Everyone knows it happens, but no one talks about it. Baker's speculative alternative storyline sets up the character of James as Mr Bennet's 'natural' son with Mrs Hill the housekeeper. And therein lies further irony. There is a male Bennet son, but he cannot be acknowledged. He even helps to run Longbourn very efficiently, but can never inherit the property.

Darcy is still the embodiment of pride when it comes to built-in, bred-in disregard for servants. Baker's tactic is different from other authors, and Simon Langton. She shows the characters *lacking* any enlightened social views or concern for those under them, unlike the authors who want to exult Jane Austen's creations. Elizabeth the social reformer and Darcy the man of the people do not figure here. Langton's invention for the scene of a Darcy who interacts with his estate workers is just that, an invention. Baker shows the 'glossy creature' from another dimension as he brushes past the 'ghost-girl'. Sarah does not blame them however; they have been born into their 'dimension' and have never questioned their privilege.

'(O)blivious to the housemaids' came 'Mr Darcy again'. The betrothals and dramas of the Bennet sisters take place in the background to the lives of the servants in *Longbourn*. The story is a 180-degree switch in the social perspective. Sarah loses James and compares her situation to Elizabeth's great fortune. The existence of James, the 'natural' son, is a clever addition to the malaise that affects the Bennets' marriage. If there were any justice, James ought to inherit Longbourn. He is not a fool like Collins. He would make a good master of the estate. Instead, all their futures are precarious because women and illegitimate children have to make way for men, however incompetent.

Elizabeth wants to take Sarah with her to Pemberley on her marriage: " …I shall want something from home about me. It would be such a comfort." Sarah is a useful object for her young mistress – a familiar domestic article – but she refuses to go with her, choosing instead to go in search of her beloved James 'Smith'. Darcy has some thoughts on this. He fixes her with his gaze, but Sarah is the only woman who resists Darcy's character and forceful personality and the insistence on her obedience. Baker shows her defiance:

> " …sense dictates that you stay."
> "No."
> He loomed closer. "This is your answer?"
> Sarah squared her shoulders.
> "You have it already, sir: I cannot stay."
>
> *Longbourn*, Chapter 19

Elizabeth is pregnant and pleads with Sarah not to leave her. The pressure on a servant to remain secure and loyal to one household was immense. But any emotional or stern appeal to her is in vain. Darcy has not noticed the 'ghost-girl' until now.

Sarah looks upon Elizabeth's swelling abdomen with some pity. She knows, in her more worldly framework, that if her mistress survives this pregnancy there will have to be more. The Darcy legacy needs sons. So, despite being poor, overlooked and in service, Sarah is relieved not to be Elizabeth – when most women would long to swap places with her. Sarah feels the intimidation from Darcy but stands her ground.

Baker emphasises another side of the hero, that of the authoritative man of property, lineage and greatness with a ruthless streak that he has learned in order to preserve his world, and he is used to being obeyed. The patrician man of influence can harbour a darker side, as we have found out, and the maid can see it. He is a giant and she is a ghost.

Darcy's clean-shaven face and good looks are something exceptional in Sarah's world, a mark of class status. To be so groomed and well-fed, healthy looking and robust was a mark of superiority, distinction and wealth.

There is also something vampire-like in Baker's descriptions of him; mythic and slightly supernatural. And when Elizabeth tries once more, unsuccessfully, to get Sarah to stay, Sarah accidentally pricks her own finger and leaves spots of blood on her needlework. A trail of blood sits on the white cap that will belong to Elizabeth's baby. If you have a feeling for omens, then this is not a good sign. Darcy cannot force Sarah to stay: "This is England, after all, and she is not a slave." But he can force Elizabeth to do his bidding, as she is his wife and his property.

Darcy the Detective: Death Comes to Pemberley

Death Comes to Pemberley (2011) by PD James takes another side-step into a different genre, and is, to give James the recognition she deserves, closer to Austen's original prose style in the first section of the novel, at least. There is, as with Baker's response to Austen, a fluidity and fluency about her approach that is only to be expected. PD James closely references the foundation story and draws certain details out to form a new plot. For example, her reflection of the characters' early experiences echoes the idea of 'first impressions' that lies within the culture of gossip that circulated around Meryton. Elizabeth was said to hate Darcy, given his slight towards her at the Assembly.

PD James lays out the basis of the conflict inherent in the relationship. Darcy's attitude from that evening in Meryton will dog him forever. Every morsel of tittle-tattle has been raked over and analysed. How could any woman, and especially Elizabeth, be happy with such a man after that? Tennant realised that the prospect of a married life at Pemberley could well be bleak and lonely and PD James agrees. She presents Elizabeth with this future also, for "Who would want to have that disagreeable face opposite you at the breakfast table for the rest of your life?" as PD James has Maria Lucas pithily put it.

Meryton gossip embellishes the story. People say that Elizabeth set out to seduce him when she spent that week at Netherfield. By placing herself in his way, she promoted the chance of intimacy. With six weeks at Hunsford she probably cemented the relationship. What other explanation could there be? How awkward must that have been, after her refusal of Mr Collins? PD James achieves quite an Austen-like tone in her voicing of the local gossip, for: 'What possible pleasure could any rational woman take in six weeks of Mr Collins' company?'

PD James develops an authentic network of rumour and gossip. Charlotte Collins, for example, has a more important role as conduit for news back to Lady Lucas in Meryton regarding Darcy's interest in Elizabeth. His repeated visits to the parsonage started suspicions circulating, with Charlotte relaying reports of his behaviour so that it was beyond question he had developed feelings for Miss Elizabeth. In addition, James places Mrs Gardiner at the centre of the conspiracy. She chose Derbyshire as a destination in order to encourage her niece's matrimonial plans.

The confluence of events in *Pride and Prejudice* is read as schemes in *Death Comes to Pemberley*. Jealousy and speculation are rampant in this sequel novel and characterise this story. The great fortune achieved by Jane and Elizabeth are viewed with suspicion. Those that could not be happy for Lizzy and

Darcy, or believe that they were truly in love, simply looked at the 'caustic' wit of the wife and the arrogance of the husband and saw that they would make each other miserable for years to come.

In this way, PD James' fluency with Austen-like socially satirical language, better than any other sequel writer's attempt, elevates this novel. It is further in evidence, for example, in the description of the sisters' double wedding. Mrs Bennet was 'seized' on the occasion with 'palpitations during the service' because of her terror that Lady Catherine might march in and break up the wedding, 'and it was not until the final blessing that she could feel secure in her triumph.' PD James' triumph was the Austen-like tone she achieved.

She also reflected the family dynamics in the same spirit as Austen. James points out that Mrs Bennet will not miss Elizabeth. Her father, of course, felt differently, and we are assured that he is a regular visitor to Pemberley's great library. The promise of Austen's conclusion, in which she briefly mapped out the characters' futures, comes true in this sequel. Darcy and Mr Bennet also take it upon themselves to educate Bingley to improve his household, 'which Mr Bennet found irksome, [as] there were few new books and periodicals to tempt him' in the Bingley marital home.

Bingley, Bennet and Darcy therefore gel convincingly in *Death Comes*. The opening phase of the novel reflects *Pride and*

Prejudice closely and offers these plausible and very satisfying plot manoeuvres. James has command of an Austen-like rhetoric and brings extra dimension to familiar characters and how their lives might progress. Because Bingley has no library – not being a big reader – and making his money 'from trade', Darcy and Mr Bennet help him accumulate one worthy of the new gentleman owner of 'Highmarten House'. Of course, the upside is that 'There are few activities so agreeable as spending a friend's money to your own satisfaction and his benefit...'. Occasionally Bingley even picks up one of the books and tries to read it. PD James reinforces the charm of Bingley in this way, and the authority of Darcy, with Mr Bennet as something of a mediating figure.

Resentment towards Elizabeth and Darcy and their fortune has built up over the intervening six years since the action of *Pride and Prejudice*, especially from the Wickhams. Lydia complains about Lizzy's 'stinginess' towards her and her mother. James continues Austen's narrative in convincing and intriguing ways, such as the Wickhams' profligacy, and foreshadows the intrigue to come.

Death Comes turns sensational, suspenseful and dark. The Lady Anne Darcy ball (in honour of Darcy's late mother) is the backdrop to the unfolding action. Elizabeth has to work to the meticulously high standards of her late mother-in-law. Laid before her is the notebook 'stamped with the Darcy crest' in which all the instructions are written in an elegant hand. There is something of Du Maurier's *Rebecca* and the second Mrs De Winter about this Elizabeth's experiences at Pemberley. The impeccable former mistress of the house haunts the place.

Over everything looms that legacy of Darcy's parents and, as in Tennant's sequel, there is immense pressure put on Elizabeth to fulfil her duty and be worthy as mistress of the estate and mother to a Darcy heir. Writers prefer this scenario in their sequel novels: the creation of anxiety and pressure for the couple, fraught with issues about social standing. To this they add family problems from the range of difficult relatives, and series of misunderstandings. All of this is designed to test Mr Darcy's love for Elizabeth even further. To this formula, PD James added her trademark murder mystery plot.

Secrets, like those concerning Mr Bennet in *Longbourn*, will out. The Darcy legacy, according to PD James, is rife with them. Foremost is the suicide in the woods when Darcy's reclusive great-grandfather shot himself. Madness, crime and family scandals give this novel a Victorian feel, with stories of bodies in the woods and suspicious goings-on. It is *Pride and Prejudice* transposed into a Victorian novel of sensation and mystery, like those by Wilkie Collins and Mary Braddon of the 1850s and 1860s. PD James used the classic ploys of the murder mystery genre, so *Death Comes* is a tale of misdirection, sleuthing and discovery.

With the opening of Book Two, unambiguously titled: 'The Body in the Woodland', the characters have a call to action. Lydia Wickham arrives at Pemberley in a speeding coach, out of which she falls, hysterically screaming: 'Wickham's dead! Denny has shot him!" It starts with this shock and escalates from there. In comes Darcy, to be a man of action and a sleuth because he carries the most authority in early nineteenth-century rural society on his own estate. Lydia's frantic outcry at the start soon proves incorrect. It is Captain Denny who is dead, and Wickham is retrieved from the woods, unconscious. Lydia's discordant complaints continue, however, 'self-serving and indiscreet' as always. As her husband lies upstairs in Pemberley, clinging to life and accused of murder, she starts stirring up gossip. She tries to remind everyone that Lizzy was 'wild' for Wickham back home in Meryton, and that she only married Darcy because of his money. Snide remarks and slander only work if there is a grain of truth in them. The shadow of Wickham and his actions will never depart. 'Was [Darcy] never to be free of George Wickham?' asks PD James. Darcy and Elizabeth know the truth – of elopements and pay-offs – but stay quiet in the face of such insults. Even Pemberley begins to feel 'alien' to him. PD James summarises Darcy's sense of self, legacy and entitlement very neatly, as he feels he is no longer master in his own house.

Challenges to Darcy's authority and masculinity come from different quarters in sequels and alternative storylines.

PD James offers these in the form of Wickham, undermining his certainty in his marriage, and Colonel Fitzwilliam who tries to undermine his mastery at Pemberley. Previously, Darcy's authority was a certainty. Sequel writers destabilise this in order to bring about crisis and conflict for the character. In *Death Comes*, when Darcy takes charge, he becomes an organised and effective investigator. When they mount the search in Pemberley's grounds on the night in question, Darcy leads and Bingley, by contrast, stays behind at the house to keep the women safe.

Cousin Roper in *Pemberley*, and then Cousin Fitzwilliam in *Death Comes*, each try to assert authority on the estate. They might try to compete with Darcy's authority, but ultimately the estate workers and household servants know only one master. Darcy is Pemberley and Pemberley is Darcy. The intrusions into his home and the mystery surrounding the body in the woods set him thinking. He looks back at his house and views it differently, PD James describes; alien and strange to him in the moonlight. She punctuates the novel with Darcy's contemplative, existential struggle about his place in the world.

He is often filled with poignant and passionate feelings about his home and family when dealing with the bleak and sordid business of Wickham, Lydia and poor, dead Denny. When searching the woodland – his land – for the body, Darcy thinks about the suicide of his great-grandfather. He thinks about his boyhood and the past. There was a huge sense of responsibility on the Darcy men, and at one point he feels sympathy for the forebear who decided he could not shoulder the burden and took his own life. PD James offers a full, sentimental backstory in this sequel as a way to build on Darcy's character and show his affinity with his troubled, tragic antecedent. Before he killed himself, he shot his dog, Soldier, and asked in his letter that the faithful animal be buried with him. But he was an embarrassment to the family, and they did not honour his final request.

Fear has reigned over much of the Darcy history. The responsibility of such wealth and status, the possible taint of madness and the melancholia that has afflicted many Darcy men – all of these things weigh heavy on him. The family rejects the unorthodox. Loyal Soldier lies alone in his woodland grave, and his master is entombed with the other Darcys. PD James reveals that Darcy's suppression of emotion and awkward ways are rooted in this family history, and Elizabeth acts as his rescuer and the 'soldier' able to fight for him.

The Taint of Madness: Jane Austen Fan Fiction Variations on Darcy's Character

The Austen sequel and alt-fiction market looked very busy into the second decade of the twenty-first century. *Death Comes* is just one of the high profile publications to date. For the indie Presumptuous Press in 2014, Alexa Adams produced a Jane Austen fan fiction sequel, *The Madness of Mr Darcy*. Less high profile, but very popular amongst fans online and in print, this good quality novel explores further the possibility of that taint of insanity. The stress and 'indoctrination' of being a Darcy causes the hero to finally crack.

Adams' *Pride and Prejudice* sequel variation begins in spring, 1813 when the Bennet family are devastated by the elopement of Lydia. This 'what if?' story asks: what if Darcy had failed to secure the marriage of Lydia and Wickham and missed his chance with Elizabeth? So, he does not track the couple down and pay Wickham off – therefore Elizabeth and he have no more contact after she leaves Derbyshire.

Instead, Wickham sold Lydia into prostitution once he tired of her. Devastated by this, Darcy could not return to Netherfield nor help to reunite Bingley and Jane. Lydia eventually returns home to Longbourn, a fallen woman. "She is mad!" exclaims Mr Bennet, after Lydia tries to claw at her mother's face. Elizabeth seems to be the only member of the family that she responds to, and so she becomes her sister's carer. Mary comments darkly: "It is as Mr Collins said,… It would have been better if she were dead."

Darcy's failure to rescue Lydia is amongst the scenes that Adams fleshes out, along the same lines as those created by

Andrew Davies for his dramatisation. These tell the back-story of Darcy and Wickham's contrasting lives, and like Davies, Adams takes us into the underworld of Regency brothels and down-at-heel neighbourhoods: 'Mr Darcy searched every brothel in London he could locate, enlisting his entire male staff in a search quite outside their traditional duties in his service.'

When Adams shows Darcy finally confronting his enemy it is in Wickham's rented lodgings, richly decorated thanks to the money he made by trafficking Lydia. Darcy '… smashed the glass… grabbed Wickham by the lapels, and pulled him to his feet. "Are you telling me you sold her?… Damn you!" Darcy roared…' and he punches Wickham in the face.

Adams is influenced by the portrayals of madness and mental distraction that abounded in Victorian fiction. Novels such as Braddon's *Lady Audley's Secret* (1862), Wilkie Collins' *The Woman in White* (1859), Charlotte Perkins Gilman's *The Yellow Wallpaper* (1892) all depict specifically female characters that suffer a mental illness or have a belief in their own madness due to incarceration, isolation or ill-treatment. If your powerful husband, such as Edward Rochester, or your family are convinced there is something wrong with you, or can convince that feeling in you, then being shut away from the world was considered the only solution. Characters are privately, secretly diagnosed, and the system was an ad hoc one of home-spun treatment mixed with paid diagnoses to hide a family's shame.

If a person could, then, theoretically be driven mad, what were, the Victorians asked, the foundations of sanity – or insanity? Many authors set out to investigate this topic in a variety of ways that touched upon social convention, sexuality, addiction, post-natal depression and melancholia, as well as psychotic episodes and violent behaviour.

In *The Madness of Mr Darcy*, Adams shows a now alcoholic and distracted hero who resorts to physical violence. Twenty years after losing his chance with Elizabeth, Darcy, now a shadowy recluse, is horrified to see Wickham turn up at Pemberley. Darcy loses control: ' …he lifted up George Wickham, hoisted him with strength no man his age should possess, and threw him, screaming, into the hungry flames.'

Both Adams and PD James construct their sequel narratives around the torment and trouble that Wickham has caused Darcy. It is a great device, to maintain the rivalry between the two men, and in *The Madness* the loss of Elizabeth and the death of Georgiana (killed on her journey to join her husband in India) compound his situation. It means he has lost everything, whilst Wickham suffers not a single twinge of conscience. So, Darcy erupts with rage in a melodramatic manifestation of revenge, casting his rival into the flames. This forces Darcy into an asylum hospital, Ramsey House, run by Dr Wilson, and he and Elizabeth finally cross paths again. This is an inventive plot twist in Adams' alt-fiction sequel.

Elizabeth had to escort Lydia to the asylum to help keep her there. After her sister's death, Elizabeth stayed on as matron because she had proved to be so competent with the patients and gained the respect of Dr Wilson. She calls herself by the more respectable 'Mrs' Bennet, as a single woman in a profession. Darcy, on hearing the name, thinks she might be connected to the Bennets of *Longbourn* but cannot be sure. Elizabeth, on hearing Mr Darcy's name, knows that this is the man she rejected many years before, and we find out how much she came to regret it.

Never has she been able to find happiness with another man. Instead, she devoted herself to care for the patients. Fortunately, even twenty years on and driven mad by grief, alcohol and the desire for revenge, 'Darcy, for all his faults, bore much the same physique he had since reaching adulthood, only broader and more imposing than ever,' Adams reassures us. Colonel Fitzwilliam still feels 'inferior' to his cousin.

To reflect again on Barlow's and Krentz's critique of romantic fiction and the Darcy legacy: 'Elizabeth's scathing refusal of his marriage proposal… forces Darcy to revaluate his own behaviour and relinquish the worst aspects of his pride…', and Adams exploited this climactic event to begin a downward spiral. She takes the opposite pathway from Austen and mires Darcy and Lizzy in an early Victorian melodrama of insanity, revenge and lost love:

' … [Elizabeth] closed her eyes firmly, yet the tears would burst even the tightest seal. Mr Darcy! After all these years! His stormy, disturbed face rose before her, just as she had last seen him in Lambton and an audible cry began to escape her lips.'

The Madness of Mr Darcy, Chapter 9

The narrative benefits from being a journey back from madness, regret and loss. In this way, *The Madness* resembles *Jane Eyre* with its themes of redemption and resurrection from the flame-ravaged wreckage of revenge and madness.

PD James, as a high profile bestseller, and Alexa Adams, popular Jane Austen fan fiction author, both manage different and interesting 'what if?' *Pride and Prejudice* sequels. They spend time with the characters and analyse the consequences of their choices. Tennant and PD James represent Pemberley as a force for good and bad in the Darcys' future. They contrast barrenness with fertility and the anxious wait for an heir and speculate what different outcomes might be imposed upon the characters. For all these sequel authors Wickham looms large, either as a force for continued corruption or as one whose influence remains a bitter torment for Darcy.

Baker's *Longbourn* adds a further fascinating departure as an alt-fiction telling of the *Pride and Prejudice* foundation. This succeeds novels such as Valerie Martin's *Mary Reilly* (1990) in telling the parallel story to a classic novel. In *Mary Reilly*, Martin narrates the action of *The Strange Case of Dr Jekyll and Mr Hyde* (1886) by Robert Louis Stevenson from the maid's point of view. Within this way of exploring of stories the material and social culture of the servant class, and a new perspective on the principle characters, are offered. In *Longbourn* Darcy is the looming, intimidating figure with a fragile wife whose future is mapped out as one of pregnancy, childbirth and exhaustion for the sake of the Master of Pemberley.

For the bicentenary series 'The Austen Project' from Harper Collins, the publishing house came up with a great concept: choose six popular contemporary writers and get them to produce an update/homage/recreation of one of Austen's six novels. One novel per year for six years, and the whole endeavour kicked off with Joanna Trollope's version of *Sense and Sensibility* in 2013. Deborah Yaffe (author of *Among the Janeites*, 2013) initially welcomed it. Many prospective readers were excited about this series. A distinguished list of authors was on board. However, Yaffe had to give a verdict on the collection so far on her blog in 2015. She titled the review 'The Austen Fiasco?' This tells us something about the results.

Trollope's *Sense and Sensibility*, Yaffe concluded, was 'pallid and unconvincing'. Val McDermid's *Northanger Abbey* (2014): 'You've got to be kidding me.' Finally, what of Alexander McCall Smith's *Emma* (2014)? It reads ' … like the Emma update he sketched on the back of a cocktail napkin during lunch with his agent and then fleshed out, just barely, during a couple of afternoons of desultory work.' However, by the time we reached the updated *Pride and Prejudice* by Curtis Sittenfeld titled *Eligible* (2016), the publicity machine hailed it as the 'must-read' novel of the summer.

Chapter 8

Expanding the boundaries: 'hate sex' and the 'Darcy problem'

High profile authors and new writers of fan fiction alike have sought to tap the potential in Austen's *Pride and Prejudice*. They prolong the narratives or add alternative perspectives to the novel, exploring the range of Darcy. There are other new versions of the story that, like Jo Baker's Longbourn, offer further embellishments and more elaborate re-tellings of the foundation narrative and sequels. A common factor identified by many of these writers of the re-tellings of the story for the modern age is the problem with Darcy. He is a difficult man. So, what modern woman in her right mind would want to be with him? Writers have looked to solve this in a number of ways.

'A Sock Puppet with a Trust Fund': Reality TV Darcy

Harper Collins' 'Austen Project' allocated the 'biggie' *Pride and Prejudice* to American bestselling author Curtis Sittenfeld. This is perhaps the luckiest – or the unluckiest – commission for any writer, ever. Emma Tennant dealt with the aftermath and fall-out from fans and critics for many years after the publication of *Pemberley*. However, it was with relief that Deborah Yaffe was able to report on her blog in May, 2016, that '*Eligible* is much, much better' than the first three updates of Austen's novels; 'It's a cheerful, light-hearted reimagining with some laugh-out-loud funny dialogue, and its playful attitude towards Austen's original makes it a lot more enjoyable than the slavishly faithful earlier instalments.' (http://www.deborahyaffe.com/blog/4586114521)

The fun starts from the outset, with Mr Bennet offering up his feelings.

> "My dear,… if a sock puppet with a trust fund and a Harvard medical degree moved here, you'd think he was meant to marry one of our girls.'
>
> *Eligible*, Part 1, Chapter 1

So says the patriarch to his good lady wife, in *Eligible* (2016), Sittenfeld's twenty-first century *Pride and Prejudice*. The Bennet girls and their suitors are all 'eligible', especially Chip Bingley. Prior to moving to the mid-western conservative Cincinnati, Ohio, this wealthy young doctor appeared on a dating show, a fictional equivalent to the US TV hit 'The Bachelor'. Reality TV match-making shows might, therefore, be the twenty-first century equivalent of coming from 'trade'. Certainly, they offer a modern-day equivalent to the drama and gossipy tension of the Regency marriage market.

Sittenfeld draws a map of equivalent culture between the source novel and this bicentennial celebration version. Only Liz and Jane have flown the family nest, an eight-bedroom 'Tudor' detached house in the suburbs of Cincinnati. They represent the east coast sensibilities in contrast to their firmly mid-western family background. Liz is a writer on a woman's magazine, and Jane a yoga instructor for wealthy New Yorkers. Lydia and Kitty spend their time working out, texting and keeping up with celebrity gossip online. Mary is an eternal student, on her second masters degree. All adult daughters, all graduates and all privileged they have careers of a sort without much staying power, such as Kitty and Lydia's stints as retail assistants at Abercrombie & Fitch that enabled a sense of what could be called 'quasi-independence'.

It is an interesting, and slightly depressing, indictment of how much female roles have not changed in 200 years. Mrs Bennet took on a 'traditional' role of motherhood and social organising. Three of the five Bennet sisters cannot afford to move out of their parents' house. The Lucas' fourth of July barbecue stands in for the Meryton Assembly at the book's opening.

The character that at first appears to be one of the more sensible and pragmatic figures is Liz Bennet, a writer for 'Mascara' beauty and fashion magazine. This employment does not exactly help her image of striving to be more than ornamental or concerned with outward appearances, however. Chip Bingley and Fitzwilliam Darcy, on the other hand, went to medical school and are a doctor and a neurosurgeon. From the outside Liz and Jane seem to be living the dream, but in fact their New York lives are quite lonely. Liz has been having an affair with married Jasper Wick for years, in the belief that he is staying in an unhappy marriage to avoid the expense of a Manhattan divorce. Jane has had a series of love affairs with handsome, wealthy men, all of which have ended in disappointment.

Liz meets Dr Darcy at the barbecue, a hospital event that she whimsically decides is a husband-hunting 'buffet', it is so chock full of eligible doctors. Sittenfeld is unambiguous about her Darcy, he is tall, dark and handsome, a rich neurosurgeon and 'stand-offish'. Jasper Wick knows him, of course, of old from their college days and is dismissive and jealous of him.

'Hate sex' is Liz's and Darcy's recourse when they get

together at first. After a sense of desperation creeps in, when she realises her parents are broke and her life has been on hold for an unattainable ideal, she resorts to venting her frustrations on Darcy's superb physique. The relationship that starts out as a cynical and superficial act of sweaty lust after a run (all the Bennet sisters except Mary share an obsession with working out) evolves into something more profound. Sittenfeld does not use Austen's free indirect style of narration, so we are effectively inside Liz's thoughts throughout almost all the novel. We know her feelings in detail, but less so about Darcy's feelings or any other character in the story's main body.

Eligible is a Liz Bennet story, with plenty of her inner dialogue as she struggles with and tries to work out her feelings for Jasper and then for Darcy. We are left for long stretches of time guessing what Darcy's thoughts and motives might be. After one particularly energetic bout of 'hate sex', however, Liz remembers that in the height of passion he had called her "my darling."' He betrays his feelings in the throes of pleasure.

There is a degree of emotional, mental, as well as sexual compatibility between the two, despite the fact that they get off to such a rocky, ambivalent start. This equivalent story-telling line for a millennial Liz Bennet, approaching forty, is satisfactory to a degree. Darcy still owns a stately family pile, Pemberley, outside Old San Francisco. He is a dutiful brother and hard-working neurosurgeon. Georgiana's chronic shyness and anxiety since the deaths of their parents manifest as an eating disorder, for which Liz can be of help as an older sister figure. Darcy finally lets us and Liz into his heart when he admits to her that he would watch her leave in her running gear after they had sex and realised he did not want her to go. He did not want it to be the last time he watched her walk away.

Despite their reticence and sense of what is proper in the face of the trashiness of reality TV, all of the Bennet, Darcy and Bingley families come together for the finale of the 'Eligible' TV show. It is not quite as simple as that, because as Jane is already forty, she has taken the plunge and used a sperm donor as a last chance to have a child when she thought that Bingley was no longer interested in her. So, pregnant with an unknown man's child, she marries the ever-agreeable Chip in a television special. The Bennets' personal lives are on display for the whole country to ogle at. However, the pay-day is worth it for all participants to save their struggling finances. The deus ex machina of Sittenfeld's novel is the all-conquering power of television to make even the most uptight family members take the cheque and swallow their pride.

The man of family pride here is the socially superior, eligible, self-sacrificing neurosurgeon with a great sense of decorum and honour. Darcy of the twenty-first century novel has a 'Liz' who declares her regret and love on reality television. *She* proposes to *him* the second time, in a happy-ever-after romance ending with a twist. He is still manly and super-rich; she can be a modern woman nestled against his hard chest after a work-out. Ultimately, they are good for each other, and together they help to secure the happiness of the extended family.

Sittenfeld writes a contemporary socially satirical novel and not a recreation of an historical past. The contemporary challenges to the conservative midwestern Bennet family status quo include Jane's pregnancy using a sperm donor, Lydia's marriage to a transgender female-to-male fitness instructor and Kitty's relationship with the Bennets' real estate agent, who is black. These happenings cause further fractures to their parents' cosy existence, which was all built on debt and an artificial sense of inherited social standing in any case. They 'aren't racist' but – what will their friends say at the country club, when they find out that Kitty's boyfriend is black?

Liz sees the alternative side to people and likes to think she brings a New Yorker's liberal sensibility to matters with her family. However, Sittenfeld causes her to inadvertently give herself away – making this an effective satire – because her sense of superiority over how cultured and accepting of diversity she is make her quite smug. Sittenfeld sums this up: '[Liz]... felt that self-congratulatory pride that heterosexual white people are known to experience due to proximate diversity.' Her two younger sisters, Kitty and Lydia, whom she dismissed as empty-headed and dully provincial, in fact turn out to be generally more accepting and honest than she; after all her affair with Jasper meant that they spent years in a lie together.

In this way Sittenfeld channels Austen's satirical tone, allowing characters to condemn themselves out of their own mouths or via their internal dialogue. In doing so, she works out the Darcy Problem for her twenty-first century characters. Liz is actually quite unpleasant, when you break it down, and that's part of the solution. Her self-satisfied prejudices about family and lovers are dismantled, and Darcy accepts her for who she is, having proven his worth by assisting her family. So, to make Darcy less disagreeable, Sittenfeld created a 'Liz Bennet' who is quite shallow and must have her bubble of self-satisfaction burst.

The fairy-tale future finally stretches out before Jane and Chip, Liz and Darcy. However, it is to Mary Bennet that Sittenfeld turned to form a coda to the main action, and again in an attempt to solve the Darcy Problem and the book's central issues of prejudice and pride. Mary is the one who occupies the author's perspective at the close of the story. As the middle child, she is criticised by parents and older siblings and mocked by younger siblings. She is derided by her mother for being dowdy and boring, but all along has been scrutinising her family 'with a near anthropological derision.' Her academic meanderings have actually had far more purpose than her sisters realised, and the author gives her the final word on their behaviour and the glorification of appearance, manners and husband-hunting:

> ' ...their elaborate fitness rituals and fakely scented lotions and the hours – nay years – they devoted to making some man see them in a particular way; they reminded her of plastic ballerinas inside music boxes, twirling in their private orbits of narcissism.'

> *Eligible*, Part 3, Chapter 181

In the 1980 *Pride and Prejudice*, Fay Weldon also offered what focus she could on the maligned middle daughter. Mary is the first of the family we see on screen, for example, compared to Andrew Davies' foregrounding of Elizabeth in the opening shots of 1995. Mary Bennet gives modern authors some scope to explore the female condition. Sittenfeld allows her a voice, and many Jane Austen fan fiction authors often feel an affinity for Mary, the forgotten sister.

Excavating Darcy: Time Travel and Magical Realism

Thoughtful, clever women and intelligent, supportive men are the aim of many authors who attempt a derivation, re-telling of or a sequel to Austen's *Pride and Prejudice*. There is a profound passion that affects these writers, and their fervour for Darcy and Elizabeth's relationship transcends inhibitions and often involves the conflation of personal experiences and feelings about Austen into fantasy-style narratives.

One such is *Project Darcy* (2013) by Jane Odiwe. The premise of this story is the question: 'who inspired Jane Austen's *Pride and Prejudice*?' and in particular the character of Darcy. In this novel a group of five undergraduates: Ellie, Jess, Martha, Liberty and Cara prepare for their lives after college in the 'real world'. Odiwe's fascination with the sisters' dynamic is common to many adaptors, and she transposes them as a group of housemates, connected by their common interests and goals for life, post-university. They are, however, far from harmonious all the time, like the Bennet sisters. As Odiwe explained in her correspondence to me:

'Writing modern equivalents to these characters is quite a challenge because they don't always translate that well, and of course, neither do the social mores of the time. The twenty-first century is very different to the nineteenth. Mr Darcy is a case in point, and is why I decided my *obvious* Darcy character wasn't going to be the man Ellie fell for, as well as providing a twist at the end of the tale.'

Jane Odiwe, via email, 2017

The 'real world' has less allure for Ellie than the Regency world that she slips into. Odiwe markets this Jane Austen fan fiction story as a 'Jane Austen time travel adventure'. It sits within that genre, and also possesses some qualities of magic realism, whereby ordinary life meshes with other-worldly and supernatural happenings. Characters' lives occupy simultaneous timelines across the centuries and their paths cross. Odiwe, like so many fans and authors, enjoys the idea of inhabiting Austen's world as well as that of her characters (there's that closeness and affinity, again, because of Austen's authorial voice). Here, the lead 'Elizabeth' character is able to do exactly that.

Ellie is on an archaeological project at Steventon, surrounded by some very handsome fellow students and celebrity archaeologists, Henry Dorsey and Will MacGourty. However, on visiting Hampshire, she becomes 'attuned' to her surroundings and slips through time to live Austen's life during the months that the young Jane enjoyed a friendship with Thomas Lefroy.

Ellie-as-Jane socialises with Tom, 200 years in the past, just as Austen did, whilst in the present she thinks she is possibly attracted to Henry Dorsey, the very privileged, tall, dark and handsome archetype. Appearances are somewhat deceptive, however, in this wish-fulfilment 'being Austen' narrative. Odiwe looks at questions of compatibility as well as physical attraction.

What is superficial and what is meaningful? Ellie is a student, an artist and a kind, intelligent woman – different from Sittenfeld's Liz Bennet. Who will she find to truly appreciate her? Odiwe enjoys researching the background lives, the domestic and the intimate spheres of Regency characters, and she engages in the process of connecting with the real historical people through settings and artefacts.

Ellie crosses time when staying in the houses and the neighbourhood frequented by Austen. Something in the 'ether' and atmosphere of the setting makes this possible. The archaeological team is digging up the rectory where Austen lived as a girl, tracing the original 'footprint' of the building. Odiwe's twenty-first century Lizzy Bennet ends up walking in the very footsteps of Austen, as the author herself experienced life. The actual world of the friends and their love lives is fractured by Ellie's forays into the past. Once there, she meets Tom: '(he) dismounted, leaping down... the white tails of his coat flapping with a snap. I'd forgotten how tall he was... Broad shoulders,... his hair reminded me of spring cowslips... he had rather too high an opinion of himself... [but] my first impressions were changing... just a little.'

Ellie-as-Jane experiences a short and thrilling love affair with him. Odiwe builds up their mutual attraction and compatibility, inspired by Claire Tomalin's 1997 biography, and elements of the Austen family history based on descendent

Diana Shervington's research. 'I loved [Jane and Tom's] story,' Odiwe wrote to me, 'and wanted to see them dance together.' As an author, historian and illustrator, Odiwe brings her personal, visual sensibilities and creativity with background research into the everyday life of the Georgian family dwelling in a country parsonage.

So, did Lefroy inspire Austen's characterisation of Darcy? Spence's *Becoming Jane Austen* is the leading speculative biographical-fiction that would have us think so. Lefroy was pale and interesting rather than tall, dark and handsome: more Keatsian 'alone and palely loitering' than Byronic. He was exceedingly shy, according to Odiwe's characterisation. However, he makes 'Miss Austen' blush with his liberal quotations from Fielding's *Tom Jones*, their favourite novel: ' …her pure and eloquent blood spoke in her cheeks… and so distinctly wrought that one might almost say her blood thought.'

In *Project Darcy*, Tom teaches Ellie-as-Jane to ride, with the associated coded references to her sexual awakening. She 'started to bounce, and then strong hands were about [her] waist, the touch of his fingers staying with [her] long after [she] was lifted to [her] seat.' Odiwe draws out the erotic possibilities in this experience that Ellie has with him, going as far as a respectable Regency lady can go: 'it was a snug fit, his thighs gripped mine, and he drew me closely to him, one arm encircling my waist.'

In a response to the heightened emotions of personal and social events Ellie slips through time to join Tom, and in the present, she realises that Henry Dorsey is starting to pay attention to her. "OMG!" declares Liberty (talking – loudly – in text speak), "Mr Dorsey has one hot body!" He is "sex on legs!" according to her friends, but Ellie's feelings are conflicted; 'falling in and out of time' only makes 'every encounter with Tom Lefroy harder for her to depart from.' She feels more a part of his world than her own. Henry Dorsey is rich and very clever, and he can dedicate his time to music and the pursuit of an intellectually satisfying academic career. But he is also rude and disparages Ellie's artistic skills. Stand-offish and rude – so far, so Darcy.

Thanks to her time-travelling exploits Ellie becomes an expert on the layout of the Steventon parsonage. As a reader and an artist, her love and affinity for Austen's world create a deeper knowledge of it than anyone else possesses, and she falls in love with the countryside and Georgian Hampshire as much as she falls for Tom. It becomes her escape and joy, a combination of bliss and enjoyment to be gained from intellectual and physical encounters in her repeated visits to the past. She experiences all the colour, beauty and charm that the surroundings of rural Regency can offer.

'Everywhere looked a blaze of colour and sparkle under glittering chandeliers as the dancers skipped and hopped, galloping down the set to reach their place in time. It was wonderful to feel his hand in mine, to catch his eye, and to have his fingers linger in the small of my back like a caress.'

Project Darcy, Chapter 20

Odiwe wanted to see them dance. When her time-travelling ceases, Ellie is bereft, like a reader who reaches the end of a favourite story, ' ...the world was a very lonely place and her heart was aching for a time and a someone who seemed so far away.'

Ellie has a choice ahead, thanks to Henry Dorsey's new-found interest in her. He decides he wants to help her career and has the connections to launch her as an artist. A tempting offer. However, Odiwe paraphrases Austen's original dialogue in an effective way to recreate the sense of discord brought about by Henry's proposal to Ellie. This heroine has a social conscience:

'I don't understand, Ellie, I've just told you that in spite of everything, I love you – I can't help myself!"

'The trouble with you, Henry, is that you think you have the right to control other people's lives – to have influence and power over them. The rich are all the same, manipulating everything from friendships to business with no one except themselves and their own ends in mind. It's disgusting!"

Project Darcy, Chapter 29

Here, Odiwe makes her contribution to solving the Darcy Problem. She described the composition process to me, and how she sees this twenty-first-century issue with the hero: 'What sensible girl… would get past the first post or put up with a Mr Darcy character after meeting him just once or twice?'

This is the crux of the problem. Does the writer introduce a redemption storyline for him, or do you replace him with an equivalent hero with better manners and people skills than the archetype? Or, like Sittenfeld, do you make Lizzy a more problematic character, hence placing Darcy in a better light? Odiwe's reasoning over her decision is clear: ' … he just seemed such an obnoxious character, I couldn't think changing him would be believable in a modern context.'

So, she included a twist to reassert the storyline of Jane and Tom. Will MacGourty, the gentle archaeologist, is the one that fulfils the role of Darcy – by stealth. The twist in the tale is that 'Dorsey' is not the true Darcy. Instead, MacGourty is the descendant of Austen's real-life Darcy, Tom Lefroy. He is Darcy by discretion and a kinsman of gentility. He has, like Tom, always been 'lovely to talk to' and full of compliments for Ellie's artwork: 'Ellie was always overwhelmed by Will's praise.' Throughout the different phases of the story Will has been the constant, respectful and unchanging presence who did not need to learn to appreciate a woman such as Ellie. We like our Darcys fully-formed in the twenty-first century.

Our Own Private Austen

Karen Joy Fowler's novel *The Jane Austen Book Club* (2004) opens with: 'Each of us has a private Austen...'. In what is a perceptive examination of characters inspired by their reading of Austen, Fowler, like Odiwe, explores growth and reconciliation, rather than redemption. This is a popular interpretation of what we now think and feel about Austen's storylines. We need a reorganisation of Austen's Regency values and mores today. Fowler summarises, with this simple opening phrase, the personal relationship that so many of us have with the author. Austen is speaking to us directly.

Bernadette, the oldest member of the book club at age sixty-seven, favours *Pride and Prejudice* and proposes to the six members that they read Austen's six novels over six months as a structure to their timetable. Of course, these six months encompass far more than simply the lifespan of a book club. It is a slice of time out of the members' lives that forces them to confront past experiences and make crucial decisions for their futures, informed by Austen. She is undoubtedly the ever-present seventh member of the group and provides them with a life code. The fifth meeting, hosted by Bernadette, is titled: 'Chapter Five: In Which we Read *Pride and Prejudice* and Listen to Bernadette.'

At the beginning of each meeting Fowler has her characters: Bernadette, Sylvia, Allegra, Prudie, Jocelyn and Grigg (the only man in the group) offer their first impressions of the novel and one another. Fowler drafts a careful construction of the lives of these California Austenites and threads the author's narratives into and through their experiences.

Before meeting to discuss *Pride and Prejudice* the group attends a dinner-dance at the Galleria of the Sacramento Public Library. The book club gathers in support of Sylvia, whose ex-husband Daniel has arrived with his new partner. Thoughtful and unhappy Prudie whose favourite novel is *Persuasion*, people-watches and broods about the couples on the dancefloor: 'Half of these… were rich men with their second wives. She based her identifications on the differential between the woman's youth and attractiveness and the man's… she disapproved.' Austen transposed to California dance assemblies.

There are a number of *Pride and Prejudice* updates set in

modern-day America, such as the 2016 Hallmark Channel movie *Unleashing Mr Darcy*, and the YouTube series from Pemberley Digital, *The Lizzie Bennet Diaries* (2012). As Sittenfeld demonstrated with contemporary Midwest and east coast US society, there are parallels that can be drawn and equivalents found for the characters in Austen's original.

Who is 'Darcy' in Fowler's novel, then? Well, she does not make it as simple as that. She approaches the narrative from the position of the group's discussions about Austen and her characters and has them investigate what makes them effective and insightful when it comes to understanding their own lives. Couples come together, separate and reunite over the period that they share the books. Bernadette, who could be called a free spirit, adores Darcy and has been married several times. Always the romantic and ever the optimist, she is sure Mr Darcy will be around the next corner. She is 'A Cockeyed Optimist' (this is one of her favourite songs) and is convinced that the Happy Ever After awaits her. At the end of the novel 'She was married again. She showed us a ring with a large aquamarine. "I really think this is the one," she said. "I love a man with vision."'

Perhaps Grigg fulfils the role of Mr Darcy? He is certainly rich enough and comes to the rescue of the lovely, lonely and damaged Jocelyn. Grigg is shy, and close to the women in his family, but in his early forties is still looking for love and an outlet for his compassion. He is very good-looking, has money and a well-developed social conscience and concern for the environment. He is another effective solution to the Darcy Problem. By contrast, Bernadette's solution to it is to always be on the look-out for romance.

Fowler's ingenuity in creating this entertaining story lies in how she blends the types and archetypes and interchanges them, and so creates combination and hybrid characters. Austen-inspired relationships are the bedrock, and she customised a new novel from that influence and goes some way towards solving the Darcy Problem for the modern reader.

Professor and Mrs Darcy

Now might be an appropriate time to take a step back from millennial fan fiction, the internet and new novels that reflect Austen's narrative to take a look at an earlier, unorthodox variation. *Darcy's Utopia* (1990) by Fay Weldon is not a novel that is ever mentioned on fan websites or internet chatrooms. It does not conform to the expectations of narrative that readers have of material that includes the charmed name of 'Darcy'. Weldon wrote this novel in a pre-1995 world after adapting *Pride and Prejudice* for the BBC in 1980, and in part used it to confront the Darcy Problem. In order to do this, she shifted the focus to a female Darcy.

One cannot help but think that Weldon, as a feminist author, as well as putting Mary Wollstoncraft's words into the mouth of her Lizzy (Elizabeth Garvie) on screen, took on further notions about relationships, morality and masculine/ feminine desires from Austen and that ten years later *Darcy's Utopia* was the result. It is a different novel from other Austen spinoffs – very different – and not as well-known as Weldon's *The Life and Loves of a She-Devil*. So, does she take the name of Darcy in vain? Is our archetype to be found within these pages? Well, sort of.

Eleanor Darcy has a mission for a Utopian society in which men will believe in two things: God and Love. She is the mistress and, later, the wife of Professor Julian Darcy, and he builds a system of 'Darcian Monetarism' or 'Darcynomics'. She is first his disciple and lover and then the leader of a Darcy religious-type cult.

In a series of probing interviews by journalists Hugo and Valerie, Eleanor takes them back to her childhood, through her various love affairs and onto her affair and marriage to Professor Darcy. Weldon's Professor Darcy heads up a social and financial revolution that fails dismally, and he ends up serving time in prison. For most of the narrative he is locked away. Instead, we focus on Eleanor as she waits for her man on the outside. Whilst doing so, she builds up her own celebrity reputation as a social revolutionary and activist. She plays off the name of Darcy.

Julian Darcy is more involved in politics than any other manifestation of the character, and his ambition is to exercise power at government level. The Darcy Problem that Weldon uncovers is the same as Odiwe: what do we make of an arrogant, obnoxious and overly entitled hero? Hugo, who writes for a prominent broadsheet, calls Eleanor 'the Bride of Rasputin'. However, like so many others before him, he has already fallen for her charm and found that he is 'bewitched' by her 'fine eyes'. In Weldon's version these are green, a witch's eyes. Whilst Professor Darcy might at first captivate colleagues and acquaintances, it is his amazing wife who eventually becomes the more powerful figure.

Despite having a passionate affair with fellow journalist Valerie and building a love nest together in the local Holiday Inn, Hugo is more concerned with the interviews conducted with Eleanor on his collection of the 'Darcy Tapes'. His brief is to produce a profile of Julian Darcy, and Valerie has to do the same for Eleanor in her magazine 'Aura'. Like Sittenfeld's Liz Bennet, Valerie is occupied with lightweight issues for women's print and fashion media. We are in that territory again, where romantic fiction, lifestyle, health, beauty and family all come in second place to the serious 'masculine' world of 'proper' news and politics. However, Weldon is on a mission to disrupt this narrative.

The late 1980s and early 1990s were, Weldon informs us, a

period in which writing, media, publishing and love were still heavily influenced by gender roles. Hugo takes on the political and economic heavyweight topics of the once mighty Julian Darcy. Valerie is to deal with the human-interest love story of the girl-from-nowhere, beautiful, home-wrecking Eleanor. Valerie also finds herself wholeheartedly embracing Eleanor's 'Darcynomics' notions: do everything in the name of love. So, she sets up home with Hugo in a hotel suite, in a way 'eloping' with him, and leaves her husband, children and responsibilities behind. She feels happy and excited for a while, because they have each other and they have room service.

The foundation of Darcynomics is a type of Marxist, co-operative-style philosophy in which everything is subordinate to love. It means embracing impulses for love and passion, but not relinquishing decorum and conscience. Therefore, Eleanor insists that Julian divorce his wife (Georgina Darcy). There is a strong thread of moralising pseudo-religious ethics in her outlook. The priests, clairvoyants, preachers and healers that populated her working-class childhood have influenced Eleanor. Now, she preaches Darcyism – a religion of chivalry, romance, charismatic leadership and self-determination.

Eleanor has been on a journey all her life. This has resulted in being the subject of media interest whilst her famous husband is imprisoned. She was born, Valerie discovers, to an unmarried mother and penniless musician father. She was named 'Apricot Ellis' because her mother was stuck for a name in the hospital and the first thing she saw was the brand name 'Apricot' on the label of her brushed cotton nightie. Little Apricot struggled through childhood and adolescence to escape poverty and her mother's alcoholism. Eleanor's family lines were further blurred because her grandmother married her father. So, when Bernard Parkin arrives in her life, she jumps at the chance to be free from the dysfunction.

Bernard is a passionate, political, devout Catholic theology student. In some ways he is Eleanor's Mr Collins. However, she marries him, and he abandons his faith and his first marriage to be with her. She changes from Apricot Ellis to Ellen Parkin. Religious still, but not conservative, they veer towards Marxism. Bernard takes up a teaching post at the University of Bridport under Julian Darcy. 'Apricot' becomes 'Ellen' who becomes 'Eleanor' as she navigates her social rise. Belinda, her school friend, recognised her ambition years before and tells Valerie she is ruthless, like a Lady Macbeth. Eleanor is more like Thackeray's Becky Sharp than Austen's Elizabeth Bennet.

Eleanor Darcy intimidates other women, including Valerie, rather like Darcy and his intimidation of others in society. Her beauty, rampant conservatism coupled with religious superstition, zeal and utopian social ideals make her confusing and fascinating to others. Here is Fay Weldon's twist on the normal telling of it. The Darcy archetype is not Julian, with his pot belly and thinning hair. Instead, it is the Devil himself as channelled by Eleanor. She believes in the presence of the Devil in the world and claims to have had a vision of 'The Dark One' in her neighbour's garden. Eleanor possesses a sinister sexual mystique and harbours occultist leanings. Valerie is afraid that whilst Hugo interviews her they have become lovers. These suspicions are well-founded. Hugo has indeed a growing passion for the bewitching green-eyed *Mrs* Darcy, against his better judgment. His struggle, too, is in vain.

Eleanor uses strange, obtuse reasoning to justify her cheating ways. She operates with her own self-serving rules for relationships. She talks in terms of lust, curses and dark forces when it comes to falling in love with the power and potency of Darcy. Eleanor likes to invoke spiritual and supernatural urges that made it inevitable she falls in love with her Mr Darcy. But Julian already has a wife, the sophisticated, beautiful woman of influence, Georgina. In Weldon's incarnation, the Darcy family sibling relationship becomes a marital one. This is another disconcerting feature. Weldon enjoys the mischief this provokes in playing with Austen's characters. Eleanor sports on Georgina's big brass bed and expensive linen sheets with Julian, cynically making her affair blatant and public. She enjoys the power and influence her sexuality gives her.

She is unpleasant to those she discards, making Bernard weep at her cruelty. Totally unsympathetic, she sneers at his teary, snotty face and compares him unfavourably to Julian's superior breeding. Julian, her Darcy, moved amongst the power brokers and politicians in the highest offices in the land, and carried a handkerchief.

Pot-bellied, with a hairy nose and yet still powerful and superior, this version of Darcy has an untouchable, unassailable career at first. When he breaks up with his wife to be with Eleanor his reputation is only enhanced, with a beautiful, young wife under his roof. Weldon, with this, goes against the grain of romantic idealism in *Darcy's Utopia*. She fills her story with social criticism about the factors that affect men's and women's lives. Darcy's reputation is undiminished among his circle, whilst Eleanor must run the gauntlet of the usual prejudices and snobbery in response to her rise. As with PD James and Tennant's versions of Elizabeth, Weldon's Eleanor confronts them and defies the pleasure they wish to take in her social downfall.

Whatever you do, Weldon's Mrs Darcy proves, you must not underestimate her survival skills. She is neither intimidated nor impressed by the life of romance and comfort. She is plain in her interviews with Valerie and Hugo:

"In Darcy's Utopia… nostalgia will be out of fashion. We will look back on the past with horror not envy and delight – we will stop our romantic nonsense about the rural tranquillity of once upon a time, which is, if you ask me, nothing but the projected fantasy of old and miserable men who, looking back into their own child-hoods, see paradise… But it isn't…"

Darcy's Utopia, 'Transcript of a Hugo/Eleanor Tape'

The message is unambiguous: do not fall for the hyped idea that somewhere the romantic ideal exists – in love, home, or some happily-ever-after future – in fact *anything* on which the brand of Cinderella-inspired popular culture is based. 'In Darcy's Utopia,' she adds, 'it will be bad form to hark back; collecting antiques for the domestic home will be outré.' Don't tell the Janeites.

For Weldon, Darcy is a concept – a talisman, a totem – of desire and romance, a religion of nostalgia and mis-taken idealism. In her cynical 'Utopia' a Darcy is an elusive personality – male, female, devil – that corrupts, lures and deceives. She tackles the Darcy Problem head on, from a socio-political perspective. For a writer who was once an adaptor of *Pride and Prejudice*, Darcy became a metaphor for everything wrong with romance. As Eleanor reveals: "What a fine fellow the Devil is, all fire and sparks and energy, but temporary…'"

Morality and Immortality: Darcy to the Rescue

Author Shannon Hale is a member of the Church of Latter-Day Saints (LDS), or as it is often known in the UK, the Mormon faith. In *Austenland* (2007), the first in a series, she explores the humorous side of the pursuit of the myth of a Prince Charming and the existence of a real Darcy. Jane Hayes, a thirty-something New Yorker, harbours an unhealthy obsession with Mr Darcy in general, and Colin Firth-as-Darcy in particular.

In the English countryside nestles the resort of 'Austenland', staffed by actors in the roles of Regency characters. Jane goes there in pursuit of her Georgian ideal and, perhaps, her own Mr Darcy. He appears in the form of Mr Nobley, a history teacher and part-time Georgian re-enactor who, it turns out, understands her loneliness and is ready to accommodate her Austen/Darcy mania. Ellie, in *Project Darcy*, could channel the reverberations of history at Steventon and fulfil the fantasy through time travel. Jane Hayes searches for thrills via the immersive holiday experience of a Regency country house party. Both characters manifest this desire for nostalgia and idealism in a narrative of romance. How Eleanor Darcy would balk at this!

Marilyn Brant, on the other hand, is an author who reinforces the strong, silent, tall, dark and handsome Darcy archetype in her novel *Pride and Prejudice and the Perfect*

Match (2013). In this there is no ambiguity. It is staunchly in the territory of romantic fiction and escapist ideals with another Dr Will Darcy, this time an ER consultant in Chicago. Both Hale's and Brant's version of Darcy, comic and romantic, share features in common. They have excellent graduate degrees and are decent, stand-up guys who come to the rescue of their respective 'Elizabeth Bennets'. The Darcy Problem in these versions is solved thanks to good education and resorting to the familiar heroic archetype with added sympathy and, in the case of Brant's version of Darcy, a sound upbringing by a dedicated single mother.

Beth Bennet in *The Perfect Match* is the object of Dr Darcy's desire, and Brant investigates social issues attached to the uncertainty of online dating and the situation of working, single mothers. Beth's doubts and fears rest upon whether any man could accept her and her son Charlie, by her first husband Pete Wickham. She is in the same situation as Darcy's mother was, and it is from this background that his pride and prejudices arise.

Dr Darcy's personal anguish stems from growing up as the son of a single mother, and he must teach himself not to draw premature conclusions about Beth. All this happens whilst his feelings for her grow into an intoxicating erotic desire, something to be expected in this genre. However, his sense of masculinity, strength, power and pride shore up a moral personality minus all cruelty. Beth is the force that subdues him. She is the Jane Eyre to his Rochester; their passion and attraction exhibits that same dynamic. From the first moment they meet they lean into one another and create a special understanding. Brant's writing of them displays all the characteristics of classic romance writing that work so well as a formula for readers' continued enjoyment. And Dr Darcy is the total package: 'After shoving his hard-earned, steel-blue Ferrari into park, he burst into the ER and called out to the head nurse "Who came in?"'

From the outset he is the brooding, passionate and dedicated hero. He has far more in common with how the archetype developed into the Victorian age. His passion is only thinly veiled: 'Will forced himself to hold back, even as he kissed her. He didn't want to scare her off, not this soon, not now when he found himself liking her so much.'

One of our favourite characteristics of any Darcy is this sense of a passion contained with difficulty. It is the moment in the novel when the original Darcy declares: "In vain have I struggled. It will not do. My feelings will not be repressed. You must allow me to tell you how ardently I admire and love you." This is the bedrock upon which the Austen variation romance novels, by Brant, Sittenfeld and others is built.

The progression of the Darcy archetype came to an inevitable point in the work of Jane Austen fan fiction/historical romance author Amanda Grange with *Mr Darcy, Vampyre* (2009). The action commences from the day of the Bennet sisters' weddings and deals with another 'what if?' – this time a Gothic storyline. The explanation for Darcy's aloof, distant and mysterious nature, along with his depths of passion, is vampirism.

Oblivious to her husband's true nature, Elizabeth is like the victims in Stoker's *Dracula*. Her wedding day is one of joy, and then in contrast to Jane and Bingley, a creeping sense of dread and threat overwhelms her:

"'So, here we are, two brides," said Elizabeth [to Jane]… suddenly, she shivered.

"What is it?" asked Jane.

Elizabeth's voice was queer.

"I don't know. I just had a strange feeling, almost a sense of foreboding."'

Mr Darcy – Vampyre, Chapter 1

She has a slow, progressive education in what it means to be married to a man who is not in fact a man, but a being of mystery and allure with deep, dark family secrets. Gothic threat and mystery bleed into what should have been Elizabeth's perfect life. For Grange, the logical development of such a man as Darcy, full of dread and desire, is to make him a vampire.

Darcy has tried to resist Elizabeth's beauty and charm, but

ultimately resorted to a marriage of painful yearning rather than be apart from her. Therein lies the Gothic torment for the couple, so much so that the 'wet shirt scene' is treated to a further erotic transformation. On their honeymoon journey through the Alps she sees her husband swimming in a lake and she joins him – nude - in the water:

'As she drew closer… she suddenly felt nervous… he had seen her… his eyes… darkened as his face flooded with desire…

"You are so beautiful," he murmured… "You are intoxicating, ravishing, exquisite."'

Mr Darcy – Vampyre, Chapter 4

Elizabeth is desperately attracted to him – she is only human, after all – and feels a tangible envelopment of some sort of spell so that she becomes mesmerised by her husband's power. They move closer to one another, but their relationship is not destined for consummation – just yet – whilst Darcy is still one of the living dead. However, Elizabeth ' … felt as though they were not two separate beings but halves of the same whole, which had long been sundered and longed to be joined.'

Amanda Grange, in an interview with me for *Fan Phenomena: Jane Austen* (2015), spoke about the 'immortal' love that she feels is contained in the relationship of Elizabeth and Darcy. It is, she considered, always ripe for reinvention and renewal in different settings and contexts because Austen achieved such a great pair of archetypal lovers. So, vampiric love is only a heartbeat away from that. Along with time-travel plots it is one of the most popular twentieth and twenty-first century fantasy genres and connected directly to the Darcy archetype with this kind of narrative and sequel writing. In Grange's hands the Darcy Problem is not so much solved as compounded, embraced even. She makes him more difficult and sends him and Elizabeth on a quest to discover a 'cure'.

Elizabeth rapidly falls under her husband's spell whenever he comes close to her: 'consumed by him, mesmerised by his breathing and the hypnotic beating of his heart.' He has the power of a mystic, psychic or Victorian mesmerist who can compel people to do his bidding. Grange's vampire version of Darcy does not exploit his power. He must resist his attraction for Elizabeth. It is too dangerous. The couple is locked in a tormented, erotic, Gothic battle.

They are like Stephenie Meyer's high school vampire/human couple, Edward and Bella of her *Twilight* series. Edward must restrain his passion around the shy, clever Bella Swan because of his fear that he might 'turn' or kill her. Edward and his 'family' of vampires have banded together because they agreed to be transformed in order to survive life-threatening situations and out of their shared morality. Grange uses a similar tactic for Darcy and Georgiana. Lady Catherine de Bourgh is their 'original'. She bit the brother and sister to save them from the Great Plague of 1665. When Darcy's eyes become dark with desire for his bride, and just as Elizabeth begins to hope that at last they might consummate their passion, Lady Catherine interrupts them. Nothing could be more effective in killing passion. She has tracked them down, outraged at his marriage outside their sect. He was, she claims, destined for her Anne 'pale and bloodless', so they could found an aristocratic vampire dynasty: "She is from an old and honourable family. She is the one who will keep the bloodlines pure…".

Elizabeth is initiated into a terrifying, competitive, erotic world with all the threats and intimidation of a sensuous, mesmeric, blood-sucking cult. Darcy defends her on their progress through Europe as they search for a cure. He fends off enemies, and at a certain point calls up a wind that swirls through the forest and vanquishes their attackers. "This is not what I imagined when we set out on our wedding tour!" acknowledges Elizabeth, 'her natural good humour reasserting itself.' Darcy introduces her to his properties in Italy, including a palace on the Grand Canal in Venice, creating a princess/Cinderella world for his wife. He must decide on a life with her, or death. Which one of them will lose their soul?

'His kiss was full of fervent desire and something more, something dangerous, something deadly. She was held by some great power, suspended in a moment of exquisite anticipation, poised between safety and danger, the known and the unknown, the natural and the supernatural.'

Mr Darcy – Vampyre, Chapter 18

Grange perfectly recreates the tone and drama of the Gothic romance and its associated tension and anxiety. The question is not whether to join the undead – it is whether to succumb to desire. There is constant hope because Darcy is still a relatively young vampire and not fully controlled by the ancient cult. He can, for example, protect Elizabeth from older, predatory vampires. Her wedding gift of a crucifix only mildly irritates his skin, but it protects him from the Vampyre Prince in a final battle.

In the hierarchy of vampire aristocracy Darcy, like Edward Cullen and his 'family', is not fully – spiritually – lost to the dark lusts of his condition. He resists the temptations that overwhelm other vampires because he maintains integrity and honour. Mr Darcy Vampyre is set apart from the rest of his kind, as he is from other men.

Austen's method was to present the romantic agony of unrequited love in her low-key and subtle fashion, contrary to the style of the Gothic novel that she so loved and which she parodied affectionately in *Northanger Abbey*, of course. Grange retraces the steps, back into that Gothic mode with its more eroticised, dramatic rendering of the desires that heroes and heroines exhibit – but must control. Here are Grange's Elizabeth and Darcy:

> ' ...his lips found her flesh again and he let out a murmur and her blood responded... he lifted his mouth from her neck, slowly, unwillingly, pulling himself away from her with every ounce of his strength...'
>
> *Mr Darcy – Vampyre*, Chapter 23

Andrew Davies' Darcy has to swim and fence to relieve the tension and heat of his desire. Grange's patrician vampire has a similar physical manifestation of the struggle with his desires:

> 'His eyes were full of pain and his body was contorted with agony, but he forced himself to walk over to the far side of the fireplace where he collapsed into a chair out of temptation's way.'
>
> *Mr Darcy – Vampyre*, Chapter 23

It is a great concept: Darcy madly in lust with Elizabeth but unable to touch her because of the danger of his passion. It harks back to Stoker's dangerous eroticism. Meyer utilised this dilemma also, at the start of the *Twilight* series, until Bella's marriage, pregnancy and 'turn' to the vampire life. Grange, Meyer and other authors have developed a fruitful exploration, using the scaffolding of the novel, with additional underlying moral codes as they Gothicise the *Pride and Prejudice* narrative.

As with Austen's Lizzy and Charlotte Brontë's Jane Eyre, the marriage of the heroine to the vampyre-Darcy proves to be his salvation. Fidelity, trust and a conviction about his inherent goodness and valour provide an excellent foundation for their love. Within the extraordinary, melodramatic, passionate and Victorianesque approaches to the narrative, Grange's stands out as a particularly effective exploration in which Elizabeth has a very active, heroic role to rescue her Darcy.

The Jane Austen Fan Fiction Community: What Makes a Great Jane Austen Fan Fiction Story?

The stormy narratives from Jane Austen fan fiction authors, such as Grange and Alexa Adams, attract readers for their combination of romance, historical research for settings, the frisson of eroticism and alternative 'what if?' storylines. They allow fans of Austen to prolong, speculate upon and consider different outcomes. If Austen had chosen any one of a number of different plotlines, where – ask fans – might the story have gone?

Alternative Darcys in print have been thrilling and entertaining us for some years, and we can include Weldon's Julian and Eleanor Darcy in their number. New additions regularly appear thanks to the growing Jane Austen fan fiction community. These writers rely on an increasing appetite for extensions of readers' favourite narrative strands from Austen's world. Many fan communities focus solely upon *Pride and Prejudice* and Lizzy and Darcy's relationship. Míra Magdó, an Austen blogger based in the UK, is a superfan and devotee of everything to do with Darcy in his various forms. Her blog, established in 2015, is called 'Obsessed with Mr Darcy' (https://obsessedwithmrdarcy.wordpress.com), and on this she regular ly reviews Jane Austen fan fiction. Because of the proliferation of the fan fiction genres devoted to *Pride and Prejudice* Míra provides a valuable service by making recommendations to her fellow readers.

If we focus on some of her reviews, we can see the features that Jane Austen fan fiction fans rely on to satisfy their love of Mr Darcy and his narratives. Discord, surprises and even heartache can constitute some of the plots and work very effectively. All twists and turns must ultimately result in harmony, resolution and a Happily Ever After that the fans approve of. Reading fan fiction is primarily intended to be fun and relaxing. It also helps if it is witty. For example, the consistently popular LL Diamond features as a favourite, with novels such as *An Unwavering Trust* (2015) in which Elizabeth's uncles appear as major protagonists. Diamond creates a sense of villainy from Uncle Gardiner, of all people the most kindly and innocuous of characters, but Míra regards this twist as not harmful to the story's integrity. It does not diminish enjoyment overall.

Jane Austen fan fiction is recognised as something of a gamble. Plot variations and expansions are a risk, especially when it comes to introducing differences in the characterisations. The potential destabilising of readers' hopes and expectations must be balanced with cathartic excitement and anguish. The ideal is something new and interesting without being inconsistent or too formulaic.

Fan fiction authorship is not an easy task to accomplish well, therefore. Míra singles out Karalynne Mackrory as an author of 'smart' and creative Jane Austen fan fiction. In highlighting the positive elements of Mackrory's work in *Yours Forevermore, Darcy* (2015) she indicates some of the pitfalls of the form:

'I have to admit I'm a bit bored that most of the variations start at Hunsford, but in this case it's not a problem at all, because the author avoids the clichés… [And] she was able to avoid the common error [that] authors tend to copy the Hunsford [first marriage proposal] scene into their book.'

Obsessed with Mr Darcy, September 2015

A slavish copy is not what Jane Austen fan fiction readers are looking for, neither do they appreciate too formulaic nor clichéd a narrative. Míra applauds Mackrory and other authors' reworking of the text. This sees segments of Austen's original dialogue and description put into a different context to draw out some added meaning for fans. In that moment it is therefore a witty reference that fans will 'get'. Varied references to the 'wet shirt' scene, for example, get worked into narratives. These variations are very flexible but must retain integrity.

Míra finds the characterisation Mackrory employs for Darcy in *Yours Forevermore* 'brilliant!' She considers the series of letters he writes as mini 'masterpieces' of fan fiction and concludes her blog with an appeal to the author:

> 'Ms Mackrory, please put aside everything – I'll take care of your kids and clean the house – and write an epistolary Jane Austen fan fiction novel.'
>
> Obsessed with Mr Darcy, September 2015

This offers a fine example of the interaction and relationships that develop between Jane Austen fan fiction writers, their reviewers and readers. Their authorship is fuelled by enthusiasm for the original novels and many have to work their writing around busy lives. They pursue it as part of the discourse around their favourite novelist and appreciative reviewers and bloggers such as Míra are crucial to this process of production and access. Her reflections can recommend the works to others, and her response can act as a prompt to authors to develop new compositions or explore more of the same.

This activity functions as a stimulus for the future productivity of fan fiction and communities online, some specifically dedicated to Darcy. The encouragement to write and reinvent is everywhere. And in so doing, authors approach different solutions to the Darcy Problem. How do you rehabilitate this adored but difficult hero?

Some authors, such as Sittenfeld and Brant, smooth out his rough edges. They recreate him as a dedicated doctor to gain immediate sympathy. He might be blunt and stand-off-ish, but that's because of the pressure he faces. A writer like Grange explains it away as a supernatural condition. He is difficult and distant for very good reason if he faces an eternity of undead torment.

Jane Odiwe takes a different tactic with *Project Darcy*. Hers is to set up a potential successor to the character, but because of the heroine's close affinity with Jane Austen we realise that Henry Dorsey is not the focus. That romantic interest is a red herring. Instead, Odiwe takes us back to the origin story in Austen's past. The gentle, clever young Irishman, Will MacGourty, is the true successor to Darcy and Tom Lefroy.

We see a more radical departure taken, characteristically,

by Fay Weldon. Instead of trying to solve the Darcy Problem she makes it a manifest part of the plot and then outdoes the hero with the heroine, Eleanor Darcy. Her religious zeal for her unkempt Professor Darcy is a form of hero-worship – ultimate mania – that seduces and troubles everyone around her. So much so, that she takes the idea of Darcy, abandons the real thing and brings in a congregation of new admirers as part of a charismatic religious cult at the novel's conclusion.

The Jane Austen fan fiction titles on Amazon and other sites often outsell other, more 'legitimate', forms of mainstream historical and romance fiction that fall into more traditional categories. The ones that acknowledge Austen's original and base their narrative on her characters have developed into a fruitful and prolific career for many new authors. They often have other commitments in their lives and so their writing is part-time. They have productive exchanges with their fans from around the world that encourage and offer support. These interrupt the solitary existence of a writer's life and help promote further creativity.

Míra highlights the specific category of *Pride and Prejudice* narratives and the exploration of Darcy in particular. We return to this focus of fandom all the time. On 'Obsessed by Mr Darcy' she celebrates the work of Victoria Kincaid and Joana Starnes. They are both very popular Jane Austen fan fiction authors and specialise in Darcy/Elizabeth spin-offs and variation narratives. Kincaid published *President Darcy* in 2017, a modern re-telling of *Pride and Prejudice* set in the White House and Washington DC. Darcy can be a 'vampyre', a neurosurgeon or President of the United States.

Míra favours Kincaid's *The Secrets of Darcy and Elizabeth* (2016), *Pride and Prejudice Proposals* (2015) and *Mr Darcy to the Rescue* (2015). The latter is a 'funny' and 'bright' book that nonetheless offers enough of an 'emotional rollercoaster' to satisfy. It is one of the characteristics of successful Jane Austen fan fiction that the authors put the characters through anguish and turmoil, for cathartic effect, before delivering a happy ending, 'Ms. Kincaid', states Míra, 'does torture Darcy and Elizabeth, but not too much.'

In the comments section to this review, Kincaid herself appears in response and shows how important this level of feedback and interaction is to her writing:

'I was touched that you enjoyed so many different aspects of the book – and you clearly 'got' what I am trying to do with the characters. As a writer, it means a lot to me when readers have the same kind of enjoyment from my books that I have gotten from other authors' works. Thanks for letting me know I hit the mark!'

(https://obsessedwithmrdarcy.wordpress.com/2015/08/08/

shelves-in-the-closet-mr-darcy-to-the-rescue-review)

Here is the shared experience, of knowing the reader 'got' what she meant to do and of letting her know she 'hit the mark.' Reader and writer understand one another and share a mutual appreciation of the ways in which Darcy ought to be portrayed. They discuss what it means to retain the 'spirit' of *Pride and Prejudice* and its enduring hero.

The abundance of Darcy types in recent fiction and fan fiction just goes to show the potency of the original and how Austen's character can be aligned into many different story forms. Romantic fiction Darcy jostles with Gothic Darcy and social satire Darcy. For Jane Austen fan fiction fans, however, a certain balance needs to be struck, and those that wish to appeal to that group of readers, specifically, are careful to follow certain parameters. But what happens when there are no boundaries? What happens with Darcy when the archetype can be amusingly, controversially and bizarrely flexible to suit the purposes of the entertainment? This is where we find some interesting alternative Darcys, hugely successful franchised Darcys, and Darcy co-opted for religious, commercial and humorous reasons. The enduring power of Darcy is next.

Chapter 9

Unwavering, enduring: Darcy – a hero for all time

Lila Stangard is not a name that readily springs to mind when talking about Mr Darcy. She was, however, in love – or thought she was – with her Darcy. But she is a silent, voiceless character. Like many young women, Lila, a college student, has a crush on a version of Mr Darcy. She discovered that he was willing to have an affair with her behind his wife's back, and on her phone he appears as 'Mr Darcy'. This is the provocative plot twist from the writers of the ABC TV thriller *How to Get Away with Murder* (2014–present).

Murderous Darcy

The first season of the show deals with the disappearance of Lila (Megan West), the discovery of her body and the eventual revelation of what she had been up to in her private life. Her Darcy, like that of Eleanor in *Darcy's Utopia*, is a college professor Sam Keating (Tom Verica). He is married to high profile attorney and law professor Annalise Keating (Viola Davis).

Lila believes in her married lover, and he understands that the name 'Darcy' is very persuasive. Sam is happy to exploit her perception of romance – her yearning – to gain her trust. She loses her virginity to him, thinks he will leave Annalise for her, and then finds out she is pregnant. She refuses to get rid of the baby and ends up murdered and left in a water tank. A fatal sequence of events awaits Lila once she becomes infatuated with 'Mr Darcy'. In this drama, Darcy is a cheating husband who uses the potency of the name to convince a young student to be lured to her death.

The cultural and sexual currency of Darcy in 2014 meant that the writers of *How to Get Away with Murder* could use the name as a device in the plot to explain why a young woman might be so beguiled and hoodwinked by a man that it ultimately leads to her murder. She hoped that the older man – rich, charming, handsome and with the added seductive power that she lost her innocence to him – would turn out to be a genuine Darcy. We feel sorry for Lila and perhaps angry at the idealism she fostered that led her towards such danger. The Victorians might have been right. Romantic aspirations for men above your station can lead to your downfall.

By using such a romantic pseudonym for their contact during the affair he insinuates to her that he 'gets it'. He understands her dream of devotion, passion, charm and bravery and eventually uses that to have her murdered. His hired killer strangles her on a rooftop. Lila, the writers show, believed – tragically and fatefully – in the existence of an everyday Darcy on her college campus. The idea that Darcy might be around the next corner is sometimes a dangerous one.

This chapter looks at different and possible future Darcys. There are many ways in which the character has departed from the original, and many angles that writers and adaptors have continued to exploit. The reading of Jane Austen is now so much a part of mainstream culture that it acts as a kind of short-hand for romantic bookishness. For example, the long running ABC family drama series *The Gilmore Girls* (2000–2007) depicts the teenage years of Rory Gilmore (Alexis Bledel) growing up in the small, idyllic, New England town of Stars Hollow (a sort of twenty-first-century American 'Cranford'). Rory (short for Lorelai) is an imaginative, sensitive soul in a coming-of-age drama, and she uses Austen, Charlotte Brontë and even Leo Tolstoy as her guides for understanding the world. Rory walks through town with her nose in a book as the drama of the neighbourhood unfolds around her.

The name of Darcy in the new century evokes a feeling and offers an archetype that anticipates a certain deep and complex response from readers and viewers. The distance between the uses of the character and the original might seem to be greater than ever the more powerful and universal the archetype becomes, but the foundation of it remains with the original.

Best in Show

Unleashing Mr Darcy (2016), a film made for the Hallmark Channel, is a 'modern-day spin' on *Pride and Prejudice* about Elizabeth Scott (Cindy Busby) and Donovan Darcy (Ryan Paevey) and their romantic entanglement amid the elite breeders and dog show scene of New York city. Elizabeth gets the chance to show King Charles spaniels and, as Hallmark states in its publicity, Darcy is 'aristocratic' and 'rude'. The mutual attraction between this Darcy and Elizabeth is complicated by the misunderstandings that occur in the dog show competition scene. Beneath the surface, however, Donovan Darcy is kind and devoted. In this movie, the ideas of posh, aristocratic and rude are conflated to mean the same thing. In 'true' Austen fashion, Hallmark claims, they have a change of heart after bad first impressions, and in this way the film stays faithful to the spirit of the story. In *Unleashing Mr Darcy* the hero appeals to romance fans and dog-lovers alike.

Kick-Ass Darcy

Writers and filmmakers have put Darcy through some bizarre variations and alternative depictions. He is usually on the side of right, however, and is rarely corrupted or tempted away from the moral path. His decency shines through. The murderous Sam Keating pretends to be Darcy to exploit a young student's romantic idealism. Even in the case of a darker and dangerous version, which portrays Sam Riley as 'Colonel Darcy' in the film of *Pride and Prejudice and Zombies* (2016), there is good reason for his solitary brutality as he patrols the English countryside: the infestation of zombie 'unmentionables'.

On screen Riley's Darcy is a leather-clad, sword-wielding warrior, ruthless in his pursuit of the 'stricken'. The zombie outbreak has been caused by colonial expansion. The over-reaching and acquisitive tactics of the British Empire have had unforeseen results. King George III was driven mad by the epic Battle of Kent against the Undead and their advance on London.

Seth Grahame-Smith's original novel (2009) translated wittily to graphic novels and the big screen. A comic, mash-up format became a quirky, satiric story. Many Janeites and Jane Austen fan fiction fans around the world had issues with the story. They found it off-putting and even felt insulted on Austen's behalf. Others found the film to be an entertaining, alt-fiction narrative. The first proposal scene at Hunsford, for example, sees Elizabeth (Lily James) in combat with Riley's Darcy. As they work through their misunderstandings, and frustration, they are perfectly matched in hand-to-hand combat. It is like a *Taming of the Shrew*-style slapstick battle between two lovers – they banter as they exchange blows.

The film version of the zombie mash-up tale has contributed to the expansion of fan culture. There are those that might not watch a variation or adaptation of Jane Austen's work but *would* watch a comic zombie movie. It also adds an extra dimension to the possibilities of Regency cosplay. Cosplay, a contraction of 'costume play', is when fans dress up as favourite characters and get together at conventions and festivals to re-enact scenes and read scripts or have a photo-shoot. The popularity of *Pride and Prejudice and Zombies* has opened up a chance for Austen fans to augment their Regency gowns with zombie-impaling katana.

The depiction of Darcy as a brooding warrior-hero has added a new twist and works very well. Sam Riley is great as this type of Darcy. He has appeared, previously, in darker and grittier roles, such as *Control* (2007) in which he played the late Ian Curtis of Joy Division, and the BBC drama *SS-GB* (2017). This show is based on Len Deighton's alt-timeline novel *SS-GB* (1978) set in 1940s London. Riley plays Douglas Archer, the shrewd Scotland Yard detective, in a Britain occupied by the Nazis who were victorious in the Battle of Britain in 1941. Instead of resisting Hitler's progress through Europe, Britain was defeated, and so Archer is drawn, reluctantly, into the resistance.

In an interview on syfy.com (February 2016) Riley talked about how he had to try and make the role of Darcy his own because of the precedent of so many famous Darcys. Perceptively, he likened it to playing Hamlet. So many actors have made their mark in the role that you have to be imaginative and new when you tackle it now. He mentioned that it was difficult to explain away the zombie-fighting Darcy to his grandmother.

An actor has to create his 'own' Darcy. In developing a zombie-Austen tale you raise the possibilities of appealing to both fanbases, although the incongruity of it is not lost on Riley and others, including his grandmother. It can also be interpreted as a story representation of just how consuming fan culture for Austen can be. The legions of flesh-eating Zombies roaming the English countryside could be interpreted in a number of ways.

Have You Met Miss Jones?

At the vanguard of adaptations and reinterpretations of Austen in popular culture at the turn of the century has, of course, been the work of Helen Fielding. The first *Bridget Jones's Diary* column started in the *Independent newspaper* in 1995. Written over the past twenty years, ever since she was inspired by the 1995 adaptation, Fielding's series of novels are: *Bridget Jones's Diary* (1996), *Bridget Jones: The Edge of Reason* (1999) and *Bridget Jones: Mad About the Boy* (2013). The books returned to the storyline of the films with *Bridget Jones's Baby: The Diaries* (2016) tie-in. The films, based on the novels and newspaper columns, employ an alternative timeline and further variations on the original: *Bridget Jones's Diary* (2001), *Bridget Jones: The Edge of Reason* (2004) and *Bridget Jones's Baby* (2016).

In the novels, Fielding employs a modern reinterpretation of Austen's novels – both *Pride and Prejudice* and *Persuasion*. Her character of Mark Darcy is a composite, based on real-life friends and, principally, Colin Firth. Firth then took on the role for the films. So, he played a character that is a version of a character he had already played, inspired by him... and so on.

The 2013 novel, *Bridget Jones: Mad About the Boy*, contains the storyline in which Mark Darcy has died and Bridget is bringing up their two children alone, now in her fifties. Prior to this telling of the story Fielding had returned to the

Independent with a new Bridget Jones column, in 2004–2005. This strand of the story chronicled Bridget's conflicting feelings about Mark and Daniel Cleaver – the Wickham character (played by Hugh Grant in the movies). The end of this strand sees the heroine pregnant with Daniel's child and contemplating her future as a parent with him. So, we see from this that Fielding experimented with a variety of outcomes for Bridget and Mark, including separation, regret, a return to her old lover and bereavement.

Bridget, in a love triangle with these two men but the ever-optimistic seeker of true love, was the driving force behind the success of the books and films. And the addition of Colin Firth as Mark Darcy did not hurt, and meant that his role grew more and more prominent. Fielding has prompted much of the Darcy mania that underpins the popular culture surrounding the character, and she has continued to supply more with the latest film and book continuations.

The 1995 founding newspaper series channelled much of the unfolding excitement for viewers of the TV series. As it was broadcast each week, there was increasing anticipation, as Fielding stated, for 'Darcy to get off with Elizabeth.' It appealed to Bridget's taste for literary romance, sexual tension and Colin Firth in a wet shirt, which is to say that it was *Fielding's* taste for all that. Bridget Jones is a thinly-disguised author surrogate.

The network of inter-connecting threads began very early

in the Bridget and Mark saga. Andrew Davies co-wrote the screenplays for the first two film adaptations. As part of the DVD extras for *The Edge of Reason* Renée Zellweger, in character as Bridget, conducted an interview with Firth, as himself. Then, on the return to print in *Mad About the Boy* (2013) and the death of Mark Darcy there was an outcry from fans. How could an author kill off Darcy – any Darcy? However, as Stephanie Merritt pointed out in her *Guardian* book review at the time, what else could Fielding have done? She explained that Bridget's purpose is to get her man. Once achieved what could happen in a sequel other than Mark's saintly death (by landmine on a mission to free aid workers in Sudan)? Bridget and Mark could not be involved in the messiness of a divorce and custody battle.

So, by 2014, Fielding had used two different storylines for the outcome of Bridget, Mark and Daniel, firstly in the newspaper series and then in the first sequel novel. In 2016 a further strand was added to the story with the release of the new film *Bridget Jones's Baby* (nicknamed '*Bridget Jones: Who's the Daddy?*' by fans online). The web of different narratives for the characters grows wider and wider. Its growth can be compared to that of fan fiction. What variations can be applied to Bridget and Mark? Fielding has tried a few 'what if?' scenarios by now. What if Bridget ends up with Mark, and what if he dies, or what if she winds up with Daniel? The possibilities tempt Fielding, like Jane Austen fan fiction authors, back into print time and again.

In *Bridget Jones's Baby* we encounter another script variation co-written by Fielding, Dan Mazer and Emma Thompson, the veteran award-winning adaptor of Austen's *Sense and Sensibility* and contributor to Joe Wright's 2005 *Pride and Prejudice* script with Deborah Moggach. Thompson also appears in the film as Bridget's sardonic obstetrician. The film explores the continuing complicated love lives of Jones and company and restores Darcy back to life – thankfully not in zombie form – instead in a replacement storyline to *Mad About the Boy*. Darcy is still a figure of worthy endeavour, of course, working in the human rights sphere. Instead of a departed Darcy, the film opens with Daniel's memorial service, coincidentally on Bridget's forty-third birthday. Cleaver is missing, believed dead, so no door is entirely closed in this franchise. Plus, there is a final clue near the end credits that suggests he will return.

Colin Firth appeared alternately baffled and exasperated in the role of this Darcy. He is older, very distinguished and still deeply in love with the frustrating character of Bridget. Each has numerous other relationships, yet their hearts belong to one another – we hope. Internet billionaire Jack Qwant (Patrick Dempsey) intervenes in this plot. Bridget has an impulsive fling with him at the Glastonbury festival. After that, she reunites – briefly – with Darcy, and shortly thereafter finds out she is pregnant. The device is one of the simplest plots but reasserts the love triangle, this time with Jack.

The continuing problems and frustrations associated with Bridget raise the enduring mystery of this version of Darcy. This has always been: what does he actually see in Bridget? She has dithered over Daniel Cleaver and then Jack, and now the paternity of her child is in question. Plus, she is something of a hedonist and a risk-taker. Kooky and awkward, undoubtedly, and with a great deal of klutzy charm, she is not unlovely in both the books and the films. So, we must fall back on the 'opposites attract' explanation for this version of Lizzy and Darcy in the Bridget Jones universe.

In Firth's portrayal, he is again the embodiment of English gentlemanliness, still (bewildering though it might be) besotted with Bridget – at least when she is in the room. As they spent so much time apart because he is a workaholic, she had always felt neglected, and once separated he did not waste any time getting married to (another) icy, glamorous and more 'suitable' candidate. Fielding is emphatic about how mismatched Darcy and Bridget still are. She makes the familiar sideswipes at tall, slim, goddess-like women, such as the collection of very young Eastern European models at Daniel's memorial service; identikit girlfriends that cause Bridget to feel even more insecure and inadequate.

Bridget is down-to-earth and funny, and that seems to be her appeal when Darcy is in her presence. Fielding's final instalment, and let's assume it is for the time being, takes us further into the realms of a millennial fairy-tale ending in which Colin finally admits his love for her (let's face it, Fielding is writing this for herself) and asks her to marry him, irrespective of the doubts over her son's paternity. According to *Guardian* film critic Peter Bradshaw, Firth seemed to be channelling the same manner in his performance as he did as George VI (in *The King's Speech*, 2010). Firth had an appearance, he suggested, whilst still handsome, that gave the viewer the impression of a 'very posh tortoise'. Awkwardness and slapstick abound in this film.

We were never meant to take Jones and company seriously, of course. Fielding's Darcy was always a knowing, post-modern critique of the original. This helped Firth to parody his period drama hero role and send himself up. He has never felt comfortable as a heartthrob. The *Bridget Jones* franchise became an exercise in gentle mockery of British costume drama and Austen adaptations with, variously, the co-operation of Andrew Davies, Crispin Bonham-Carter, Hugh Grant, Jim Broadbent and Emma Thompson.

Patrick Dempsey as Jack, the convenient billionaire, is Bridget's potential 'Prince Charming' match, especially when he gets down on one knee and offers up her shoe that has got stuck in the Glastonbury mud. Dempsey has played such characters before, in Disney's *Enchanted* (2007) and most notably as Dr Derek 'McDreamy' Shepherd on ABC's *Grey's Anatomy* (2005–present) from seasons one to eleven. Like Firth, Dempsey gets cast to type.

However, reunited with Darcy before he flies out to Khartoum (be careful of those landmines, Colin!) Bridget realises that he still means more to her than anyone else. But the point remains that his important job and responsibilities left her 'mostly alone' throughout their time together. Thanks to her useless (biodegradable!) condoms she has to involve both men in her life, in order to discover which one she wants to be with as father of her child. Being Bridget, though, the paternity issue is made more and more complex by the fact that she cannot choose because she likes them both and does not want to hurt either of them. Her situation is compounded because at forty-three she will be a 'geriatric' mother.

Darcy, in his job, must defend a Pussy Riot-style activist group ('Poonani') in a human rights case. His deadpan responses to the lewd topics discussed in court are classic Mark Darcy. Bridget's dilemma increases as her due date looms and she appeals to Darcy to think about her as much as he does his work. In order to be together, they have to be honest about what they want. Bridget: "Knights in shining armour don't exist anymore – or do they?" and Mark: "Bridget, you know

I find emotional declarations difficult." This latter remark is something of an understatement, but perfect modern Darcy.

Bridget's waters actually break *on* him when she goes into labour. He is forced to carry her to the hospital because they are stuck in a traffic jam: "Good god, Bridget – you're immense!" She reaches for Darcy's hand when she is in the throes of giving birth, as their son comes into the world. This is the most significant moment. To whom do you turn for comfort and reassurance when things get real?

At forty-three and a new mother, Bridget finally grows up, sort of. And with Jack in attendance, she marries Darcy, in a satisfactory conclusion to this part of the series. The resolution that cinema audiences seek requires a neat storyline with a Happy Ever After. Bridget's goals are finally realised, and the knight in shining armour finally comes to her rescue. After twenty years of turmoil and uncertainty, they marry in a suitably Regency location and setting – picturesque eighteenth-century gardens – with their son in their arms. And his name? William, of course!

It seemed like a bizarre choice when, in December 2016, BBC Radio 4's *Woman's Hour* included Bridget Jones on its Women's Power List for the last seventy years. The full seven names, one per decade, were: Margaret Thatcher, Germaine Greer, Beyoncé Knowles, Barbara Castle, Helen Brook, Jayaben Desai and... the fictional Bridget Jones. A chaotic, stressed, exasperating, fictional diarist (and not her creator Helen Fielding) joined six other women whose careers informed and helped to shape women's lives through music, social activism, academia, politics and trade unionism. She was included as an important and influential character for women precisely because she was a divisive choice that would attract debate. As one of the programme's contributors said of her: 'She bust in and gave voice to single, drunk, fun-loving', flawed women, the 'normal state for a British woman without shame,' imperfect 'and a bit of a failure'.

She has entered slang as synonymous with big knickers and 'doing a Bridget Jones' such as being too hungover to go into work, feeling dowdy compared to a boyfriend's ex, or showing yourself up at a public event because of what you wear, how you act or how much you have to drink. Helen Fielding reacted to Bridget's inclusion on the Power List, saying that it was an honour for her to be included. Her creation is undoubtedly lovable, claims Fielding, and is a resilient, non-judgmental, sincere soul. Bridget is an example of the person we truly are, plagued by the notion of how we ought to be.

This does stand up as a rationale for including her on the *Woman's Hour* seventieth anniversary list, because it gives us a chance to reflect on how the character operates and echoes social anxiety. There is another key reason why she emerged on the list, not articulated openly by those who chose or defined what female influence is. That reason is hope. Hope remains for Bridget throughout all her haphazard adventures that Darcy still loves her. Contrary to her devil-may-care attitude towards relationships, Bridget is deep down a romantic, hopeful, quite traditional person who, when she discovers that Darcy wants her and she is 'the one', is blissfully happy.

'Mr Douchey'

The transmedia production company Pemberley Digital has also employed long-running, extended storylines that build upon a popular culture thread for their format of shows on YouTube. Writer/producer Bernie Su is behind the Digital Emmy-award winning show, the *Lizzie Bennet Diaries* (2012). This adaptation consists of 100 episodes of around five minutes each. So, the cumulative output of the channel equals a feature film length re-telling of a modern *Pride and Prejudice*.

The dramatisation opens with Lizzie having to struggle with her future, working through student debt and trying to get on with her family. She juggles the pressures of establishing her online reputation as a vlogger and coping with her mother's insistence that she get married, against a backdrop of her emergent relationship with the infuriating and charming Darcy.

Daniel Vincent Gordh as Darcy stars opposite Ashley

Clements as Lizzie. He is attired in preppy-style clothes (braces and bowties with a neat sleeveless jumper) and has an archaic and somewhat exaggerated sense of social class. Despite the fact that he operates a successful millennial transmedia company, the fictional 'Pemberley Digital', he is something of an incongruous figure, and a slight anachronism beside the other contemporary equivalents to Austen's characters.

Lizzie is an expressive, gregarious arts graduate with a pastime of vlogging (based on the format used by Canadian You-Tube star Lilly Singh, aka 'Supergirl') in which she comments on her life and performs in character as members of her family – such as her parents. Her friend, confidante, director and editor Charlotte Lu assists her in this project. By contrast, Darcy, the head of a successful tech company, still insists on sending Lizzie a handwritten letter when the time comes for him to apologise. Lizzie is taken aback with the handwritten, wax-sealed letter, in 'cursive?' script. This Darcy is an old-fashioned guy, a man out of his time.

Gordh's Darcy could be an American relative of Fielding's Mark Darcy. He admits to difficulty in expressing his feelings. Lizzie calls him robotic on camera. However, he causes her to question her attitude to disclosure and discretion on social media. Darcy is a mature, understanding and ambitious kind of guy but lacks emotional insight, and so he and Lizzie, again, make a perfect match. They act as a counterbalance to one another.

The 100 episodes unfold against a setting of graduate students managing debt and new careers and businesses with Charlotte, Darcy, Gigi Darcy (his sister) and Bing Lee embarking upon ventures in digital media and inventing their roles in the new multimedia industries. Lydia is the twenty-one-year-old younger sister from hell, who runs off to Vegas at New Year. That city perfectly doubles for Regency Brighton and Gretna Green.

In contrast, Lizzie's graduate supervisor, Dr Gardiner, sends her to San Francisco to shadow the team at Pemberley Digital. Darcy's company is a fairy-tale landscape of innovative millennial entrepreneurship in a beautiful setting that encourages creativity, a twenty-first century equivalent of an estate in Derbyshire. Curtis Sittenfeld's Dr Darcy also lives in a San Francisco-based Pemberley. It is an appropriate location for a modern-day American Darcy, it seems – just enough tradition coupled with modern style and innovation. At the Pemberley Digital HQ Lizzie meets Gigi and is confident that she has avoided Darcy because she 'Twitter-stalked' him to make sure he was still in LA. Their paths inevitably cross, and it is at his idyllic business centre that she realises her feelings for him.

In Episode eighty, 'Hypermediation in New Media' by Margaret Dunlap, Lizzie has to call upon Darcy to role play with her and act as himself in her video. This is a method used in the vlogging style of 'Supergirl' Lilly Singh. Lizzie and Darcy role play as themselves and it makes for an interesting conceit. This is the 'hypermediation' of the title. Artificiality and role play act as therapy and give them insight into their relationship, and they end up counselling one another with renewed perspective. A story-within-a-story enables characters to capture this knowledge. Hamlet explains this before the performance of 'The Mousetrap': 'The play's the thing with which I'll catch the conscience of a king.'

Episode 83 of the *Lizzie Bennet Diaries* continues the gradual thawing out of the Lizzie/Darcy relationship, with Darcy's proximity to her (demonstrated by a shot of him in tight trousers) making her nervous. He takes her seriously when she is shadowing the team at Pemberley Digital, and they start to have fun together. Gordh's Darcy steadily comes out of his shell, and the more self-aware he becomes the less prejudiced and shy he is.

The short, episodic nature of the videos works very well for the story and helps it to unfold in direct, pithy bursts. It helps too that the cast members put in excellent performances. It is a tightly written and beautifully produced series made on a low budget, and with strategic use of social media platforms it links fans to the story. This interactive experience and audience feedback were key features to the Pemberley Digital production model. Viewers are encouraged to post comments and participate in the online discussions via

Twitter, Facebook and their own blogs and vlogs. Lizzie's disclosure across the many episodes, self-consciously broadcast with her co-producer/director/editor Charlotte (played by actor/playwright Julia Cho) proves to be a very useful means for Darcy to understand her character.

The *Lizzie Bennet Diaries* adaptation is very interesting in the way in which it unpicks the questions of privacy, intimacy, self-disclosure and publicity across new media platforms. Is it right for Lizzie to do what she does, revealing so much about herself and her family? Will it not jeopardise future relationships for her and her sisters? Surely her parents will be offended by the pantomimic way in which Charlotte and Lizzie depict them? These are concerns that also resonate for Regency characters. What will people think? In the Regency period, if a young woman took a lone carriage ride with a man (as in *Northanger Abbey* and *Sense and Sensibility*) they were taking a huge risk. What do you do if your youngest daughter absconds to a resort city (Las Vegas) or a notorious barrack-town (Brighton) and gets into trouble?

In Episode ninety-nine, 'Future Talk' by Jay Bushman, Darcy has the chance to speak out and show what a cute boyfriend he makes. He has moved on from a place where Lydia taunts him, as 'Mr Douchey' or the 'Darcinator'. They have all accomplished a lot since Episode one and engaged in self-examination via the use of uploaded videos. Even Lydia. She and Lizzie have both matured in their relationship as sisters and become quite close, unlike almost every other version of *Pride and Prejudice* from the original to the present. In Episode ninety-nine, Darcy's questions directly reflect the novel's original dialogue: "when did you discover your feelings had changed?" And then we cut, as the passionate kisses between the couple are edited out.

The romantic life of the new couple flourishes, and their careers go from strength to strength. The future looks very bright, with this Happy Ever After, feel-good ending. Darcy wants to offer Lizzie a job in his department at Pemberley Digital. However, this twenty-first-century Lizzie does not need the man in her life to keep her and set her up. She does not want, as she puts it, to 'date the boss'. Thanks to her vlog, Lizzie has enough backers and interested clients in San Francisco for her to set up her own media business. She can be her own boss and close to Darcy as they decide on their future together.

Episode 100, 'The End', written by the series' originator and producer/director Bernie Su, extends the story whilst completing and rounding things off, and offers a further platform for growth via the hypermediation factor with its foreshadowing of new productions to come. Su went on to produce *Welcome to Sanditon*, adapted from Austen's unpublished novel, in which Gigi Darcy has her sequel story, and we get to hear more about Darcy and Lizzie's relationship and how it grows.

All the characters admit how they have changed and grown as the resolution comes around. Darcy is not afraid to talk about their relationship on or off camera.

When all is said and done this new generation of *Pride and Prejudice* characters as media producers 'get it' also. They have built their relationships on the development of social media platforms, Su shows us in this adaptation, and as long as things remain positive and supportive, they are happy to communicate and share online. They reveal all, or almost all, of their feelings and emotions in hindsight thanks to this method of disclosure and confession. It is, in effect, the epistolary novel played out online.

The *Bridget Jones* franchise and the *Lizzie Bennet Diaries* are of a type. As well as having the confessional intimacy of a young woman keeping a type of diary or journal, they both look at the story adaptations as updates that describe a world of hypermediatisation, with their ever-expanding web of story possibilities. Characters never die. They play themselves and speak in different voices, and writers and actors engage in a series of performances that defy categorisation. Is Rénee Zellweger (as Bridget) conducting an interview with Colin Firth (as himself) on the DVD extras of *Bridget Jones* a parody or piece of satire? It can be understood in a number of ways and looked at as offering greater subtext, or amusing tangents to the background story of production.

Mad About the Boy

The connections and expanding story webs of new media and adaptations have close associations with late-eighteenth and nineteenth-century narrative, publishing and literary culture. In addition to such schemes as the one Austen was involved with to raise money for Frances Burney's new novel, there was much interaction with authors and readers that helped to shape different publications. As well as the support via subscription, authors' responsiveness to readers' enthusiasms was key to catering to their desires and satisfying the market. Readers were not slow to write to newspapers or magazines to let the publishers, authors and subscription libraries know what they thought. Even Charles Dickens is known to have changed the ending of *Great Expectations* (1861) on the advice of novelist Edward Bulwer Lytton. Bulwer felt strongly that the reading public had to see the hero and heroine united at the end. Dickens' original ending was published posthumously by John Forster, his life-long friend, in his biography *The Life of Charles Dickens* (1873).

Readers have always wanted to have their say about favourite stories and characters. They can now do so with great ease through online fan communities. This has energised the whole fan fiction market and its interactions and developments. This has its highs and lows for authors. Readers can be demanding, hyper-critical and even cruelly disparaging as well as supportive, constructive and appreciative.

A set of characters and readers that have been under-represented in British literary culture and have historically had to keep a low profile are members of the LGBTQ community. The identities and experiences of these characters had to be coded at certain times throughout history and conveyed via subtext and insinuation. In *Lost in Austen*, the explanation for Miss Bingley's characteristic discontent is the fact that she cannot honestly articulate her attraction for other women. So, a life in the closet has resulted in bitterness. Now, fan fiction authors and adaptors are more at liberty to show the expression of desires amongst Georgian and Regency characters that depart from the solely heterosexual and offer a more authentic picture of the range of human relationships.

Has there been a 'queered' version of *Pride and Prejudice*? Well, Jo Baker in *Longbourn* offered an alternative narrative for Mr Hill, the Bennets' servant, as a gay man in a marriage of convenience with Mrs Hill, the housekeeper. This situation protects them both because she is the mother of Mr Bennet's 'natural' son. Does such a subtext apply to Darcy and his desires? It certainly exists in fan theory and the analysis of what might be these literary subtexts.

On moviepilot.com, Caroline Cawley offers a four-fold theory that looks for the gay subtext in the relationships that

Darcy has. This is mostly based upon the aesthetic of, and the casting decisions for, the 2005 film adaptation. She prefaces her mini-essay with a warning for fans to stop reading if they do not want Mr Darcy 'ruined'. She is familiar enough with fan culture to know that some readers will take personal offence.

It is not quite that drastic, however. The editing style of scenes from the film is drawn upon to represent a channel for interpretation. This is then applied to the characters' motivations. Cawley finds Darcy's reluctance to be paired with Anne and his fondness for Colonel Fitzwilliam's company to be a giveaway about his true sexuality. Secondly, there is the gorgeous Charles Bingley. Darcy, simply, loves Bingley, and his moodiness and sternness stems from his jealousy of Bingley's attraction to Jane. And that is why thirdly, he sabotages their relationship. Cawley claims, however, that he has a change of heart after a while and cannot see the heartbroken Bingley pine for Jane, so he sorts things out for them. He would rather be lonely than see Bingley miserable.

The final part of the four-fold theory of homosexual subtext in *Pride and Prejudice* is the threat from Wickham. The handsome childhood friend, suggests Cawley, provokes further jealousy. Darcy's attraction to Wickham began as part of his sexual awakening, which is why he could not stand to see him attempt to court Georgiana. Elizabeth agreed to marry Darcy in the end as a matter of money, convenience and respectability.

They are fond of one another, but the reasoning in this essay is that Darcy is gay and it will never be a love match. This, in a nutshell, is turn-of-the-twentieth century Queer Theory applied to *Pride and Prejudice*. This is the term coined by critic and film studies theorist Teresa de Lauretis at UC Santa Cruz in 1990, to describe the interpretation of culture in this way.

Queer Theory analyses the 'mismatches' that exist in culture and media 'between sex, gender and desire,' Annamarie Jagose explains in *Queer Theory: An Introduction* (1996, NYU Press). It asks us to think that even though characters progress in a seemingly effortless fashion towards heterosexual marriage (the 'normal' state), is this an authentic conclusion for their identity and *actual* desires, as the author has realised them? So, an author might represent a character in a coded way in the story – suggesting their desires through certain behaviour or descriptions. The 'what if?' scenario applied to sexuality and difference in *Pride and Prejudice* takes a partial cue from Queer Theory.

As far-fetched as Cawley's ideas might sound (and they are meant to) they are based on theoretical fan studies – they demonstrate how Darcy, and Austen, are employed and understood as part of popular culture. We know, for example, that LGBTQ communities over the centuries were unable to articulate their desires at various times, legally and morally speaking, and occupied a marginalised place in society that endured oppression, punishment and execution. By employing Queer Theory to push the boundaries of interpretation of *Pride and Prejudice*, it shows that Austen has become an unassailable figure in culture whose characters can be used, and useful, to represent alternative perspectives and marginalised voices. Queer Theory gets us to apply a cross-examination of possible subtexts, during which we might hear the messages of some of these silenced voices and decipher their coded meanings.

This theoretical reading applied to Austen, in a cultural-historical context, does show some interesting features, not in pursuit of homoeroticism and desire, but the question of male intimacy and friendship. It is not all about trying to discern the romantic or sexual subtext between male characters. What Austen did, and did very well, was imply the male intimacy between Darcy and Bingley and other male characters, such as Captain Wentworth and his comrades in *Persuasion*. Kind men make for good intimates, confidants and eventually husbands. Although Austen is known for the virtual absence of any male–male exchanges, the implications she offered in letters and reported conversations, and how events transpire, display the communicative and supportive aspects of male friendships.

Georgian men, we have come to realise, can be shown to contradict the uptight masculine stereotypes of the age.

Bingley and Darcy, Brandon, Knightly, Edmund Bertram and Captain Wentworth all provide great potential for scriptwriters. Viewers and fans have enjoyed the 'fleshing out' process of these characters that created a range of articulate, sensitive lovers, and the roles are ready-made for actors, as Firth explained, thanks to the foundation that Austen supplies. She has contributed to the way in which male characters are depicted in a variety of guises throughout popular culture.

A growing branch of Regency romance, and romance authorship in general, is that openly gay characters feature more and more in mainstream titles. The risks are highlighted nonetheless, by authors such as Ava March (*Object of His Desire*, 2009 and *Bound to Him*, 2009) to show just how dangerous it was for men to express feelings of love and desire for one another in the Georgian and Regency period. The 'unnatural' love between men did result in arrest, prosecution and punishment in many cases. So, the Happily Ever After resolution of 'MM' (male–male) Regency romances is a difficult strategy to resolve. As March wrote on her blog in 2009:

' …a HEA in a Regency-set romance is possible, but it is a challenge to craft one that is realistic to the time period. Personally, I find the HEA the hardest part of a gay historical romance, but also the most satisfying element of the story. If a relationship can survive in the

Regency, then it must be very strong and meant to be. A true love match.'

www.avamarch.com

She makes a compelling argument here about love against the odds, the absolute bedrock of romantic fiction. For Austen's contemporary readers the love affair between Darcy and Elizabeth was certainly, as Darcy emphatically reminded her at Hunsford, against social convention. Now, authors can directly articulate the status and story of previously unheard voices of characters that must strive against even greater odds. Love across the social divide is now matched by love across the divides of sexual preference and its expression.

March and other Regency MM romance writers, such as historian Catherine Curzon (*Life in the Georgian Court*, 2016) who writes fiction as Willow Winsham (*The Star of Versailles*, 2017) resort to the use of high social class to shield their characters from persecution. To arrive at a Happily Ever After, MM romance protagonists have titles and means, much as they do in Austen's heterosexual love unions. This results in some protection away from the prying eyes of society and the law. Male love affairs can, therefore, attain *their* degree of security and privacy in these escapist narratives, that try to defy history and challenge the prevailing literary traditions. As March reminds us, her writing life was prompted by her 'fantasies involving Bingley and Darcy':

' ...I think Mr Darcy just epitomised the Regency period. I've said it before and I'll say it again, it really is a shame Mr Darcy and Mr Bingley never hooked up. They would have been so great together!!'

www.avamarch.com

Be Careful What You Wish For...

Thanks to this universal desire for escapism in romantic narratives, fans are enthusiastic to engage in immersive storytelling experiences. This is depicted in the TV comedy-drama *Lost in Austen*, in which Amanda (Jemima Rooper) exits her twenty-first-century life through a portal in her bathroom and swaps places with Lizzy Bennet. Therefore, Amanda destabilises the novel's storyline because of her foreknowledge and insight into events. This meddling by a modern character brings fan theories to life, and sees characters express different and unsettling new feelings and witness anachronistic goings-on. As a substitute for Lizzy Bennet, the suggestion is that you too, dear reader, can experience your deepest desires if you want them enough.

Amanda has to navigate her way through the story, unfortunately having a huge effect on the plot as she goes along. For example, she French kisses Mr Bingley at the Meryton Assembly, which astonishes him and leads him to pursue her instead of Jane. This then leaves Jane available for marriage to Mr Collins when he arrives at Longbourn and so, naturally, as the dutiful eldest daughter, she accepts his offer. Thus, begins the huge tangle that Amanda must try to unravel. To be immersed in the novel, then, is perhaps the ultimate fantasy for the fan, but it comes at a price. You can mess things up and find that a horribly comic situation transpires.

Latter-Day Darcy

As we have seen, the Latter-Day Saints' church community in the USA has witnessed a flowering of writing that champions Austen and the values of true and enduring love. In channelling Austen, Shannon Hale and Stephenie Meyer reiterate many of the resolutions that readers find most satisfying. Where there might now be some greater flexibility for LDS members' lifestyles, there remain some traditional restrictions on bad language, sexual or immoral content and imbibing caffeine, nicotine and alcohol.

The Mormon faith takes a famously strict line on the importance of marriage, and the compatibility of faith with the endurance of love. One aspect of their beliefs is that marriage on earth reflects the celestial marriage that endures after death. So, a couple that is united in their lifetime remains so as they pass to the spirit afterlife. This is why Meyer depicts the eternal vampire-love of Bella and Edward in the *Twilight* novels. The vampire state – as a virtuous one – stands in for conversion to the Mormon religion. It is why Meyer's vampires do not burn up in the sunlight. Instead they sparkle, because of their heavenly state. They are forever young, beautiful and in love.

It is clear to see, then, that Austen's novels and especially *Pride and Prejudice* have a huge appeal to LDS authors and readers. Romance authors who belong to the church have a great template to follow when it comes to Georgian rules of etiquette and purity before marriage (at least where women are concerned). It comprises a combination of morality, romance and some mild rebellion in the pursuit of happiness. Austen can be read as a sort of advocate for these values and the importance of family life at the centre of society. So, when LDS production company Camera 40 was looking for a project, it was natural for them to alight upon *Pride and Prejudice* for an adaptation in 2003.

Pride and Prejudice: A Latter-Day Comedy, written by Anne Black, Jason Faller and Katherine Swigert, starred Kam Heskin and Orlando Seale as Elizabeth and Darcy. A group of students, house-sharing in Provo, Utah, are our Bennet sister equivalents. Lydia is the wealthy daughter of the house's owner, and her younger sister Kitty, in this version, is her sidekick in mischief and husband-hunting. They live by the rules of *The Pink*

Bible: How to Bring Your Man to His Knees by Louisa Hurst. This vacuous text has no appeal for the other housemates: the serious-minded Mary, international student Jane from Argentina and the perky-yet-bookish Elizabeth, a graduate student with ambitions to be a writer.

Lydia's pet pug is called 'Austen'. Curtis Sittenfeld's depiction of the two youngest Bennet girls in *Eligible* bears more than a passing resemblance to these versions of Kitty and Lydia, with their slavish sense of entitlement and fragrant lifestyle of consumerism, keep-fit and romance. Awkward, shy Mary is shown getting a strike in the scene at the bowling alley in which she gives advice to 'Jack' Wickham on his technique whilst Jane and Elizabeth discuss their romantic prospects. Mary is in her element there, much as Sittenfeld's Mary is in *Eligible* – leading a secret life with her bowling league. The similarities of this film to Sittenfeld's later updated *Pride and Prejudice* are, like Mary's bowling form, striking.

Pride and Prejudice: A Latter-Day Comedy is a stab at a sort of feminist-inspired satire from an LDS production. Lizzy writes 'Napoleonic techno-romances', a genre a little like Victorian steampunk; her own invention of fantasy Georgian adventures. She runs into the seemingly pretentious Englishman Darcy who works for the publisher that is interested in her novels. He is into French existentialism, and therefore comes across as a total jerk from the start.

The emphasis of *The Pink Bible* and conservative Mormons, such as Mr Collins, is on fulfilment via marriage. However, as the action builds, there is more to this film than simply an LDS-endorsed romantic comedy. Whilst the action is quite stilted at times there are some charming and amusing moments. Captions punctuate the action, for example, including direct quotations from Austen that send up the characters' devotion to the girly *Pink Bible*.

There is a sense of (mild) rebellion in this movie that challenges the typical view of the Mormon lifestyle. The young women resist reactionary opinions that tell them to be grateful for male attention and prepared to give up their education and career for marriage and motherhood. Elizabeth wants a balance between these roles. Lydia escapes to Vegas with Wickham. That city, again, stands in for Brighton or Gretna as it does in the *Lizzie Bennet Diaries*. It is the location for a frenetic chase at the film's finale to *prevent* Lydia from making a disastrous marriage to Wickham at the Chapel o' Love. In contrast to the world of Regency risk it is better for Lydia *not* to enter into a marriage than it is for her to marry in order to save face.

Gallant Darcy races to her rescue and even tackles Wickham to the ground at the altar. Darcy, the intellectual, is a *gentle*man and characteristically socially awkward. So much so, that he would far rather sit by himself in his classic car and read poetry than mix with people at a party. So, his act of wrestling with

Wickham, like Colin Firth's drag-out fight with Hugh Grant as Daniel Cleaver in the finale scene of *Bridget Jones's Diary*, is evidence of his feelings for Lizzy. To risk losing his dignity in public shows how far he will go for her.

LDS orthodoxy requires a certain moral outlook and standard. In the film some characters still refer to 'living in sin', and there is an emphasis on honour, trustworthiness and fidelity that is comparable with Austen's view of the world. Good prospects and a strong work ethic, plus a sense of family, are highly valued. Darcy, therefore, fits the bill and becomes an excellent modern-day hero for a conservative-leaning religious denomination.

This film can travel beyond the community, however, as most of the LDS references are incidental to the story. It is amusing to see Lizzy's and Jane's 'hangovers' for example, which – in the absence of the banned tobacco and alcohol – are induced by ice-cream and pizza. Of all the adaptations and updates of *Pride and Prejudice*, this version offers a consolation to the middle 'sister', Mary. She ends up with Collins, after a makeover, and achieves her Happily Ever After – finally.

Shannon Hale makes little or no direct reference to her LDS faith in her books, and the adaptation of *Austenland* into a movie (2013) by Hale and LDS director Jerusha Hess (*Napoleon Dynamite*, 2004) is far more mainstream. In it, JJ

Feild (Henry Tilney from the small-screen *Northanger Abbey*, 2007) plays the Darcy stand-in, Mr Nobley. He, like Darcy, is a fish out of water as a history professor moonlighting for extra money at his aunt's wacky, Austen-themed holiday resort. In this hotchpotch of dinner parties, assemblies, hunting, carriage rides and card games, guests experience a mocked-up Regency-lite experience. Hale and Hess point out that the unreal, deceptive imitation of Austen and her values are a poor substitute and only lead to disillusion and disappointment. Actors who suggest sincerity and conviction surround Jane Hayes and the other visitors, but 'Austenland' is ultimately a façade. This heroine's dream of a Regency/Austen romantic fulfilment is not, of course, possible.

These writers and directors show how the romantic fantasy is unreal, and the perception of Austen as simply a romantic novelist is also false. Austen's satire and the satirical effect of her work on society are still relevant, they suggest. *Austenland*, the movie, is a broad, comic exploration of romantic disillusion with some great bawdy jokes, and far removed, it seems, from its Austenesque or LDS roots. However, the silliness and affection with which Hess explored US-fan obsession with Darcy and Englishness shine through.

Jennifer Coolidge (*Legally Blonde, Best in Show*) plays 'Elizabeth Charming' (they all have to adopt Regency-sounding fairy-tale names when at *Austenland*) who is headed to the

'Darcy Place', as she calls it. When Jane chips in with a reference to the actual novel, Coolidge comes back with "What's that?" The only frame of reference her character has is that of Colin-Firth-as-Darcy and the concept of 'Darcy' as a hero and romantic archetype.

Jane Hayes (Keri Russell) might purport to be a literature fan and know the novel, but she mainly watches and re-watches the 1995 series. When her real-world boyfriend attempts to get romantic on the sofa whilst they watch it, she elbows him away with: "Shh, this is the best part." He leaves in frustration and punches the head of the cardboard figure of Firth-as-Darcy on the way out. Jane lovingly repairs it with a kiss after he leaves.

Jane's all-consuming passion for the fictional Darcy and Regency fantasy distracts her from the potential true love that is right under her nose in the form of Mr Nobley. Russell as Jane and Feild as Nobley make a sweet couple. She has to wean herself off her obsession and discover real, honest emotion. Her total immersion in the romantic fictional world even extends to the legend *Darcy Was Here* displayed above her bed. She eventually realises that her facile response to Austen's work is no different from Miss 'Charming' and her pursuit of the 'Mr Darcy guys'. So, Jane must learn to re-evaluate her approach to relationships.

The Evolution of Darcy

Authors and screenwriters now regularly address this divide over the reception of Austen's work. Darcy is such a potent force that he sometimes presents a serious distraction from a full understanding or appreciation of the novel. Many writers light-heartedly explore the constructs and contexts now imposed on Austen's work and the character of Darcy. Witty and playful interpretations have begun to proliferate in the early twenty-first century.

In that fashion comes the 2016–17 UK tour of *Mr Darcy Loses the Plot* by Maggie Fox and Sue Ryding, who together are LipService Theatre Company. Fox and Ryding's previous theatrical interpretations of great literature include *Doreen Grey*, *Giddy About Gaskell* and *Withering Looks*. So, it was only a matter of time before Jane Austen received the LipService treatment, and there was no better time than in 2017, the year of her bicentenary. Fox plays Darcy in this silly deconstruction of the novel and its dramatisations. She is perhaps the first and only female Darcy on stage – or screen – to date.

Paulina Helgeson, the Swedish translator of Austen's letters, spoke to me recently about the nature of her work. Austen's is a truly global fan culture, and Helgeson described what she does as both a translation of Austen's words and her character, from the first-hand accounts of her letters. This offers Swedish readers a perspective on the person that can cross both cultural and language boundaries. Once translated into a foreign language – with the nuances and context also transposed – more and more readers around the world begin to 'get it'. They too can see Austen as a familiar and friendly persona with so much to say to the world.

There are many voices and many means by which Austen and her best-loved archetypal hero Darcy have come to us over the last 200 years. GH Lewes, Walter Scott and Charlotte Brontë critiqued the original novel, with both positive and negative responses. Admiration and imitation developed and proliferated with Charlotte and Emily, Mrs Gaskell and Bram Stoker, and onto Orczy and Heyer, then Helen Fielding, Marilyn Brant and Curtis Sittenfeld. Simon Langton (the 1995 director) and Andrew Davies (screenwriter), with the co operation of Colin Firth, have probably had the greatest influence on the culture after Austen herself.

More and more, like Shakespeare, Austen is re-invented and infiltrates multiple aspects of world culture, from the vampires, zombie-hunters and surgeons of popular novels and screenplays, to *Bride and Prejudice* (2004), the satirical musical reimaging of the story by Gurinder Chadha, set in twenty-first-century India. Austen's work is robust enough to travel, with rewards to be gained from repeated readings, viewings and adaptation. We recreate an Austen for our time.

The relationship we have with her is best demonstrated by the longing, obsession, affinity and mania that so many fans have for Darcy. The expression of this appears in twelve-foot-high statues in the middle of a lake, in cookie cutters of his profile and Christmas ornaments, on 'I ♥ Darcy' tote bags from the Jane Austen Centre in Bath, on the Darcy mugs that regularly sell out in the gift shop of The Austen House Museum in Chawton, and in repeated and obsessive viewings of films, TV shows and online videos. The yearning for Darcy is shown in his representation as a judge at a dog show, a heart surgeon, a time-traveller, a human rights lawyer, a publisher or a zombie killer.

And why? Why has he taken hold and seized the popular imagination?

Darcy enables us to critique our relationships. He can be realised in a number of ways, but retains the character arc from social awkwardness to insight to true love. Darcy gives, mostly female, writers the opportunity to reiterate substance over surface. The Darcy archetype repeatedly falls for the edgy, slightly rebellious, intelligent heroine, wanting her in preference to the glamorous, upper-class socialites. He enables writers to represent stories that circulate around change for the better, redemption, men with means who seek sincerity over superficiality, and strong heroes who can say: "I'm sorry, I was wrong."

In addition, if certain features are emphasised over others then this allows writers to deal with the Darcy Problem. This ranges from the socially awkward and taciturn with Daniel Vincent Gordh in the *Lizzie Bennet Diaries*, to Matthew Macfadyen's gentle, devoted brother concerned with social responsibility, to the disappointingly snobbish Henry Dorsey in *Project Darcy*.

Influenced by Darcy, John Thornton in *North and South* is the working-class, chivalrous, modern man who carries the unconscious heroine into the parlour where he kneels beside her, trembling with anguish that she might be dead. Then there are the difficult men of the Brontë sisters' stories, who lie and deceive, exhibit cruelty and anger, and on to Dracula – the Prince of Darkness. Sometimes a pure and virtuous soul is needed to deal with this hero's darkness, and at other times something less subtle, like a stake through the heart and a mouth stuffed with garlic, does the trick.

The use of the Darcy archetype allows criticism and examination of relationships, and for 200 years many writers have interrogated what his power and enduring appeal might mean. It constitutes his attractiveness and wealth, which is enough at one end of the spectrum: representing the simplicity of the fairy-tale construct of Prince Charming. Other elements of his appeal involve his challenge to social conventions and the choice of marriage for love instead of financial or familial alliance. So, the Darcy archetype is often his own man, willing to take risks and prepared to risk personal harm or disgrace for the one he loves.

Heterosexual or homosexual, a man of family pride or a man of business, he is the hero that shows his inner sensitivity beneath the tough, proud, awkward, sometimes cruel, exterior.

Cookie-cutter souvenirs and Darcy on the Hallmark Channel are all very well. Darcy as the influence for other prominent writers cements his significance in a commercial and cultural context. And it goes further. Within the serious context of political scandals in the USA in 2017, the Darcy-type appeared.

James Comey, former head of the FBI, answered questions before a congressional committee in Washington DC after his shock dismissal in May 2017. President Donald Trump took this step of firing him, as stories broke about misdeeds during the 2016 presidential campaign. In defence of his reputation and interactions with the President, Comey swore to tell the truth before Congress. This tall, dignified, all-American law enforcement official was described as an 'unlikely sex symbol' by Lizzie Crocker of 'The Daily Beast' news website. She interpreted the events in American politics through the lens of the English author and that of director Simon Langton with her article in June, 2017: 'James Comey is the Sex Symbol America Needs Right Now.' In the divisive tribal atmosphere of the USA after the election, people began to look for heroes.

Comey exhibited 'integrity, emotional complexity, and quiet but certain confidence' during his testimony, according to Crocker. With his 'imposing physical stature' he had the 'alluring masculinity' displayed by 'sex symbols like Mr Darcy in *Pride and Prejudice* (particularly Colin Firth as Mr Darcy in the BBC's *Pride and Prejudice*).' (https://www.thedaily-beast.com/james-comey-is-the-sex-symbol-america-needs-right-now)

Darcy, then, is an immediate symbol for an ideal of authority, honesty and protection. It is very telling that when people look for an image of security, heroism and positive masculine attributes and desirability, they turn to Austen and her hero. Wherever heroes might go and however they might be manifest in years to come, Darcy can – and will – endure.

Further reading, viewing and inspiration

Non-fiction

The Making of Jane Austen, Devoney Looser (Johns Hopkins University Press, 2017)
Jane Austen: The Secret Radical, Helena Kelly (Icon Books, 2016)
Jane Austen's England, A Travel Guide, Karin Quint (ACC Art Books, 2019)
Mr Darcy's Guide to Pemberley, JB Grantham (Independent, 2017)
Be More Jane, Sophie Andrews (CICO Books, 2019)
Jane Austen at Home, Lucy Worsley (Hodder & Stoughton, 2017)

Fiction

The Particular Charm of Miss Jane Austen, Cass Grafton & Ada Bright (Paperback: Brown Dog Books, 2016; eBook 2nd edition: Canelo, 2019)
The Jane Austen Project, Kathleen Flynn (Harper Perennial, 2017)
Mr Darcy's Diary, Amanda Grange (Sourcebooks, 2007)
The Falmouth Connection: A Pride and Prejudice Variation, Joana Starnes (Independent, 2014)

Blogs

Laughing With Lizzie https://laughingwithlizzie.blogspot.com/
Jane Austen's World https://janeaustensworld.wordpress.com/
Darcyholic Diversions https://darcyholic.blogspot.com/
Jane Austen Variations http://austenvariations.com/
All Things Jane Austen https://allthingsjaneausten.net/
Austenesque Reviews https://austenesquereviews.com/
Obsessed With Mr Darcy https://obsessedwithmrdarcy.wordpress.com/
My Jane Austen Book Club http://thesecretunderstandingofthehearts.
blogspot.com/
From Pemberley to Milton https://frompemberleytomilton.
wordpress.com/

Films & TV

Miss Austen Regrets (2008)
Pride and Prejudice – Atlanta (2019)
Marrying Mr Darcy (2018)
Pride, Prejudice and Mistletoe (2018)
Jane Austen: Behind Closed Doors (2017)

Acknowledgements

Thanks to: my agent, Sara Keane; Jane Odiwe; Amanda Grange; Marilyn Brant; Jocelyn Harris; *Persuasions Online*, the JASNA publication; Cassandra Grafton (author, aka Sandra Platt); Míra Magdó; Jackie Herring (Director of the Jane Austen Festival, Bath); The Jane Austen Centre, Bath; Joan Mossop (Director of the Hampshire Regency Week); The Jane Austen House Museum, Chawton; The Chawton House & Library Trust, Hampshire; Julian Platt; Simon Langton; Paulina Helgeson; Dick Claésson; Birgitta Johansson Lindh; Alexa Adams; Rita Watts; Victoria Kincaid; Deborah Yaffe; LL Diamond; Alice Rees and all at Endeavour Quill; and my family Andrew, Alexander and Antony.

Acknowledgements

About the Author

Dr Gabrielle Malcolm is an academic, artist, author and script writer who regularly researches and writes about Jane Austen's continuing influence on popular culture. She is the author/editor of several books on English literature and writing, including a study of Jane Austen fan phenomena.

Gabrielle with The Colin Firth Shirt

About the Author